T0129091

PRAISE FOR
Headhunters on My Doorstep

"Like Bill Bryson, Troost deftly combines humor, commentary, and education. . . . A splendid travel memoir."
—*Booklist* (Starred Review)

"[Troost] crafts exquisite paragraphs that capture the seductive beauty of the islands. . . . Laugh-out-loud wit. . . . Troost is an insightful guide, who can see beyond the superficial shimmer to the complexities underneath. . . . A celebration of persistence."
—*National Geographic Traveler*

"Maarten Troost . . . has done it again: He has created a masterful travelogue that is informative, funny, and introspective; authors are fortunate if they can accomplish any one of those three feats. . . . If you don't enjoy this book there is something wrong with you. Troost displays a level of sophistication rarely found in travel writing. His humor is spot on, and one needs humor when reading about the loss of indigenous culture in the Marquesas, the urban sprawl of Tahiti, and the notion that Kiribati as a nation may soon be subsumed by the Pacific Ocean. Acquire this book by any means possible."

—*Library Journal*

"Troost's language rings true. The author candidly, humorously probes the nether regions of his addiction along with the temptations he encountered during his journey. . . . Troost's sly wit permeates the narrative, propelling his saga out of the ranks of many recovery memoirs. . . . A rambunctious, intimate trip well worth the armchair time."

—*Kirkus Reviews* (Starred Review)

"Evocative, funny. . . . Troost is an excellent travel narrator, clever, bold, and full of captivating visual details. His personal story of recovery is also powerfully told and will surely resonate with many readers." —PublishersWeekly.com

"Delightful, hilarious, and filled with wisdom grounded in an engaging sense of humor." —BookBrowse.com

Sylvia Troost

J. Maarten Troost was born in the Nether-
lands and has lived in Canada, the Czech Re-
public, Kiribati, Vanuatu, Fiji, and the United
States. He is the author of *The Sex Lives of
Cannibals*, *Getting Stoned with Savages*, *Lost on
Planet China*, and *Headhunters on My Doorstep*.
He currently lives with his family in Wash-
ington, DC.

HEADHUNTERS
ON MY
DOORSTEP

A True Treasure Island Ghost Story

J. MAARTEN
TROOST

GOTHAM BOOKS

GOTHAM BOOKS
Published by the Penguin Group
Penguin Group (USA) LLC
375 Hudson Street
New York, New York 10014

USA | Canada | UK | Ireland | Australia | New Zealand | India | South Africa | China
penguin.com
A Penguin Random House Company

Previously published as a Gotham Books hardcover

First trade paperback printing, June 2014

Gotham Books and the skyscraper logo are trademarks of Penguin Group (USA) LLC

Copyright © 2013 by J. Maarten Troost

Penguin supports copyright. Copyright fuels creativity, encourages diverse voices, promotes free speech, and creates a vibrant culture. Thank you for buying an authorized edition of this book and for complying with copyright laws by not reproducing, scanning, or distributing any part of it in any form without permission. You are supporting writers and allowing Penguin to continue to publish books for every reader.

The Library of Congress has cataloged the hardcover edition of this book as follows:

Troost, J. Maarten.
Headhunters on my doorstep : a true treasure island ghost story / J. Maarten Troost.
pages cm
Summary: "The bestselling author of *The Sex Lives of Cannibals* recounts his latest hilarious misadventures in the South Pacific, following in the footsteps of his unlikely idol, Robert Louis Stevenson. *Headhunters on My Doorstep* chronicles Troost's return to the South Pacific after his struggle with alcoholism and time in rehab left him numb to life. Deciding to retrace the path once traveled by the author of *Treasure Island*, Troost follows Stevenson to the Marquesas, the Tuamotus, Tahiti, the Gilberts, and Samoa, tumbling from one comic misadventure to another as he confronts his newfound sobriety. Troost gradually awakens to the beauty of life and reconnects with his family and the world." –Provided by publisher.
ISBN 978-1-59240-789-7 (hardback) 978-1-59240-873-3 (paperback)
1. Troost, J. Maarten—Travel—Oceania. 2. Oceania—Description and travel. 3. Stevenson, Robert Louis, 1850-1894. Treasure Island. 4. Recovering alcoholics—Biography.
I. Title.
DU23.5.T76 2013
919.504—dc23   2013011908

Set in Janson Text · Designed by Spring Hoteling

While the author has made every effort to provide accurate telephone numbers and Internet addresses at the time of publication, neither the publisher nor the author assumes any responsibility for errors, or for changes that occur after publication. Further, the publisher does not have any control over and does not assume any responsibility for author or third-party Web sites or their content.

Penguin is committed to publishing works of quality and integrity.
In that spirit, we are proud to offer this book to our readers;
however, the story, the experiences, and the words
are the author's alone.

For Lukas and Samuel

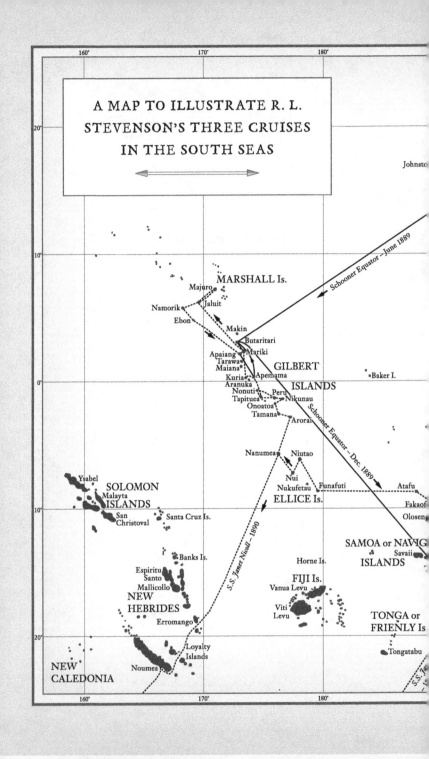

A MAP TO ILLUSTRATE R. L.
STEVENSON'S THREE CRUISES
IN THE SOUTH SEAS

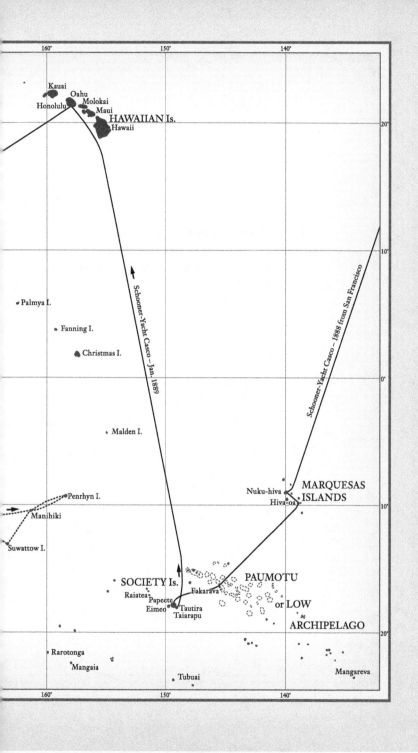

I never knew the world was so amusing.

—*Robert Louis Stevenson, 1889*

Chapter One

Everyone has problems. Spend a few moments catching up with friends and you're likely to hear a litany of catastrophes.

"I lost my job at the prison," one might say.

"I'm going to prison," says another.

"I'm about to lose my home."

"I blew mine up to collect the insurance."

"My ferret died."

"I ate mine."

". . ."

"Long story."

Tales of woe had become inescapable. What were once simple quandaries now seemed to come equipped with trapdoors. One misstep and you'd tumble into the chute of doom, where demotions became terminations, homeowners became squatters, and Little Bandit was no longer safe. I was no exception. I too had problems. Multitudes of problems. If something could go wrong, it usually did. The only law that seemed to apply to me was Mr. Murphy's. For a long while, decades even, the sun had shone upon me. Life had been an effortless glide.

I'd traveled the world, married my soul mate, sired two strapping boys, and wrote books that—I've been confidently informed—landed on the bestseller list in Eugene, Oregon. I couldn't explain why good things happened to me. They just did. But then, like a bad Chinese proverb, my good fortune evaporated like a spilled Slurpee in a Phoenix parking lot. *Everything that could go wrong . . .* was not a thought I dared to finish. It could always get worse, and usually it did.

What'd happened? I wondered. Good luck seeks no antecedent, but bad luck demands an inquest. Was it simply written in the cosmos? Did the yin of happiness necessitate the yang of misery? Could it simply be bad karma? No, I thought, as I reflected on the causes of my misfortune. Behind every event, every circumstance, lay a cold, hard trail of facts. I needed only to follow the breadcrumbs of past experience to bring me to the source of my tribulations. And there, sadly, I found something immense and unmovable:

Continents.

Bad things happened to me on large land masses. Terrible things.

This was a most unfortunate realization, of course. How I'd hoped to discover an unhappy childhood, an unjust prison sentence, or a soul-scarring bout of acne to explain the recent trajectory of my life. Who wants to blame their woes on something as inalterable as the North American tectonic plate? After all, continents are—at the very least—nice to look at. I too could admire majestic, snow-glazed mountains, the rivers that flowed with the tide of history, the buzz of the megacity. I am, for the record, appreciative of boreal forests and rain forests, deserts, and the vast expanse of the northern tundra. I like New York *and* Los Angeles, as well as Mumbai, Shanghai, and Dubai. I am fond of small towns. Also apple pie and yak, though not together. All this can be found on continents. But, alas, experience tells me that if I'm not surrounded by an ocean, my life crumbles like a stale cookie.

It's true.

Take my most recent sojourn in North America. I'd protected my well-being by living on a peninsula. Surrounded by water on three sides, I navigated the perils of the modern world, and whenever events or situations threatened to leave my eyes agog and my head a-splitting, I retreated to a rented sailboat, where secure in a finite space surrounded by the infinite blue of the ocean, I navigated pitching waves and morning fog with an aplomb that failed me on dry land. On water I was free and sure; on land I felt like a lost fish. But then, chasing a job, I moved deeper into the continent, distant from familiar waters and sandy dunes, and there I fell.

Into the bottle to be precise. This wasn't entirely unexpected. In retrospect, it was probably a foregone conclusion. I'd always had a temperamental shut-off valve. Open-minded to the mind-altering, I'd long ago learned to be wary of the seductive offerings of both the street and the pharmacy. I'd known that drugs could be *a problem* and that it was best to dispense with the experimentation early on. I pretty much maxed out on magic mushrooms. Instead, I'd settled into the steady companionship of pint glasses and decanters. Like everyone. It was normal, no? A few beers at the bar; wine with dinner. It was all good. In fact, hard liquor was a no-no in my world—until, eventually, it wasn't, and there was that unknown moment when the proverbial invisible line was crossed, when everything started to tumble with a terrifying ferocity, and despite untold As-God-Is-My-Witness promises to get this under control, to show some restraint, I couldn't. I couldn't stop. Not until my wife, bless her, deposited me at rehab, where, sedated with Librium, I learned that lucky-ducky that I was, I had a fatal brain disease and should I ever pick up a drink again I might as well put five bullets in a six-shooter and shove it down my piehole.

So this was bad. And it happened on a continent. In my mind, the case was closed.

Now hold on right there, someone might say. Do you mean to suggest that there was a link between the pint of vodka you kept tucked in your sock during the last month of your drinking and the fact that you inhabited a continent?

Yes, I do. And furthermore, having noted the correlation between large landmasses and big problems in my own personal life—the larger, the bigger—I gave thanks every day that I didn't inhabit Asia, where I undoubtedly would have ended up a crackhead in Pyongyang. It's important to think positively, I figure. It *could* be worse. Aware now that my well-being depended on my proximity to an ocean, I made a point not to travel deeper into the country lest I get run over by a hog-feed truck in Iowa or catch Ebola in Omaha. You can't be too careful.

It has, of course, invariably been pointed out to me that my reasoning is a trifle thin and specious (Hello, Father Mark!), and that perhaps I ought to dig deep and conduct a *searching and fearless moral inventory*. Well, I did do that. Beyond the dismal lack of presence at the end there, when the drink became the end-all be-all of my day—unforgiveable, all things considered— I discovered that, in all likelihood, I am not as evil as Simon Cowell, but not nearly so good as Oprah Winfrey, which probably makes me average, morally speaking. Reading the scientific literature on the neurobiology of addiction, as I did with the fervency of a medical student, I discovered that deep in my noggin, I simply had an amygdala that hummed a little differently than most. Addiction is a brain disease. You either have it or you don't. It can gestate for years, but once it awakens it will kick your butt thoroughly and mercilessly. And so it did with me. That it did so on a continent, however, I felt was not entirely coincidental.

The reason I am not entirely in jest about this last point is that, rose-tinted glasses or not, I am able to do a little compare-and-contrast. Some years earlier, I lived on the sun-dappled atolls of Micronesia and the high islands of Melanesia. Like most good things, my time in the South Pacific was accidental. I certainly didn't know anything about the region. Can anyone name the leaders of Niue, or Tuvalu, or Vanuatu? Does anyone even know where these places are? Anyone? Anyone? Bueller? Bueller? I too had not an inkling. I'd found myself on the far side of the world because one evening, during grad school, I'd gone to a keg party, where I'd met a woman and become smitten, and because it seemed like an excellent idea at the time, I'd followed her out to Kiribati—the end of the world—where she'd landed a job with an NGO because no one else wanted to work on a remote, drought-stricken, heat-blasted sliver of rock just a notch above the equator and worlds removed from anywhere. While Sylvia occupied her days building composting toilets—*atollettes* she called them—and growing sad little vegetable gardens, I was busy *surviving*. I'd envisioned a rustic Club Med, a *South Pacific* musical, *Survivor*-lite. Life on a remote island in the equatorial Pacific would be like a Corona commercial, I'd thought.

Of course, it turned out differently. "To picture Kiribati," I'd written at the time:

> Imagine that the continental U.S. were to conveniently disappear leaving only Baltimore and a vast swath of very blue ocean in its place. Now chop up Baltimore into thirty-three pieces, place a neighborhood where

Maine used to be, another where California once was, and so on until you have thirty-three pieces of Baltimore dispersed in such a way that 32/33 of Baltimorians will never attend an Orioles game again. Now take away electricity, running water, toilets, television, restaurants, buildings, and airplanes (except for two very old prop planes, tended by people who have no word for "maintenance"). Replace with thatch. Flatten all land into a uniform two feet above sea level. Toy with islands by melting polar ice caps. Add palm trees. Sprinkle with hepatitis A, B, and C. Stir in dengue fever and intestinal parasites. Take away doctors. Isolate and bake at a constant temperature of 100 degrees Fahrenheit. The result is the Republic of Kiribati.

This was home. And I grew to like it. Moving from North America to an atoll was like being transported from the lush cacophony of Saint Peter's Basilica to the austerity of the Bodhi Tree. You get used to it. True, there were times when I would have endured the amputation of my left foot by a rusty hacksaw in exchange for a decent meal, a cool breeze, and news of stirrings beyond the breakers. More often than not, when Sylvia got home from doing her good deeds, we'd typically have a conversation that went something like this:

Sylvia: What's for dinner, honey?
Me: Rotten shark, weevils, and rice boiled in seawater.
Sylvia: Oh, good. I was getting so tired of Filet Mignon with the Truffled Mushroom Ragout.

Then, two thousand miles from the nearest cow and oceans removed from a mushroom, we'd laugh dementedly. But the laughter would be true. Perhaps suffering from Stockholm syndrome, we'd adjusted to our peculiar reality. Once I'd accepted the inherent isolation of island life, when I'd internalized a world demarcated by a fringing reef and the rolling waves of the Pacific, I lived life as God intended me to live—slowly and weirdly, among coconut palms and breadfruit trees, in a timeless place where each morning, as I sipped my toddy, I could confidently pencil in a dose of misadventure and a tonic of bewilderment. I felt, more than anything, at home on a South Seas isle, and I shared with Pacific Islanders their bafflement at the hurry-hurry ways of those unfortunate enough to live far away from the balmy waters of the South Seas. This was my world—happy mostly, kind of kooky, and strangely beguiling.

Indeed, we liked it so much that, having learned where it was, we went on to live in Vanuatu, the oddest island nation in Melanesia—volcanoes, cargo cults, a hundred languages, mind-molting kava—before settling for a spell in Fiji—coups, championship rugby, fearsome chiefs, coups—where we felt sufficiently at home to have our first child, whom we now lovingly refer to as our anchor baby for when the SHTF in the West. The Pacific, we learned, is its own vast universe; each island a star, and our lives revolved contentedly around its languid rhythms, coups and crappy food notwithstanding. Unsurprisingly, I would later think very fondly of these distant places, their palm-fringed beaches lapped by the emerald waters of a lagoon, the cragged eminence of a volcanic isle, the ancient songs voiced by islanders whose ways had changed little since the first exiles washed ashore. It wasn't long until I'd gaze at the big blue space of a world map with finger-gnawing longing. Of course my pining was motivated by pure, unadulterated escapism, but I'd always answered that with an enthusiastic *so what?*

While drinking yourself into rehab is evidence of escapism gone horribly wrong, the desire to experience the far side of the world reflects the optimistic hope that a little skull-jarring dissonance could stir the soul. Falling off the map, I knew, could be good for you.

And so, as I adjusted to the post-drinking landscape, which, early on, felt about as weird and unsettling as finding myself on the planet Tatooine, I decided to read the early literature on the South Seas. Evidently, in the eighteenth and nineteenth centuries nothing aroused the ardent spirits of readers enduring the slate-gray skies of northern climes quite like tales from the sunny South Pacific. When De Bougainville, captain of the first French ship to circumnavigate, published his *Voyage Around the World* in 1771, his descriptions of the sublime beauty and easy love of Tahitian women gave rise to the enduring legend of Polynesia as an Edenic paradise before the Fall. And it is no wonder, really. Imagine reading De Bougainville's torrid descriptions on a frigid night in Lyons. "The young girl negligently allowed her loincloth to fall to the ground," he wrote, describing a Tahitian lass who'd climbed aboard his ship, "and appeared to all eyes as Venus showed herself to the Phrygian shepherd. She had the Goddess's celestial form." Or how about this, courtesy of Philibert Commerçon, the botanist on board the *Étoile*? "Here, modesty and prudery lose their tyranny. The act of procreation is an act of religion; its preludes are encouraged by the voices and songs of the assembled people, and its end is greeted by universal applause." Public sex? Clapping? No wonder the pith-helmeted fascination with the South Pacific. This was shocking stuff for its day. Even in the unflappable Captain Cook's journals, you can almost feel the man blush as he describes the hip-shaking *Otea*, which he calls the "indecent dance."

For the next hundred years the literature on the South

Pacific rarely deviated from the same sultry script. It was the *Girls Gone Wild* of its day. Herman Melville, in *Typee*, his largely fictional account of being marooned on one of the Marquesas Islands, lauded the cheerful immodesty of the island's female inhabitants—"bathing in company with troops of girls formed one of my chief amusements," he wrote—though watching them dance, he observed, "was almost too much for a quiet, sober-minded, modest young man like myself." One day, while gliding in a canoe with the Polynesian nymph Fayaway, he noted her "happy idea. With a wild exclamation of delight, she disengaged her ample robe of tappa . . . and spreading it out like a sail, stood erect with upraised arms in the head of the canoe. We American sailors pride ourselves upon our straight clean spars, but a prettier little mast than Fayaway made was never shipped a-board of any craft." Are you wincing? Clearly, he saved the nuance for the whale.

R. M. Ballantyne's *The Coral Island*, Charles Stoddard's *South Sea Idylls*, even Paul Gauguin's *Noa Noa* all continued to feed the popular imagination of islands inhabited by winsome, available women and savage headhunters. Which is fine. Nothing wrong with that. I'm all for the titillating yarn. But among the early books on Oceania, none rang particularly true to me. Where was the rawness of the Pacific, the withering heat, the poisonous reef, the giant centipedes, the roaring westerlies? And where were the human beings? The islanders depicted in these pages had all the complexity of a coconut frond. It hadn't been written yet, but nineteenth-century literature on the South Pacific already seemed like a PG-13 derivative of *Mutiny on the Bounty*, tidily cinematic with mature themes.

Apparently, I wasn't the only one to have noticed that so much of the era's writings on the South Seas read like the gauzy, Technicolor pantings of a fevered sentimentalist. "Everybody else who has tried," observed one perceptive reader, "got carried away by the romance, and ended in a kind of sugar candy sham epic." Then, as if in a dare, the writer confidently asserts: "You will know more about the South Seas after you have read my little tale than if you had read a library."

Here was Robert Louis Stevenson. He was, I'm embarrassed to admit, a stranger to me. I knew, of course, that at some point in his life the author of *Treasure Island* had become a creature of the Pacific. When I'd lived on the sun-blasted atolls of Kiribati, I'd been aware that Stevenson was of that small tribe of foreigners who'd once weathered its shores—the few, the proud. And when I'd settled in Monterey, I was dimly cognizant that he was somehow tangentially associated with the town. A plastic-sheathed menu at a Cannery Row restaurant would inform visitors that the day's specials included *Calamari à la Robert Louis Stevenson* alongside *John Steinbeck's Famous Clam Chowder.* But I'd never actually read him. His books, in my mind, were homework, the sort of thing you'd be assigned to read for an eighth-grade book report. He was someone you were supposed to read for your edification, and much as my ten-year-old son scrunches his nose at *Huckleberry Finn* while counting the days for the next Rick Riordan book, I passed on *The Strange Case of Dr. Jekyll and Mr. Hyde* in favor of, well, anything but the musty prose of some muttonchopped Victorian. Robert Louis Stevenson, I thought, was boring. He was stuffy. He was probably English.

So I was an idiot. Perhaps it was the lingering effects of the drink, the harrumphing triumphalism often found deep inside the second or third bottle of Pinot Noir. But as the months rolled by and the cobwebs lifted, as I returned to earth from whatever awful orbit I'd been inhabiting, I found myself strangely attached to this, ahem, Scotsman. Perhaps it was the descriptions of him. Robert Louis Stevenson, a contemporary noted, was prone to "smoking cigarettes without intermission except when coughing and kissing." Wasn't RLS some kind of weak-lunged, tubercular, sickly waif, the sort of unfortunate that was said to be suffering from *consumption*? Encountering Stevenson on a beach in the South Pacific, a missionary observed that he strode barefoot, "dressed in a shabby suit of white flannels that had seen many better days, a white drill yachting cap, a cigarette in his mouth." I liked the cut of the man. In fact, I sort of dressed like him. While I no longer smoke—inexplicably, I'd taken up long-distance running; something had to give—I recognized immediately a kindred spirit. Robert Louis Stevenson, I sensed, was animated by the *fuck-it*s.

How else to explain the moment he found himself aboard the *Casco*, a ninety-foot schooner, he'd chartered in San Francisco? Imagine the scene: Stevenson, five foot ten and weighing all of ninety-eight pounds, standing on the bow of a rich man's pleasure yacht, his only experience at sea a short jaunt around the Hebrides, a lazy meander through the rivers and canals of France, and two Atlantic crossings on board ships ten times the size of the *Casco*. He wouldn't know it, of course, but once he escaped the shadow of California he'd never set foot on a continent again, unless you count Australia, which—let's be honest here—is just a large island. For two years he'd voyage among the Marquesas, the mysterious soaring islands that are the bedrock of Polynesian culture; the Tuamotu Islands, the Dangerous Archipelago where slivers of land encircle luminous lagoons alive with sharks and manta rays; and the Gilbert Islands, my erstwhile stomping grounds in Kiribati, as remote in my day as it was in Stevenson's. He'd build his home in Samoa, call it Vailima, and dress his staff in tartan lavalavas, and write of his escapades and encounters in the fabled South Seas with an earthy realism that defied the twittering primness of the Victorian era (official motto: We are not amused).

But why go all the way to the South Pacific? He was an ill man when he'd boarded the *Casco*. Half resigned to an existence as the perpetual patient, ceaselessly nursed and fussed over, he'd told people that he decided to decamp for distant islands to restore his health, which had been failing since the day he was born. While it certainly made sense for a man prone to lung infections and fever to depart cold and damp Edinburgh—I reach for a scarf just thinking about Scotland—he'd already long ago assumed the itinerant life, wandering the European continent before setting forth for America in pursuit of a woman. Now, this I understood. You meet someone, they end up on the other side of the planet, you go follow them. It's called stalking, and sometimes it works. Stevenson married Fanny Osbourne, an American divorcée ten years his senior, and after several years in Europe, they returned to the United States. While spending a winter in upstate New York, where he began *The Master of Ballantrae*, it occurred to him that it might be an excellent idea to set forth for the South Seas. Well, *duh*, you think. That's what everyone says after spending a winter in upstate New York. But why go, really?

Of course, it was relief from his lung-splattering cough that he was seeking. It's what brought him to the Adirondacks in the first place. It was that same quest that caused Stevenson to move to England, and to France, and to Switzerland, and to California. It was the reason he gave for boarding the *Casco*. No doubt this was true. Illness, as only the sick know, is maddening. But, in his letters, one senses another motive for the long journey to the South Seas. "I travel not to go anywhere, but to go," he wrote. "I travel for travel's sake. The great affair is to move." He was irrepressibly restless, a born wanderer. He traveled, I thought, not because he was ill, but in spite of his health. He was, he noted, prepared "to visit like a ghost, and be carried like a bale." Frail or hardy, Robert Louis Stevenson had the twinkling eye of the nomad. To be still was to languish.

And yet, a few years later, after what he'd planned as a seven-month sojourn to the South Pacific had become the odyssey of his lifetime, he wrote from his home in Samoa: "Few men who come to the islands leave them":

> They grow grey where they alighted; the palm shades and the trade-wind fans them till they die, perhaps cherishing to the last the fancy of a visit home, which is rarely made, more rarely enjoyed, and yet more rarely repeated. No part of the world exerts the same attractive power upon the visitor.

The rootless exile had found his place in the lush islands of the South Seas. He'd become known as Tusitala, the teller of tales. Among his readers in England, there was little love for his dispatches from the Pacific. Where was the serialized fiction, the colorful yarns, that'd made him famous? What on earth would compel a gentleman to live among cannibals and heathens? Stevenson, true to his character, cared not for the opinions of London society. The vagabond had settled in the distant backwaters of Empire, where he immersed himself like a highborn chief, signing his letters as *the well-pleased South Sea islander.*

What happened, I wondered, after he passed through the Golden Gates of San Francisco? Roaming the South Pacific as his fancy dictated, Stevenson lived like a jaunty beachcomber, flitting from island to island, the warm breezes offering him the sustenance that would carry him through his remaining years. It wasn't merely a lazy idyll that he'd inhabited. Rarely did he write about beaches and ukuleles. He did not, as far as I could tell, spend much time in tiki bars. The mai tai remained unknown to him. Indeed, he'd come to know the Pacific as a "stir-about of epochs and races, barbarisms and civilizations, virtues and crimes." Drama there was aplenty. But what did he find there, in what realm of experience did he now live, that caused this man, racked by illness, to embrace his world with such saucer-eyed glee? "The whole tale of my life is better to me than any poem," he'd write. Were the restorative powers of Oceania so great that a sick man could reclaim a life of wonder? Could a person, adrift in the continental world, find redemption on the temperate islands of the Pacific?

I pondered this question for a long time. It'd been a year since I crossed borders other than those found in my own mind, and suddenly the world beyond seemed alive and inviting. I reached into my bookshelf and finally pulled out Stevenson's *In the South Seas*, and as I did so I felt a lean hand grip mine, and soon I was aloft, floating over arid plains and towering mountains, the night a whirl of stars and motion, until at last I was set down on the deck of a boat rolling in the swell of the blue blue sea.

Chapter Two

You don't quite realize how imponderably vast the Pacific is until you are upon it, rolling in a ten-foot swell, legs splayed, accompanied only by the occasional porpoise or Wandering Albatross, the air redolent of ocean spray, the fumes of a diesel engine, and the faint odor of a landlubber's vomit. Out here, the smell is vaguely metallic, like blood, and there is not a hint of the continental world anywhere, except possibly in the dormitory sink, where one of your half-dozen cabin mates has expelled lunch. Turn your gaze to starboard and it is exactly like the vista offered from the portside railings of your vessel, a million shades of blue extending toward an infinite horizon, a heaving panorama where waves are singular and entrancing, pulsating bursts of energy that only hint at mysterious forces and faraway storms. Standing on the deck you feel like a remora, a furtive stowaway, as if you shouldn't really be here at all.

But this was exactly where I wanted to be. Ever since I was a kid, my life has been marked by the sweet incongruity of travel. One moment I'm in some East Coast metropolis, grinding out days, the white noise of contemporary American life enveloping my world like an encroaching dome—a cacophony of grim economic stats and dismal politics with an occasional Kardashian popping up like a bobble-headed gopher in an arcade game—and suddenly I'm on a boat in the marble-blue South Seas. I picked up my phone, pleased to see that I had precisely zero bars, and then saw an albatross fly low. There is a topography to the ocean, and as I watched the bird disappear in an ever-shifting seascape of peaks and valleys, I felt pleasantly stunned by the change in my environment. Not forty-eight hours previous, I was nursing a café mocha in the departure lounge at LAX, quietly tapping out the last e-mails, utterly uncertain where I'd be a week hence, and now here I was, acquiring my sea legs on a flat-bottomed boat plying the great expanse of the South Pacific. Some say it's all about the journey, that the wonders of travel should be revealed layer by layer, like the peeling of an onion. I do not subscribe to this. Give me the adrenaline shot, the caffeinated jolt, the pleasure buzz that takes me from A to Z in the shortest time possible. I'll concede right here at the top that my wiring might be a little defunct.

I'd set out, as much as possible, to replicate Stevenson's journey through the great sweep of the Pacific, sailing with the tide from San Francisco Bay and tumbling down the arc of the planet until we crossed the equator with a great huzzah and found a steady current to the Marquesas. From there, I would make my way to Tahiti and the emerald lagoons of the Tuamotus and then fall off the map in the Gilberts before emerging in Samoa, where I'd make my pilgrimage to the great man's grave on the summit of Mount Vaea. But immediately I encountered obstacles. Stevenson, of course, had chartered a well-appointed ninety-foot schooner to sail the great distance between California and Polynesia. He did this because, if only for a spell, he was loaded. A New York City newspaper publisher backed up the money wagon at Stevenson's front door and said, *Go, write what you see, send us a letter from time to time.* When I read that I'd wept a little as I thought of newspapers today, which barely cover the cost of a pastry at Cinnabon during a layover in Denver. Then I got over it and got all practical-like.

It was January, cyclone season in the South Pacific. There were no sailboats departing California for the islands at this time of year, at least none with a sane captain. I'd briefly considered tracking down one such Ahab, determined to impose his will over nature, and offer to crew for him, but then rejected it out of hand when I recalled the cyclones I experienced in Vanuatu—the felled trees, the crumpled homes, the dozens of sunken boats in the harbor, their masts peaking above the surface like forlorn tombstones. What would it be like to endure such a tempest at sea? I didn't really want to know. Death, I figured, is like a coiled snake. It'll get you in the end. Why provoke it?

Nor was it possible to hitch a ride to Nuku Hiva, Stevenson's first landfall, on a commercial ship. There are thousands of container vessels plying the waters between the Americas and Asia, but not one calls on the Marquesas, not even to pick up some bananas. I know this because I checked ship manifests from Canada to Chile. This swath of the Pacific—a wet cosmos so remote and underpopulated that the only thing you're likely to see afloat is an occasional exhausted seabird or a weathered flip-flop—is the last corner of the world to remain immune from the trade flows of globalization. It is lonely out here.

It wasn't always thus, of course. Back in Stevenson's day, in the 1880s, when the tales and exploits of Captain Cook, the drama on board the *Bounty*, and the lurid romanticism of De Bougainville's prose were just freshly mythologized, thousands set forth for the sun-speckled islands of the South Pacific. Oceania was brimming with vessels carrying whalers, traders, explorers, missionaries, and blackbirders—slavers that descended on the islands to ferry laborers to Peruvian mines and Australian sugar and cotton plantations. Others came for breadfruit, sandalwood, and bêche-de-mer, turd-like reef-cleaners prized as a delicacy in China. They came for the guano, dried bird dung, found on the most isolated islands and noted for its excellent qualities as a fertilizer and as an ingredient in gunpowder. Many came for the sperm whales and hunted them to within a whisker of extinction. Planters, like those romanticized in James Michener's *South Pacific*, converted immense swaths of ancestral lands into coconut factories, supplying the world with its need for copra. Hundreds of emissaries were dispatched to the islands to proclaim them protectorates and colonies and that henceforth they would be ruled from Paris, London, Berlin, or Washington. It was for their own good, the locals were told.

Ships to the South Pacific there were aplenty, ferrying dreamers to the islands, lured by the promise of wealth, empire, or everlasting life in the hereafter. If there is such a thing as a sea-highway, this was it. In our imagination—or at least mine—*Robinson Crusoe* typified the South Seas dream, the solitary explorer, marooned, living in an uncharted world, unencumbered by the weight of history. But even in Stevenson's day, Defoe's tale was one hundred and seventy years old. Many islands remained unmapped, and yet already they carried the whiff of possibility, the promise of exploration and conquest. Of course, one man's dream inevitably becomes another man's curse. Bring a ship full of rats, pigs, and unwashed men from the Midlands, or Brittany, or Prussia, or New Bedford, and anchor it off an island in the South Seas that'd spent the previous millennia or so in utter isolation from the world beyond the reef, and the result is biological mayhem. Tuberculosis, pneumonia, plague, smallpox, elephantitis, syphilis, and a host of other ailments decimated the indigenous population of the South Pacific. On many islands, a 90 percent mortality rate was common. When the first Russian to circumnavigate the globe, Admiral Adam Johann von Krusenstern, visited the Marquesas in 1804, he estimated a population of 100,000 people. By 1926, there were but a mere 1,500 Marquesans left.

Seeking to explain this desultory state, Stevenson framed the problem thus: "Where there have been fewest changes, important or unimportant, salutary or hurtful, there the race survives. Where there have been the most, important or unimportant, salutary or hurtful, there it perishes." Insightful, no? And yet not even Stevenson could have envisioned what would befall the islands in the years ahead.

By the 1930s, the Japanese decided that, come to think of it, they'd like to have an empire too, and we all know what happened next. The Imperial Army deployed troops throughout a huge swath of the Pacific, building fortifications in Papua New Guinea, the Solomon Islands, Micronesia, the Marshalls, and the Gilbert and Ellice Islands, ensuring that any approach to Japan would have to be fought one sandbar at a time. The subsequent fighting was among the most brutal the world has ever known. Accounts of that era, however—riveting and appalling as they are—rarely mention what, precisely, the locals may have experienced during the war, and as a result you sort of assume that they were in the bleachers, mere spectators. This wasn't true at all, but perhaps this lack of attention to the islanders' experience was a kind of foreshadowing, because after 1945 it was as if a dream had ended. For more than a hundred years, the South Pacific had fired the imagination of imperialists and romanticists, and then, suddenly, the flame died, and the islands faded into the obscurity from whence they came. True, from time to time, some great power—the United States, Great Britain, France—would nuke an atoll just to make sure things were still hunky-dory with their nuclear arsenal, and dreamers still roamed the islands with visions of eco-resorts and coffee plantations, but mostly the South Pacific reverted to what it'd always been, a sleepy backwater on the far side of the world.

This, ultimately, was what drew me to the more remote corners of Oceania. It is difficult to disappear on earth today, but if you are so inclined, few places can match the isolation offered by the islands of the South Seas. Here, I'd thought, I'd find Stevenson's idealized world, the places with the fewest changes, important or unimportant, salutary or hurtful. Of course, not so long ago, many of these isles were nearly extinct of people and more than a few were bombed to the edge of oblivion, but leave something alone for long enough, and it will return to its natural state, like a seedling on the slopes of Mount St. Helens or a colony of cranes in the DMZ. People, I'd thought, would thrive in unexpected ways in lands unreached by iPhones and container ships. Of course, such places are few and far between, and to find them requires hacking through the jungles of Amazonia or dogsledding across the frozen Arctic tundra or climbing the precipitous slopes of the Himalayas or . . .

. . . or you could fly to Tahiti on the red-eye from LAX.

Which is what I'd done. For a brief moment, as I accepted the flowered garland on board Air Tahiti Nui and settled in to a double feature starring Juliette Binoche while perusing *Paris Match*—and particularly as I tried to refrain from making googly eyes at a short-skirted Tahitian flight attendant named Hotette—I thought, perhaps, Robert Louis Stevenson would have disapproved, and that I should have constructed a raft like the *Kon-Tiki* to take me to Polynesia. Somewhere down there, I'd thought, as we crossed the ocean, Robert Louis Stevenson endured mountainous seas while subsiding on cabin biscuits, whereas I'm up here being served tea by Hotette, she of the gravity-defying curves and melodic voice, and then I figured that being attended to by a beautiful Tahitian woman with a resonant name was in itself a kind of old-school South Seas anthropological experience, and so it was good, and acceptable, and a kind of immersion experience all its own.

I'd flown to Papeete, the administrative capital of French Polynesia, because it was the only place I'd find a boat to the Marquesas. And it was there that I found the *Aranui III*, a 360-foot cargo ship and the only vessel to carry passengers to the more remote islands among France's far-flung possessions in the Pacific. The *Aranui*, as I soon learned from a guesthouse owner, was scheduled to depart the following day, and as I rushed to the harbor to book passage, it didn't take long until I felt strangely elevated at the prospect of leaving Papeete so soon. This puts me in good company, of course. Stevenson despised Papeete; Gauguin fled from it, and writers ever since have been tripping over themselves to figure out new ways to describe the many ways in which Papeete disappoints. This always struck me as unfair. It wasn't as if the Tahitians themselves had decided to one day abandon a charming seaside village of wood and thatch and replace it with chintzy office towers, traffic circles, oven-like churches, filthy sidewalks, and, near the port, cylindrical fuel storage depots that looked like unhatched eggs shading French naval vessels that exuded nothing but malice, and a megacruise ship that merely looked ridiculous, like a Viennese wedding cake melting in the jungle. This was a town built by my kind, travelers who had arrived with hearts full of romance or bile, often both, and found that what they really wanted was a place that offered a decent baguette, a café that served a cup of coffee, a dozen taverns and discos, a brothel, an ATM, a store where you can buy those snowflake *thingys*, perhaps with a maiden in a coconut bra wiggling the hula, and a few ornate administrative buildings to make it all seem classy.

I'd be back, I knew, and I'd traveled enough to know that first impressions often belie something far stranger or wondrous, but I felt that no journey following in the footsteps of Robert Louis Stevenson should begin here. I'd wanted to experience the splendor that he'd felt upon reaching his first landfall in Nuku Hiva after a forty-five-day sail, and so I'd picked up my pace as I wandered through the incessant cacophony of traffic, passing offices, cafés, at least two McDonalds franchises, a Peugeot dealership, and shops selling crap to herds of cruise ship passengers, stopping only to have a gander at the war memorials that the French sprinkle among their possessions like a dog marking its territory. AUX ENFANTS DE LA POLYNÉSIE FRANÇAISE—MORTS AUX CHAMPS D'HONNEUR read one placard listing those lost in Korea, Indochina, Madagascar, and North Africa. Another memorialized all the Polynesians killed in World War I—MORTS POUR LA FRANCE. Throw in a harbor slick with pollution, add copious amounts of spray paint, soak it all in shirt-drenching humidity, and the result, aesthetically speaking, is the very sort of urban hellhole that one flees for the islands. Were it not for the serrated peaks of Moorea, a bewitching sight, looming in the near distance, you'd think you were still a long distance yet from the mythical South Pacific. And so it was with undisguised glee that I'd learned that it was still possible to find a berth on board the *Aranui*, which reared above a wharf in the industrial harbor, its crane steadily loading cargo into its hold.

"*Bon*," I said to the Tahitian clerk inside the ship's HQ, a squat office building surrounded by warehouses, after he'd assured me there was ample room on board. "*Et c'est combien?*" I was feeling a jet-lagged giddiness, the kind of euphoria that occurs when a plan starts to come together. I'd arrived in the Marquesas by ship, just as Robert Louis Stevenson had, and while it wouldn't be in a ninety-foot schooner with a velvet and brass stateroom, it would do. The clerk tapped at a calculator. When he was done, he flipped it around so I could see. I had only a passing acquaintance with the Polynesian franc and the number displayed meant nothing to me. It was, however, immense, the sort of sum astronomers bandy about when describing earth's distance to faraway galaxies, and for a brief moment I felt a pang of worry. I asked if he happened to have the day's exchange rates handy and when he finished with his arithmetic, converting the sum into US dollars, he again thrust the calculator toward me.

"Are you shitting me?" I said after a long, considered pause.

"*Pardon, monsieur?*"

The number was hideous to behold. I'd turned to look out the window, where a crane was loading bags of cement into the *Aranui*'s cavernous hold. It's a freighter, I thought, not the *Queen Mary*. There was, as far as I could see, no casino on board. Nor an Olympic-size swimming pool. Or a spa. Or shops that sell Thomas Kinkade prints. Or anything else that I imagined would be standard on a ship with such a lofty price tag. I've owned cars that cost less than what they were asking. Now that I think about it, the birth of my children cost less than a voyage on the *Aranui*. Forgo this trip, and I could have two more, three if they're delivered in Fiji.

"*C'est trop cher pour moi*," I finally said and asked, if it wasn't too much trouble, if could I just sleep outdoors, under the stars like the Polynesians of yore, and in exchange I'd swab decks and peel *pommes de terres* and otherwise strive to make myself useful.

The clerk looked upon me sadly, pursed his lips, and suggested that perhaps monsieur would prefer a berth in the ship's dormitory. It was, he noted, a third of the price of a regular cabin and probably more suitable for someone of my disposition. Actually, my disposition was inclined to inquire whether he was aware that there was a global recession going on, and did he not think that these prices were a trifle high? And didn't he think it ridiculous that the croissant I'd had that morning cost ten bucks? And come to think of it, didn't he think it weird that we were speaking French, and even stranger that we were at this very moment actually *in* France? Was he not aware that nearly every colony in the world achieved independence, I don't know, sixty years ago, and yet Tahiti remained as French as Bordeaux? Did he listen to Johnny Hallyday? Did he think Jerry Lewis was funny? But I let it go. "The great affair is to move," Stevenson wrote. Exactly so. I was on the move, and if it meant enduring snoring, sleepwalking, and seeing strangers in their underpants, so be it.

And so it came to be that I found myself steaming toward the Marquesas in the company of six strangers, which was fine, except perhaps on that first day, given the prodigious amount of vomiting. Humanity, I believe, is divided between those who get seasick and those who don't. I am, evidently, not particularly blessed genetically, but this I know: I don't puke at sea. Alas, the same could not be said of my new roommates, a young female air force officer from Nantes and a family of cheerful gnomes from Lyon.

"*Ça va bien, Maarten?*" Edgar had said after we made introductions, as he would every time we encountered each other, whether in the dining hall or outside the shower stall. He was seventy-five years old, the patriarch, and his hair tumbled below his neck, Dungeons and Dragons style. I suspected 1974 was a very fine year for Edgar, and he had seen no need to move on. He spoke with a raspy, phlegmatic voice that suggested a pretty serious nicotine habit back in the day. In clogs, he stood approximately four foot ten.

"Oui. Ça va très bien. Et vous?"

"Merveilleux," he said, and then as the ship rolled in the swell he lurched toward a sink and hurled the remnants of lunch. When he was done, he wiped the corners of his mouth with a handkerchief and explained that it had long been his dream to sail to the Marquesas. Dreams, he said, while pale and smelling of regurgitated chicken, do sometimes come true and this, he concluded, was how we endure the tragedy, the comedy, of life, and for a moment I was reminded of why I love the French—not even blowing chunks will ruin *la grande romance* of it all.

Our doorless room had a stench that would make even a hungry hyena whimper and so I left Edgar and his elven kinfolk and stepped outside, leaned against the railing, and took in the splendor of the ocean. We had sailed early that morning, leaving the sheltered lagoon of Tahiti and the hillside sprawl of Papeete and, under a blazing sun, made our way to the northeast, near the equator, beginning a fourteen-day roundtrip journey to the Marquesas, where we would unload the ship of its cargo of food, water, beer, and building materials and carry back fruit, copra, cars repossessed by the banks, and a whole lot of seawater to fill the ballast. I nodded my greetings to the extravagantly tattooed Marquesan crew—their quarters were next to ours on the lowest deck—and spent a long while gazing out to sea. Most of the ship was off limits and I spent a few minutes trying to ascertain where, precisely, the other passengers were standing. Many, I suspected, were inside their cabins, suffering and moaning as the ship pitched and rolled in a heavy swell, but a few braved the upper decks. I know this because from time to time I could hear someone above me retch and for the briefest moment a blob of vomit would cascade over the side until it exploded like a cluster bomb in the wind. I empathized with their suffering, but frankly, nothing could diminish the bliss I felt as the lofty, verdant peaks of Tahiti and Moorea disappeared over the horizon. I have never tired of the sensation of seeing land recede from my vision. Something elemental takes over, a kind of universal awareness of the beauty and fragility of life. It induced no fear in me. As we crested a large roller, I felt as if I could feel the pulse—the *thump, thump*—of earth's rhythm. This, I thought, gazing around my world, my eyes attuned to the waves, searching for those really big ones, the ones that come pitching and howling, those huge bastards that elicit awestruck wonder, and as they pass leave you with a really stupid grin plastered to your face, was perfect.

And yet, something felt wrong. I detected a disturbance in the Force. It was as if, despite the gasp-inducing beauty, there remained some dark undercurrent, a malevolent, unseen predator hovering just below the surface, seeking a victim. My senses were suddenly in overdrive. I could feel a clammy sweat on my hands. This sweeping panorama, the endless blue seascape, dissipated, replaced by the narrowest tunnel vision. My heart thumped and my mind churned, considering possibilities. I felt an overwhelming need, my entire being thrummed with desire. What I wanted, more than anything, more than life itself, was a fucking drink.

This happened from time to time. One moment I'm a happy, healthy, productive member of society, paying bills, cooking tasty and nutritious meals for my family, playing catch with my boys, watching *The Daily Show* with my wife, and then, all of a sudden, my brain sends a message that says, *Hey, might be a good idea to tuck a pint of vodka into your sock and head out to an alley and drink yourself into oblivion.* It's the oddest thing. And it never ceased to surprise me. I'd always thought quitting drinking would be a fairly straightforward endeavor. There comes a day when you just can't take it anymore—feeling constantly miserable, the habitual seeking of relief through drink, discovering, again, that it doesn't work anymore, drinking more just to make sure, rinse, repeat, the beginning of consequences, followed by capital-C Consequences, vows to never drink again, drinking, feeling miserable and so on and so forth—until that moment arrives when you just give up, when you step out of the boxing ring, because that's what it feels like at this point, going toe to toe with a bottle, determined to emerge as some kind of victor, bruised yet triumphant, and every night of course, it is your own personal ass that is whupped, and finally you say *No mas.* This, I had thought, would be followed by a few weeks of unpleasantness, and then, Boom, you're done and you move on with life. And then, again and again, you discover why they call alcoholism cunning, baffling, and powerful. Your brain, it turns out, is your mortal enemy.

This, for me, was unsettling. Up to this point, I'd had a long, fruitful relationship with my brain and felt no reason to question its dictates. *Eat this*, my neurotransmitters would say when confronted with a heaping platter of barbecued frog in Shanghai. Good idea, I'd say, and smack my lips in delight. *Why don't you . . . go to college?* Gee willikers, that sounded like a great idea. My skull was full of helpful tips: *Scratch your knee.*

Duck, or you'll be hit in the head with a baseball. Write a love letter to your wife. Move to the end of the world. We had heaps of fun, my brain and I, and so when it started to tell me to *go ahead, open up that third bottle of wine,* I blithely followed along. When objections were raised about this sudden spike in my alcohol consumption, my noggin had a ready solution: *Hide some vodka in the office closet.* Excellent idea, I'd thought.

Standing on the deck, I tried to let the moment pass, to step back and let the desire dissipate like froth on a wave. That's what you're supposed to do. Intellect over emotion. I'm an alcoholic, therefore I can't drink. Play the tape forward. If I drink—best-case scenario—I emerge ten years later, a decade-long blackout. Where? I don't know. Thailand? Nairobi? A trailer in East Texas? Folsom State Prison? Certainly not at home. I'd pull out of it with a throbbing cranium and think, briefly, *What the fuck just happened?* and then catch sight of myself in the mirror and note with some surprise that somewhere along the way I acquired gray hair and a Mike Tyson tribal face tattoo. And then it would be off to some boot-camp rehab, followed by a lengthy stay in an ass-kicking halfway house, and years of unreturned phone calls: *This time will be different. I promise.* Worst-case scenario? I have a beer and a few hours later tumble over the banister, my last words a slurry *Vive la France,* as I end my days as shark chum.

But my brain was unrelenting:

You've been doing this sobriety thing for eleven months. Good for you. Why don't you take a little break. You deserve it. You can be sober again tomorrow.

Think of how good it would be. A frothy beer or two on the deck as the sun goes down in tropical grandeur. Wine with dinner. Perhaps a nice red from the Médoc. Good company. Easy conversation. You know your French is better after you've had a few. Drinks at the bar. Johnnie Walker with a few perfect ice cubes. You know you want to.

It wasn't so bad. Think of all the good times you had while drink-ing. These spirit-sucking fun-haters are trying to take it away from you. You're a bon vivant!

No one will ever know.

On and on it went. It's tiresome doing battle with your head. You'd like to just walk away, but of course you can't. There's no hiding. I tried staring off into the distance, forcing my eyes to search for a last glimpse of Moorea, but I saw noth-ing but the beads of condensation dripping down a bottle of Hinano, the Tahitian brew. It's probably shit beer, I thought, but still I imagined taking a long pull.

It suddenly occurred to me that this might be a mistake. It had been months since I had felt a craving of such intensity. Perhaps I wasn't ready for this. Should I have waited longer before setting off to traipse around the South Pacific? They—the proverbial *they*—tell alkies not to do anything at all for at least a year or two once the last bottle has been emptied. Don't move. Don't change jobs. Don't divorce, the assumption being you have some kind of choice in the matter. Needless to say, hooking up with the really hot heroin addict from Wednesday's step meeting is also a no-no. Two sick*ees* don't make a well*ee*, they say. They are full of such pithy aphorisms. Take it one day at a time. Let go and let God. Do the next right thing. Live life on life's terms. Easy does it. My brain was turning into a bum-per sticker and every time I thought, no, this is not my life, I'd think of the moment when I first started to fill empty water bottles with vodka and I'd go to another meeting. I picked up chips—thirty days, sixty days, six months, nine months—and reclaimed my life as a husband and father. "If you ever drink again," my wife had said, "I'll turn you into a eunuch."

This snapped me awake. There was much to lose. My eyes regained their focus as I saw my friend the albatross swoop low for another pass. I took a deep breath and tried not to think of the bar three decks above. What exactly was transpiring here? A craving, sure. A bad one, no doubt. But why now? Was it the impending approach of five o'clock, a rooster's crow for lushes everywhere? Not likely, I thought. Happy hour had long ago lost its frisson. Christopher Hitchens once said that he drinks "because it makes other people less boring." I'd read a lot of Hitchens when I was trying to justify my drinking. If he could write like that, I reckoned, while getting blotto every day, well then, everything must be just peachy with me. Of course, when I finally did stop drinking I discovered the other side of that equation: When you're sober, drinkers are curiously boring. For a long while I could only walk by a bar at dusk with finger-gnawing longing. I'd hear the laughter and the clink of glasses—or even catch a waft of stale beer and Lysol—and I'd have to quicken my pace. I'll never have fun again, I'd think, as I hurried home to my steaming cup of herbal tea. But after a few months, when I finally felt confident that I was unlikely to start pounding shots of Jägermeister, I'd occasionally meet friends at a pub. As I sipped a club soda, I'd immediately scope out those who belonged to my tribe—the solitary drinkers hunched over their phones, the anxious woman with the shaky hands waiting for her pinot grigio, the two college students on their third pitcher, the bartender sneaking shots—and I'd feel a special camaraderie. It's like gaydar for alcoholics. And then, as the alcohol started to take its toll and people began repeating the same stories and their eyes got glassy and their coordination started to wither, and there in the corner, the woman who just slipped off her barstool, I'd think, no, I don't really miss this and I'd think of myself as cured. Done. Finished. No worries.

But still the cravings came. Not often, but enough to scare the shit out of me. On the one hand, I could be a great father, a loving husband, a successful something, or, on the other, I could have a drink, and there'd be moments when the choice was paralyzing. Think logically, I told myself as I gripped the handrail. What's causing this? Was it the prospect of spending a couple of weeks confined on a ship full of French people? Not likely, I thought. I like the French. They live life as if every moment was consequential. Spend enough time with them, and you'll eat tastier food, you'll dress better, and your conversation will be elevated, although you'll acquire this strange tic wherein you start using your face as a punctuation mark. The French do, however, drink like every alcoholic wishes he could drink—moderately, daily, with great ceremony, which is irritating. If they could just drink like Russians, that would be fine. There's nothing like seeing others get shitfaced to help keep you sober.

But I had reconciled myself to the fact that there are in fact normal drinkers. *Freak*, I used to think whenever I saw someone leave a half-empty wineglass. No longer. Perhaps they're allergic to peanuts. I happen to be allergic to alcohol. *C'est la vie*. And yet, I couldn't pretend that everything was fine, that I'd reconciled my condition with my situation. Three flights of stairs above me there was a bar. I wanted—really, really wanted—to climb those stairs.

Finally it dawned on me why I was feeling so squirrely. I had boarded the ship at seven thirty that morning, having huffed my backpack the two miles it took to get from my guesthouse to the wharf, and when I climbed the gangplank I was handed a plastic cup of juice. Great, I thought. I'm thirsty. I brought the cup to my lips and then smelled something odd, like it was mixed with turpentine.

"*C'est quoi ça?*" I asked.

Rum punch.

Who the fuck drinks rum at seven thirty in the morning?

What was this? A booze cruise? A convention of active alcoholics? Maybe I should have read the brochure. You've heard of *Leaving Las Vegas*. Come experience *Leaving Papeete*. The only people I know who've turned to Captain Morgan for a pick-me-up in the early A.M. are late-stage alcoholics who pour it into their coffee mugs to stave off the shakes, the palpitating anxiety, the early onset of delirium tremens, seeking to forestall impending death and/or hospitalization. And now here I was, with a cup of rum punch in my hands, handed to me with a nod and a wink. Good times, bro. Time to get your buzz on. And it got worse . . . well, depending on your perspective. There was free wine at lunch. Entire bottles. Red and white. Now, I'm sure many, right at this very moment, have left the page to book their vacations, but for those still reading, let me say that setting down a couple of opened bottles of wine right in front of a newly recovered alcoholic, the kind of alcoholic who once thought of himself as a bit of a connoisseur, is like handing a pipe to a crackhead. I read the labels, a white Bourgogne and a Rhône red, and then read them again. That alcoholic voice inside my brain, usually a devilish whisper, was now pounding the drums, doing the rumba, putting on a party hat and shimmying on the dance floor. *Come on*, it said. *Drink it.*

So it had been that kind of day. Challenging. It wasn't simply that there was alcohol on board, but rather a kind of electricity that encouraged me to drink alcoholically. Rum with breakfast. A couple of bottles of wine with lunch. My body is wired for that. What to do? I steadied myself as the boat pitched over a wave and then headed inside to the stairs. Up or down. Up or down. Choices. Choices.

I headed down, into the bowels of the ship, unsure of what I was looking for. There was the laundry room. Did I have any laundry that needed to be done? I could do laundry. Wash. Fold clothes. Some kind of mindless Zen-like task. The machines were complicated European models. I studied the instructions. But I didn't really have much that needed washing and so I moved on. Another door. I opened it. A gym. Hello.

It was tiny. There were some free weights, a couple of Stair-Masters, and a treadmill. I crab-walked inside and flicked on the lights. I was at water level and could see the waves smashing and foaming against the porthole windows. I unlatched the weights from where they'd been secured, grabbed what I needed, and sat on the bench press and started lifting, all the while gazing at the treadmill. Could I run on a machine in a pitching sea? I was aching for a run. Ever since rehab, it's what I'd done. A couple of miles at first. Then four, seven, ten, fourteen, eighteen, even twenty-mile runs when the mood hit. I'd lost thirty pounds in two months and felt more physically fit than I had in years. Of course, I shredded my Achilles tendons—I could even hear them snapping (*pop, pop*)—but they healed, more or less, and I kept running. I'd never jogged on a treadmill, however, regarding them as expensive contraptions for dilettantes. I'd become a purist, pounding trails and pavement in wilting heat and bone-shivering cold. Someone once told me that I was simply replacing one addiction for another and that I wasn't quite *getting the program*. I ignored him and started adding hills to my runs. All I craved was a run, and here at least was an urge I could satisfy.

I took off my flip-flops and decided to run barefoot. I flipped the machine on, let it gather speed, began to jog, and was pitched off by the next wave. I got back on and tried again. The same thing happened. But soon I found a rhythm. I got a sense of the waves and how they'd impact the boat. It was like running among the hills of San Francisco after you've had way too much to drink, the upper body lurching in one direction, pinballing through the air, carried by an indefinable momentum, and the legs scooting and halting and twisting to keep from having the whole edifice come crashing down. This, I discovered, was right up my skill set. The kilometers—it was a French model—ticked by—three, four, seven—and soon I felt that happy, calming surge of endorphins, my brain and body aglow in a sense of well-being. Suddenly, finally, I felt good.

But you know what would be really good right now?

This would be my brain talking again. What? I answered wearily.

A cigarette.

And this, alas, I found irresistible.

Chapter Three

Every child has a hero. Or at least they should—a person whose attributes and accomplishments are so prodigious and compelling that they stoke a kid's imagination, shaping and molding a burgeoning consciousness, subtly altering the course of their life in weird and unpredictable ways. You never know who's going to step up to the hero plate, of course. Every kid is different. For some it's a ball player—the Joe Namath of yore giving way to the Robert Griffin III of today (a great trade IMHO; Namath was a punk, RG3 is a rock star). For others, it's a Steve Jobs or Oprah Winfrey, entrepreneurs who transformed the world and in the process revamped their own difficult beginnings into lives full of rainbows and unicorns. Parents, of course, seek to influence who their child's heroes are, which is why, around the dinner table, young Jacob and Isabella are sometimes regaled with stories describing the lives of Sally Ride or Barack Obama, demonstrating what a wonderful country this is, a place where little girls can grow up to be astronauts and little Muslim boys from Kenya can one day become president. But really, you never know what's going to stick. Leave them be with the television remote one day, and the next thing you know they're cursing like sailors, exclaiming about the necessity of spray tans and six-pack abs, and all of a sudden a decade is lost as they model their young adult lives on Snooki and "The Situation." It's a perilous world out there.

My own personal childhood hero was Thor Heyerdahl, the great Norwegian adventurer, and the original Most Interesting Man in the World. I'm not exactly sure how this came about— probably some combination of early exposure to Indiana Jones and the *Raiders of the Lost Ark* franchise, the presence of *National Geographic* magazine in our home, and a fortuitous encounter with *Kon-Tiki: Across the Pacific by Raft* during my formative years back in the Neolithic Age. This was before the advent of Facebook and *Call of Duty: Black Ops*, when bored children still perused their parents' bookshelves, hoping to find an illicit collection of *Penthouse Letters* or even *Scruples*, but settling for anything that sounded exotic. I devoured Heyerdahl's books— *Kon-Tiki, The Ra Expeditions, The Tigris Expedition*—and even when I learned that he'd been mistaken about everything— Polynesia was settled via Asia, not South America as Heyerdahl maintained; the ancient Egyptians did not sail to North America—my estimation of him only increased. Despite overwhelming evidence to the contrary, he'd stubbornly held on to his beliefs, creating his own reality, one that was far more interesting and lively than the humdrum offerings of the mainstream world. This was a man I understood.

On board the *Aranui*, I spent much of my time reading Heyerdahl's *Fatu Hiva: Back to Nature*. Initially published in Norway in 1938, *Back to Nature* recounts Heyerdahl's first great adventure, when he and his new bride up and left their comfy, bourgeois existence in a hamlet in Scandinavia and set forth for the Marquesas, to an island, as he writes, "renowned for cannibalism and fornication." He had auditioned potential wives, dropping them when he sensed a lack of enthusiasm for his grand plan, which was to "run away from bureaucracy, technology, and the grip of twentieth-century civilization," until he met a young woman of a similar disposition—Liv, who would go on to be the first of his three wives. "What do you think about turning back to nature?" he'd asked her.

"Then it would have to be all the way," she'd replied, demonstrating that both she and Thor must have been really stoned at the time, because no one talks like that unless they've had a blunt or two. Off they went to Fatu Hiva, the southernmost island in the Marquesas, to live off the bounty of the land, breathing in the heady aroma of the tropics, and otherwise cavorting as if they were on the set of *The Blue Lagoon*. Ten pages in and I could already hear the faint echo of my adolescent brain. *This*, I thought, *should be good.*

As I lost my myself in Heyerdahl's world, the ocean had calmed, and it wasn't long before the smell of vomit that had prevailed throughout dissipated, replaced by the fragrant offerings of whatever Muana, the ship's waiter and resident tattooist for those so inclined, carried on his trays. There were only two other solitary travelers—my roommate, Yvette, who proclaimed her dislike of Bora Bora ("They were speaking Tahitian. We are in France. They should be speaking French.")—and an impeccably groomed Swiss banker, who could usually be found on the uppermost deck, smoking Cohibas, while plotting ways to launder the money of the criminally rich and devising new and creative means to destroy the world, as bankers are wont to do.

The other passengers were largely older—I felt like a pup— and they sported shirts that bragged of prior expeditions across the Sahara, cycling treks in Tibet, and cruises up tributaries of the Amazon. Some carried binoculars, members of the birder cult who could spot the differences between a red-footed booby and a red-vented bulbul. They were invariably interesting. I spoke to a central banker who'd penned two books on Napoleon and a retired French naval pilot who had survived not one, not two, but three plane crashes. They were, by and large, members of the luckiest generation the world has ever known, baby-boomer European pensioners who came of age in the post-war years with guaranteed jobs, heaps of benefits, oodles of vacation time, early retirement, and superannuation payments that ensured a comfortable, prosperous existence till the end of their days. From time to time, because I'm that kind of person, I'd note the 50 percent of Spain's youth that could not find jobs, the riots in Greece, the Italians who could not afford to leave home until the age of forty, and the youthful Irish families who'd lost hope and were again emigrating as their forefathers had done in generations past. Everyone agreed that this was *vraiment dommage*—very sad, a true crisis—and went back to perusing the wine list, searching for better offerings than the house table wine. I didn't begrudge them their good fortune, of course. Live long enough, and eventually you learn that so much of life is pure serendipity.

The ship was largely lorded over by George, an affable Romanian engineer who strutted about like a haughty sovereign. He'd been there from the beginning, in a shipyard on the Danube, six hundred miles from the Black Sea, where the *Aranui III* had been constructed. The owners, a Tahitian-Chinese family that had run the business since buying the first *Aranui* in Australia in 1947, had searched far and wide for a new ship, and no one, not the Chinese, not the Germans, nor the French, could match the price offered by George for a cargo vessel with a shallow draft capable of taking passengers and material on the Tahiti-Marquesas run. "We started building in 2004," he said, "and finished in eighteen months. And you know what?" he said, waving his finger. "It floated!" He beamed at this. "I came for six months. It's now ten years. Tahitian time. So it goes."

I liked George. Out here, he said, waving toward the immensity of the ocean, you have to forget your identity. We are just people, and there are not very many of us in this part of the South Pacific. In ten years, he'd seen only seven other ships. Even the whales avoided this place. In Monterey, I saw whales— grays and humpbacks and orcas, the occasional Blue—nearly every week, viewing them from a pine-forested ridge or from a sailboat. But in this remote expanse of the South Seas, they were strangely absent. George said he'd encountered them just three times in his decade at sea. And so it was just us out here, a small crew and perhaps 125 passengers.

Mostly, however, I sought out the company of Mareile, a soft-spoken Swiss archeologist who had lent me the Heyerdahl book. "He was wrong about everything," she had noted. "But he pushed people to think, to try to figure out the mystery of the Marquesas. He arrived there forty years after your Stevenson, when things were very grim."

Mareile lived in Tahiti, and from time to time joined the voyage as a resident expert. She used to sail full-time—two weeks on, a week at home—but had recently scaled back her travels. "It was lousy for my marriage," she declared.

I sought her out because, despite having lived in the South Pacific for five years, I knew next to nothing about the Marquesas. Look at a map and no island group is as peripheral as this one, no small feat in a region that defines marginal. One would assume that by now, in the twenty-first century, there'd be some kind of cohesion to Oceania, a unifying theme. They do, after all, face many of the same issues, like climate change. You'd think that when confronted with rising sea levels, which are projected to rise upward of three feet over the next century, rendering many of the islands, in particular the atoll nations, uninhabitable, that perhaps the region's leaders would unite, speak with one voice, nice and loud, and say something like HEY YOU CHINESE PEOPLE WITH YOUR POLLUTING FACTORIES AND YOU AMERICANS WITH YOUR CADILLAC ESCALADES AND YOU INDIANS WITH YOUR COAL-FIRED POWER PLANTS AND ALL YOU BIG RICH COUNTRIES SPEWING CRAP INTO THE AIR, YOU'RE KILLING US OUT HERE, but, no, there's none of that, which is part of the charm, I suppose, the fact that the islands remain distinct, even kind of unaware of each other, but perplexing all the same. These countries and territories just do not have anything to do with each other, which is why it's possible—even if you've lived in three of these nations—to still think of the Marquesas as somehow off the map, a terra incognito, a blank slate upon which I could only project a giant question mark.

Fortunately, I had Mareile to turn to. I was interested in the ancestry of the Marquesans. And really, how could you not be? Perhaps no island group is more *out there* than this one. How on earth did anyone get there? And why, exactly, did the first Pacific Islanders, whose ancestry can be traced to the Eurasian landmass, leave the continents in the first place? What was wrong with Asia? Not big enough?

What we know is this: Sixty thousand years ago, during the Pleistocene Era, when much of the northern hemisphere was encrusted with a thick layer of glacial ice, a hardy troop of early humans somehow managed to transport themselves from the Eurasian landmass to Australia, Papua New Guinea, and the islands of Indonesia. For decades, this feat had confounded scientists. This was millennia before any known group of humans was constructing boats of any kind, much less the sturdy vessels with sails and rudders needed for a blue water passage, no matter how short the distance. Perhaps, it was thought, these humans had rafts. And let's say one day there was a storm, a tempest that blew a raft or two to Northern Queensland, and upon these rafts were enough men and women with sufficient genetic diversity to populate a continent and several large islands. This, for some years, was the prevailing theory. How else to explain the miraculous appearance of humans on islands in the South Pacific?

The truth is even more arresting. Those early vagabonds, the restless souls forever searching for the better place, walked to the isles. It's true. It's uncanny, isn't it, how they were able to just amble from a continent to an island? Like Jesus. From Africa to Europe to Asia, our ancestors were roamers, carelessly wandering as far as their hairy legs would take them, searching for a better meal and a nicer view, and what finer place than a beach hut overlooking a balmy seascape in the South Seas.

Except there was no sea. Not there in any event. Not then. Here we have a most unusual circumstance. Humans got there—Australia, Papua New Guinea, parts of Indonesia— before they became islands. From roughly 2.6 million years ago until 11,700 BC, give or take a year, sea levels were approximately three hundred feet lower than they are today, enabling restless humans to wander from Africa to Europe to Asia and onward, with some heading north to Siberia and across a land bridge to Alaska and the Americas—which must have been heaps of fun to do during an Ice Age—and others, the lucky ones, making their way to the south, to Australia/PNG/ Indonesia. And then, because the earth can be temperamental, impulsive, overcome by sudden urges to rearrange things, the ocean rose, swiftly, without warning, isolating our hardy bands of hominids on their new islands. You can imagine the scene:

"Hey, Fred, come look at this."

"What is it, Barney?"

"Look. All of a sudden, we're surrounded by an ocean."

"Well, shit. I promised Wilma I'd take her to China for Christmas. Now what do I do?"

Build a boat, of course. Which, five thousand years ago, is exactly what our intrepid band of explorers did. But did they head back to Asia? No, they did not. They set sail for the east, into the unknown, their vessels pointed toward the horizon, where sky and water intersected and blurred. Why not? Something must be over there, right? Let's check it out. How big could this ocean be? And they kept going, these crazy people, who we now call the Lapita, and they discovered New Caledonia, the Solomon Islands, Vanuatu, Fiji, Tonga, and kept sailing until they arrived all the way out in Samoa. How do we know this? Pottery. That's right. While the English were still playing with stones, our Lapita were cruising the South Seas in mega-yachts, colonizing the island universe and, in their spare time, firing up the kiln to craft vases and jars.

But then things get murky. Word had gotten out, apparently. The islands were no longer a secret. And now the migrations came in waves. We don't quite know from where. The Philippines? Taiwan? Yunnan? Vietnam? Linguistic and bacterial evidence points us toward Taiwan as the likely wellspring that sent forth the hardy, seafaring people that eventually found and settled Polynesia and Micronesia, but no one knows if this was the only source of plucky folk willing to sail over the horizon or just one of several. In any event, here were a different people, newly arrived on the scene, and they too had wandering ways, finding their way to Samoa, which has long been regarded as the stepping stone to the hinter-islands of Oceania. No one knows what happened when our new arrivals encountered the

Lapita. Did they fight? Or were they presented with a cake frosted with a decorative, swirly WELCOME, NEW NEIGHBOR greeting? Did they date and mingle? Or did they devour each other? We have no way of being sure. But onward they sailed, to Tuvalu and Kiribati, to Tahiti and the Tuamotus, to Hawaii and Easter Island, and finally to the Marquesas, whereupon they ran out of roaming room, there being nothing left to find in the Pacific. And what's really extraordinary is that they were able to sail to the Marquesas some two thousand years ago, back when Jesus couldn't even find a boat to cross Lake Galilee.

"Actually," Mareile said, "recent studies show that the Marquesas weren't populated until about AD 1000."

Oh.

Which brings us to Viking times. Still damn impressive.

"And that the first Marquesans didn't come from Samoa or anywhere else in Polynesia. Rather, they originated in Southeast Asia and migrated through Micronesia."

Really? That can't be right, can it? That would make the I-Kiribati the forefathers of the Marquesans.

It is an ocean of mystery.

But surely, these first Marquesan settlers were refugees, exiles banished from their home island, sent on their way with a few coconuts and breadfruit, cast out of their communities and forced to scour the ocean. That's how I'd always envisioned it. A little trouble at home and off to sea they went.

"Nope," Mareile corrected me. "They were explorers, and once they'd found the Marquesas, they headed back to their home islands and then returned with their families."

Ah. But why didn't everyone go? I mean, do you have any idea what it's like to live on an atoll, the thin crust of an undersea volcano, an island that wasn't really an island at all, just a faint suggestion of land, not more than a few feet above sea level, often drought ridden and heat blasted, where lagoon and ocean nearly merge? It's hard. And then to hear about these high, fertile islands to the east? Of course, you emigrate.

But how did she know all this? How could she be so sure?

"It's what the rats have been telling us."

I'd found the Rat Whisperer apparently. Rodents never spoke to me. They merely regarded me with an appraising eye, but Mareile, it appeared, had crossed the human-rat communication divide. She told me of the research that was being done on the Polynesian rat, often described as the only mammal endemic to the South Pacific, but really, it's a creature that's as indigenous to the islands as we are. They were, for better or worse, the constant companions of the great Pacific navigators of yore, accompanying these fearless travelers from ship to ship, island to island. Most of the cultures that arose in the Pacific did so with a strong oral tradition, passing down stories through the generations, but of course many of the old tales are now lost forever, victim of the same diseases that decimated the populations in island groups like the Marquesas. And so people like Mareile turn to the entrails of rotting vermin, coaxing the story of the Pacific out through DNA analysis and a careful examination of stomach contents.

"But really," Mareile continued, "we still know so little about the ancient Marquesans. They had about seven hundred years to develop their culture, and then the Europeans arrived and so much was lost. I find myself envying Heyerdahl. He, at least, had a chance to see some of the old Marquesas. Are you finding his book helpful?"

"Oh yes," I said. Except, I thought, I found it helpful for entirely different reasons.

Chapter Four

One of the interesting things about sobriety is how your perception of people, places, and things changes. It's like you get a do-over in life, and now you inhabit an entirely different being. Drunk You liked the color black; Sober You likes periwinkle. Drunk You liked England; Sober You prefers India. Drunk You liked Henry Miller; Sober You thinks he's a dick. Drunk You never ate sweets; Sober You is a raging chocoholic.

And so it is with Thor Heyerdahl. Not that I couldn't relate to his tale of departing the continental world for a mysterious island on the other side of the planet. In fact I could relate to it all too well. Run away from civilization? Where do I sign up? I too had felt the siren song of escapism, the urgent desire to say to the world *I'm outta here* and depart for a sunny shore on the far side of the world. For me, however, this had been no idle dream. I too had met a woman of similar thinking, albeit someone who would only engage in bat-shit crazy endeavors in a sane, thoughtful, responsible manner, and moved with her to an atoll in the equatorial Pacific. I soon learned, of course, that paradise would forever remain a day's sail away, that islands, even balmy, tropical ones, are real places with real people with real problems, and eventually I'd seek my escapism through far easier and more efficient means. For Heyerdahl, however—at least the youthful Thor on display in the pages of *Back to Nature*, the first long-haired, bearded hippie as he'd come to describe himself—reality would always be forged, manipulated, and molded into the same romantic ideal. You read passages such as this:

> Once upon a time, a hundred thousand Polynesians were supposed to have lived in the Marquesas group. Today, a mere 2,000 were left, with only a handful of white men. The Polynesian islanders were dying out at a tremendous rate. And Fatu Hiva was the most luxuriant island in the South Seas. If 98,000 had disappeared, there had to be room for the two of us.

And you think, well yeah, I guess there'd be space, but must you be such a self-absorbed clod? Of course, this was written before World War II, so maybe the extermination of a people wasn't regarded as quite the faux pas that it is today, but still, a little empathy please. But it never comes. We read of lepers and islanders afflicted with elephantitis; we meet, briefly, an elderly missionary and a wizened, old cannibal living by himself, the last of his tribe; but they, in Heyerdahl's eyes, have less life than the tikis he stumbles upon in the jungle, evidence, in his mind, of Incan travels to the Marquesas. Even Liv comes across as nothing more than a decorative plaything. It was all about him, his adventures, his theories, his happiness.

Now, of course, I completely understood the narcissism. I'd always thought of myself as a simpatico kind of person, but just a year previous I too was all about me—specifically, my need for a drink—and just as Heyerdahl could only perceive things through the lens of his own fantasies, I too could only live through the prism of the bottle. *Polynesia was settled by indigenous South Americans*, Heyerdahl would declare over and over again, whereas I would think, *Everything would be better with another shot of vodka*, and I'd do it over and over again. The end result, in its own strange way, is remarkably similar: It's a boring way to spend the day and it gets kind of tiresome for the people around you, though—I may be going out on a limb here—I suspect most would still prefer the company of the free-thinking contrarian to the vodka-sodden alcoholic. Just a hunch.

And so, after three days of sailing, as we approached the southern Marquesas, I resolved to take a different attitude to the islands. I'd already decided to jump ship in Nuku Hiva. I had no idea what would follow, just that it seemed like a good idea. There is a fine line between the tourist and the traveler, and it didn't take long to figure out that as long as I remained on the boat, I would be on the wrong side of that divide. But in the meantime, I'd have some time on the other Marquesan Islands, isles unvisited by Stevenson, and it seemed necessary to have a plan, an objective. I looked at the itinerary—we'd have a day in Fatu Hiva, a morning in Ua Pua, an afternoon on the north shore of Tahuata, and so on and so forth, far too little time to get familiar with the islands—and concluded that I needed a disciplined approach. Heyerdahl was looking for freedom. I was looking for limits. Heyerdahl saw the Marquesas as a refuge from civilization. I saw them as a cross-training, multi-use obstacle course.

This makes me a shallow person, I realize. Here I was, on the very periphery of the known world, approaching islands steeped in mystery and romance, and I prepared by studying maps, searching not for ancient ruins or prominent headlands offering grand vistas, but rather for trails and roads I could run. Every evening, during the golden hour of sunset, as most of the passengers headed upstairs to the bar I descended into the entrails of the boat, settling into the gym, which I had come to think of as mine alone, until one day I was joined by a Swiss woman of indeterminate age—thirty-five? forty? forty-five? I can rarely tell, anymore—but, clearly, a woman who was fit. I know this because her workout attire consisted of a leotard, nothing more, revealing chiseled guns for arms and the kind of marbled legs more commonly found on Olympic gymnasts. She was a StairMaster junkie, I soon discerned, and as I nodded my greetings I wondered if she was of my tribe. I would sometimes speculate about the people I encountered running fourteen miles at dawn until I began to meet some of these very same people in church basements. I had always imagined your typical twelve-step meeting as occurring in some grim, darkened chamber full of cigarette smoke, bad coffee, and doughnuts, filled with fat, spiteful old men telling you to take the cotton out of your ears and stuff it into your mouth and listen for a change, *why don'tcha*, but these days, you're more likely to find a meeting in a smoke-free hall serving herbal tea, filled with people discussing Bikram Yoga and their latest marathon time. This made sense to me, of course. Try as we might, the word *moderation* leaves many of us scratching our heads. Why run one mile when you can run ten? Why do half an hour of sun salutations when you can do ninety minutes of pretzel-like contortions in a 105 degree sauna? More is better. Always.

Wait, I can hear someone say. Isn't recovery from addiction supposed to be all about finding serenity and some kind of inner peace? Well, yeah, but did you know for every year you used your substance of choice, it takes about a month for your brain to heal? For some of us, that adds up to a lot of months. In rehab, upon learning this, you could feel the collective groan. These had been sharp minds when it came to math; all those years of measuring grams and ounces, calculating cash flow, pilfering savings accounts, the extended cost/benefit analysis involved in choosing between a pint of Popov and a bottle of Grey Goose—this was a crowd that would have aced advanced calculus were it not for the hangovers—and now, in a nanosecond of well-honed mental gymnastics it'd suddenly dawned on most of us that we weren't looking at twenty-eight days of brain-scrubbing, from which we'd emerge like a cherubic bodhisattva or Hindu ascetic, but rather at months and years of unsettling feelings and occasional, monstrous cravings. Well, that sucks, I'd thought, and for the first time I'd begun to envy the heroin addicts. You have about five years of injecting black tar until you hit the wall, when the veins recede and the abscesses deepen, when your tolerance has reached the point where no matter how much you inject, you can no longer get high—the dragon is gone forever—but of course you can't stop, because withdrawal is such a motherfucker, and now you have to choose: OD or get clean. Choose the latter and the brain is up and running again in five short months. Lucky folks, indeed.

Now think of the alcoholic. In rehab, we'd played an exciting game called Guess the Addiction. Whenever a newcomer slinked into the dining hall, there'd be a moment of collective silence as we'd appraise our new comrade, and then we'd engage in furious scribbling, the goal being to ascertain their substance of choice, age, and hometown. I personally was awful at this, but my roommate Pin Cushion (heroin addict) was a superstar. It was as if he were a sage, an oracle, who with a mere glance could discern everyone's darkest secrets. "Twenty-four," he'd say, as a young blonde shuffled in. "Xanax and Vicodin. Montclair, New Jersey." And he'd nail it. "Fifty-eight," he'd move on, as an older gentleman wandered in, baffled to find himself here. "Anesthesiologist. Fentanyl. Washington, DC." He was like a mystic, pointing out the pill poppers, the tweakers, the smack-addled, the coke fiends with the bloody noses.

But no one needed any help discerning the alcoholics. In they shuffled; the women typically in their thirties or forties, wondering how the evening glass of chardonnay had descended into the coffee cup of vodka hurriedly gulped down during the morning commute, followed by a breath mint and a quick spray of perfume until the lunchtime nip; the men, more likely in their forties or fifties, whether Hells Angels bikers who'd been intervened upon by fellow gang members, Big Law partners, or airline pilots; usually admitted under the threat of a job termination or divorce, sauntering in full of attitude and self-pity; and all easily identified by the broken capillaries in their noses, the gin-blossom hue to their faces, and the alcohol bloat around their guts. And then there were the really horrifying cases, the end-stage alcoholics, who'd arrive skinny and jaundiced, their guts distended with fluid, who'd mosey about afflicted with disfiguring edema in their legs and a grotesque case of ascites, marking their remaining weeks until either a liver transplant could be found or, more likely, they'd disappear and a counselor would announce that, sadly, another had been lost to the disease.

The street-drug addicts were typically young. Coke, heroin, crack; they hit hard and fast. Rare is the middle-aged junkie. No, scratch that. There are no middle-aged junkies. Keith Richards? He's been off heroin for thirty years. Nick Cave? Clean since the nineties. Lou Reed since the eighties. Trent Reznor hit the wall in 2001. Iggy Pop's been clean forever. He's sixty-seven. You don't get abs like that while freebasing. Nikki

Sixx of Mötley Crüe? Technically speaking, he died twice from overdosing, but I suppose it doesn't really count since he's now coming up on eleven years sober. A quick search tells me that many of those bad boys from the eighties—from Slash to Tommy Lee—are now sober, though God only knows what Axl Rose is up to these days.

But what of the other drug-addled rock stars? Dead. People speak of the curse of twenty-seven—Jim Morrison, Jimi Hendrix, Kurt Cobain, Janis Joplin—but it's so limiting. What of Jay Bennett, guitarist for Wilco, and Mikey Welsh of Weezer, and Johnny Thunders of the New York Dolls, and Shannon Hoon of Blind Melon, and Hillel Slovak of the Red Hot Chili Peppers, and Dee Dee Ramone of the Ramones, and Bobby Sheehan of Blues Traveler, and Sid Vicious of the Sex Pistols, and Kristen Pfaff of Hole, and Bradley Nowell of Sublime, and God help you if you were ever a member of Alice in Chains—two down so far. Shall we go on? Rob Pilatus of Milli Vanilli. Milli Vanilli! And perhaps most tragically, Vinnie Taylor of Sha Na Na. You can't even write about music without kicking the bucket—Lester Bangs, the best music critic of all time, OD'd at thirty-six. So, kids, remember, there's no such thing as recreational IV drug use. Nice suburban boys and girls get scooped out of Dumpsters every day.

But these days, of course, it's the pharmaceutical companies that are enabling a whole new class of junkie; the well-to-do kids on Adderall and other uppers, the anxiety-ridden moms on benzos like Xanax and Klonopin, the chronic pain sufferers on OxyContin, which they then sell on to the opiate addicts for rent money, and when those addicts can't afford Oxys they move on to heroin, 'cause it's cheaper.

And the doctors? They're just middlemen. Every nineteen minutes in this country, someone—Heath Ledger, for instance—dies from an overdose of prescription meds. Roughly 10 percent of the US population is addiction prone they say, though I think that's a meaningless number. Some substances will ensnare your brain no matter how wholesome you are. Let a nice Mormon like Mitt Romney smoke crack a few times, or shoot dope, or be prescribed Oxys for a recurring injury, and I guarantee you that within a month he'll be giving blowjobs in an alley to fund his habit. (Okay, maybe a year. He's got those accounts in the Caymans.)

And then there are the old-school alkies. I recall when I'd first heard that Amy Winehouse song—"They tried to make me go to rehab and I said no, no, no." Even then, that voice, those lyrics, hit me like a wall of bricks. *Whoa*, I thought, what's going on in the pop universe? A rich, smoky voice singing a tune that felt honest, a little disturbing, but with a clarity that I hadn't heard since I was a wee tyke on a tricycle listening to Stevie Nicks (recovering Klonopin addict, incidentally). And then, because I'm far too oblivious to pay attention to Top 40 radio—do they even call it that anymore?—I paid no more mind to her until she was dead. And it wasn't drugs, but, according to the early reports I'd read, *alcohol withdrawal*. That was an enlightening discovery. Opiate addicts bitch and moan about withdrawal, but it won't kill them; meanwhile, the hard-core alcoholics die, their last vision a hallucinogenic spider crawling into their eyeballs as their bodies convulse and roll into bone-shattering contortions during delirium tremens. No fun that. It's no wonder that every year a quarter of a million Americans are hospitalized for alcohol withdrawal.

For most alcoholics, it typically takes years until they earn their seat in rehab. I calculated that from the first moment I took a drink until the last, twenty-four years had passed. The first fifteen were great. I loved bars and dinner parties and beers at sunset, and save for the occasional head-shattering hangover, the time ticked by with nothing more than the warm glow of a life well lived. During the following five years, however, drinking had settled into habitual monotony. It's five o'clock. Time for a beer. We're having salmon for dinner. Better open up a sauvignon blanc. Slowly, the ease and comfort I'd always felt with the pop of a cork dissipated, replaced with nothing at all, and now suddenly my brain clicked over to the other side, the line had been irrevocably crossed, and soon I was quietly obsessing about the next bottle to be opened, wondering whether this would be the one to bring on the warm glow of yore. And it never came. The alcohol had stopped working. And this irritated me to no end. "I never saw you drunk during this time," my wife would later note. Well, it certainly wasn't for lack of trying. My tolerance, always high, now increased exponentially, and yet I'd never hit the sweet spot, the moment when I was suffused with a cheery warmth. Within a few short years, though, I'd undergo the physiological change that marks the terminal alcoholic. I'd become dependent on the drink. I never developed the shakes. I never drank while I worked. But come 3:00, 4:00 P.M. my head would feel like a belt was rapidly tightening around it, my anxiety levels would skyrocket, my usual mellow disposition would undergo a Dr. Jekyll–like transformation, and I'd become a short-tempered asshole until I'd had a drink or ten, and suddenly I'd feel "normal," no better, no worse.

Until vodka entered the picture. Everyone's seen that twenty-point questionnaire given to determine whether or not you're an alcoholic. By the time you've been institutionalized, you've aced that exam. But frankly, I believe there should be a twenty-first question—Have you recently switched to vodka? It is, in my experience, the beginning of the end, and now, for me, the effects of alcohol became unpredictable. On some days I'd sneak a pint or two and no one would be the wiser. I could function, speak clearly, and because I'd taken up yoga, hold an extended Eagle Pose without even a wobble. On other nights, however, after a few discreet shots of vodka, I'd slur my words, my gait would widen as I'd careen from one hallway wall to another, and finally, as I plopped onto the couch, I'd spend the rest of the night thinking of all the cool stuff I'd do if I wasn't so fucked up. So the weeks would pass.

And then I quit. On my own.

It hurt for a few days. Insomnia, of course. Sheet-soaking night sweats. My BP soaring like a brick had been fastened onto an accelerator. And then it was over. I attended the dawn meetings in Carmel, California, and liked them just fine. No hand-holding. No Lord's Prayer. Must be a West Coast thing. Just the Serenity Prayer at the end, which is a fine prayer. I met people with tales no worse, no better than mine, save for the DUIs, the divorces, the jail terms, the carnage that I'd so far avoided, and I felt pleased to be among a group of disparate people all united by a shared allergy to alcohol. I paid no mind to these Steps and Promises that people kept yakking about, and in the evenings I popped open a nonalcoholic beer— Buckler or Beck's N.A., typically—and rejoiced in my sobriety. After thirty days, I decided that this was all well and good, but really, must we go through life without an occasional buzz? It was then that I decided to reward my good behavior by getting a Medical Marijuana License. This, of course, was a brilliant idea. A little problem with the drinkee-drinkee? Why not turn to weed? It's *medicinal*. All natural. Organic. It could only be good for you. Woody Harrelson says so.

I found myself moseying on up to Santa Cruz, where I met with a "doctor," mumbled something about back pain and insomnia, and because California is a wonderfully enlightened state, I was soon in possession of a laminated ID card that enabled me to buy the finest herb that the great horticulturalists of Humboldt County were able to produce. With license in hand, I used my phone to Google the nearest pot dispensary— no shortage of choices in Santa Cruz—and soon I was met by a couple of twenty-something kids with glazed, dilated 8-ball eyes, wearing officious-looking white lab coats that they must have stolen from an old set of *Doogie Howser, M.D.*, and who kindly walked me through all the different varietals of cannabis. Not having followed advances in the marijuana industry since, like, 1993, this was a revelation to me. Was I interested in the euphoria-inducing Sativa strains or in the mellow, blissful Indica varietals? I ventured to guess that I was likely an Indica-man myself, and as my helpful cannabis technicians filled my order—little baggies of Afghan Kush, Purple Buddha, Death Star, and Yoda OG—they thoughtfully added a pre-rolled joint of Blueberry Kush, a freebie. "We . . . uh . . . value your . . . um . . . you know . . . like business . . . and stuff." And then they'd returned to their brownies, the crumbs tumbling down their lab coats.

So now I was happy. I'd stopped drinking. I was reliably sober, alert, and pleasant during the day, and after I read the evening stories to my kids, I'd head out to the deck and fire up the bong. "I think, this, uh, sobriety thing is really working," I'd tell my wife moments later, as I slunk deeper into the couch. "Yep. Yes, indeed. Best thing I ever did. Quit drinking." She'd look upon me with stoic blankness. "But you know what would be really good right now?" I'd say, tapping my belly as her eyebrows arched in anticipation. "Tacos." And now there'd be a flicker in her eyes as she looked at her watch and realized with a sigh that it was too late to call the divorce lawyer.

Meanwhile, of course, I'm thinking I'm all cutesy and smart, having beaten back the alcohol demon, except of course there was a very good reason why I hadn't smoked weed in twenty years. I didn't actually like getting high. It's just not my thing. I'm a monogamist. The only plant I loved was the grape-vine.

The inevitable happened, of course. I'd gotten some bad news and relapsed on a pint of Sam Adams and a bottle of pinot noir, and so began the last five months of my drinking, which would include a transcontinental move from California to the East Coast, where my wife, who'd been consulting from home for a few years, landed a proper job, having concluded that I was well on my way to becoming an unreliable fuckwit and that it was best to take matters into her own hands, which she did, eventually delivering the ultimatum: Leave now or go to rehab.

It's a lovely story, isn't it? It irks me to this day that I didn't manage to quit on my own like my own personal sober hero, Duff McKagan, bassist for Guns N' Roses, whose drinking was so legendary that he became the inspiration for Duff Beer, the preferred beverage of Homer Simpson, and who eventually landed in the hospital when his ten bottles-of-wine-a-day habit caused his pancreas to blow up. When he was discharged, he hopped on a bike, started eating his veggies, and never looked back. Enough, he said, and it was so. I, however, had picked up again and soon it got me once more, and it became something even more monstrous—the drink revealed itself for what it truly was for all those years, just fattening me up for the slaugh-ter, all semblance of control now shattered—and then I ran out of choices until there was nothing left but to be locked up somewhere for a month. It is what it is and it takes what it takes.

So now here I was, nearly twelve months sober, alone for the first time in a faraway place on a boatful of booze. According to my back-of-the-envelope calculations, twenty-four years of drinking entailed twenty-four months of brain-mending. I told you I was good at math. With a little more forehead-scrunching deliberation, I figured I was halfway there. I had no idea where *there* was, just that it was surely better than the place from whence I'd come.

The technical term for this cerebral metamorphosis is neuroplasticity, which is now my favorite word ever. After re-hab, I plunged into the science of addiction, and now, in the next life, I hope to come back as a neuroscientist. Who knew that the space between your ears could be so interesting? I'd always thought that the brain peaked around the age of seven and then it was all downhill from there. One day you're creating Lego spaceships, building pagodas made out of twigs, learning languages, and sixty years later you're lying prone on a La-Z-Boy watching Sean Hannity, the brain cells curdling as you gear up for the War on Christmas. This turns out not to be the case. Or rather, it's not inevitable that you become a crusty old fart who spends every Thanksgiving bitterly complaining about how Jack Kennedy's daddy stole the election in Illinois. The brain is mutable, constantly adapting and evolving as it processes new stimuli. This for an addict/alcoholic is good news because our brains are basically fucked. Have you ever seen an MRI of an end-stage alcoholic's cerebrum? It's ghastly. Alcohol, no matter how you dress it up, whether in a fruity cocktail glass with a little umbrella or in a wineglass, is essentially ethanol, the same thing we use in sanitizers to kill bacteria. Pour enough of it onto your brain and you turn your noggin into something that looks like a hideously deformed molten doughnut, the booze literally melting the brain from the inside out.

Now hopefully you've quit before that happens, but in the meantime your prefrontal cortex—responding to years of alcohol and drugs—has pretty much abandoned its original mission, which is to act as the CEO of your being, the executive in charge of decision making. This is the rational part of you, the voice that does the internal cost-benefit analysis, judiciously measuring the likely consequences of a course of action and sternly clamping down on destructive impulses. It's the voice that says, yes, we are going to study for that history exam, and, no, we're not going to max out our credit card on a diamond nose stud. Drugs and alcohol completely mess up the prefrontal cortex, however. All those neural pathways that were meant to allow you to live a productive, happy, balanced life become redirected, and now it's your reptilian brain—the amygdala—that assumes the pilot's seat. And your inner lizard is indeed a lounge lizard. He wants to feel good *now*. People often wonder why on earth an alcoholic or addict continues to use despite all these, shall we say, adverse consequences. It's because our own personal planes have been hijacked by fucking lizards. Have you ever tried to reason with a Komodo dragon? Exactly. Ain't nothing stopping him from his fix.

But then you quit, most often due to some particularly bad adverse consequence, and then it's all good, right? This is where the really depressing part comes in. Your brain is so messed up that you cannot properly feel pleasure. Not for a long time. On its own, your brain produces a certain amount of dopamine naturally. It's the little smiley face on your day, the happy neurotransmitter that causes you to laugh at cat videos on YouTube. Your brain tends to regulate your dopamine at a fairly fixed level, which is why normal people never get tired of cat videos. It's also why they don't drink too much or mainline heroin into their genitals. Something in the genetic code of the alcoholic/addict, however, causes their dopamine levels to spike to stratospheric levels as soon as they encounter the substance their bodies were wired for. You never hear of stories that begin with: "Gosh, the first time I drank/snorted/inhaled/swallowed/ injected, I really hated it. It was yucky and it made me feel icky." No, what you hear about that first encounter with their particular substance of choice is how the heavens opened, the sun shone, Handel's *Messiah* and the trumpets of angels greeted them as they attained a whole new level of consciousness, and for the first time, they felt the grace of God. Seriously. But what's really happening is a rush of dopamine flooding the brain. And you want more. And then you have more. And then your brain goes, hey, wait a minute, there is just way too much dopamine floating around in here. So, to keep things in balance, it decides to produce less and less of it on its own, which creates its own vicious feedback loop as the addict/alcoholic seeks to compensate for the brain's stubborn unwillingness to get back on the dopamine assembly line by ingesting more of the substance, leading, of course, to the brain's own dopamine assembly workers basically going on strike, like they lived in France or something.

And these dopamine transmitters? They are difficult to rouse out of their slumber. They will not be hurried. There is no magic pill for them. Prozac and the like are useless. In rehab, we had a neurobiologist tell us that not even sex will equate the dopamine rush that the addict/alcoholic feels when using. Really? Were we that pathetic? The only thing is time, the good doctor assured us. Well, someone asked, what if we had vigorous sex with our partners five times a day? Would that speed up the dopamine normalization process? No, he informed us. That was just so sad we all agreed. What strange mutant creatures we had become.

Fortunately, in the interim, while our brains normalized, there were a few things we could do to help mosey things along.

It turns out that those early twelve-steppers back in the 1930s were on to something with their suggestion that it might be a good idea to develop some kind of relationship with a Higher Power. This is what trips a lot of people up, of course. Do you mean to say, I thought early on, that my sobriety is somehow dependent on my settling, right here and now, essentially five thousand years of religious conflict and sectarian strife, and that I had to choose a well-defined interpretation of God, a corresponding religion, a subgenus denomination, and a particular congregation/community, otherwise I'm destined to die a gutter-drunk? No, dipshit, I was told. Just find whatever floats your boat, whether Buddha, Ganesh, Jesus, Satan, your family, your group, the Nature Goddess, whatever. Just make it be something larger than yourself and every day toss a little prayer balloon its way. And if that doesn't work for you, then learn how to meditate. The point here is to transform your selfish, self-absorbed ass into someone that connects with a living world in all its wonder and glory. No one gives a shit about anyone's particular religion; it's all about spirituality, dude.

Because I was totally geeking out on neuroplasticity I'd decided to look this up—ye have so little faith, I was told, not for the first time—but indeed it's true. MRIs taken of the brains of Zen Buddhists in deep meditation and Franciscan monks immersed in prayer all light up like a Christmas tree in the prefrontal cortex, which for the addict/alcoholic in rehab, of course, has long ago gone as dark as North Korea. So I decided to do both. I meditated for me and I prayed for you, and now sometimes whole hours would pass without an evil thought.

And yet I still missed that kinetic buzz, that surge of something, the rush of pleasure and calm that accompanied drinking back when it still worked. This is called euphoric recall, when the addict/alcoholic conveniently skips over the last, miserable days of their using, and lets their mind wander back in time, to the nights when all it took was two or three glasses of a really good red zinfandel to get their groove on.

Fortunately, while my dopamine transmitters were still a little wobbly, I could depend on good old reliable endorphins to give me the kick that I craved. And like so many who had only recently ended their relationship with their substance of choice, I too found myself spending enormous amounts of time at the Bikram Yoga studio, the gym, or, especially, the running trails, pursuing the endorphin high with all the devotion of the addict. The fact that this also entailed pain and suffering was an extra-special bonus, given that I was generally feeling guilty and repentant, and so I liked the medieval hair-shirt element involved in pushing myself to the point of cracking.

So to say that I was eager to get off the boat and commit to some hardy endorphin-stimulating exercise would be an understatement. That intense craving I'd had just a few days prior left me tremulous with worry. It would be so easy, I knew, to relapse here, on a small ship in the middle of nowhere, filled with people drinking from noon to night, like vacationers without a worry in the world, passing the time over long wine-soaked lunches and dinners because there wasn't much else to do. This, I knew, was not an ideal milieu for me. From time to time, my brain would zap me a message: *Hey*, it said, *how about we change our no-drinking rule to no-drinking-on-terra-firma? That could work, right? That would free up boats, airplanes, and inner tubes. What do you say?* After a few days of this, I was fairly frothing like a racehorse locked in the gate, looking forward to nothing more than a long trek on a dirt trail.

But then, standing on the deck during the first blue wisp of dawn, as we cruised slowly into the bay at Omoa, one of two small settlements on the island of Fatu Hiva, for a brief moment all thoughts of strenuous exertion left me as the first morning rays of sunlight illuminated what, I thought, could very well be the most beautiful island in the world, and now I was grateful to be sober, because if I'd been drinking, there's no fucking way I'd be up this early.

Chapter Five

Robert Louis Stevenson, upon sighting the Marquesas, associated the experience with the loss of one's virginity. Actually, technically speaking, he said that it "touched a virginity of sense," but since I make no claim to being any kind of official biographer, I feel free to extrapolate. In any event, Fatu Hiva is that breathtaking, provided of course that you equate the loss of your virginity with something that was beautiful and novel, which changed you forever, and not with something that was sad, pathetic, and fumbling, which left you thinking, *Wait, that's it?* But Fatu Hiva, encountering it, seeing it, inhaling it, is like an entirely new sensory experience. It is unlike any island I have ever seen.

It wasn't merely the light. Dawn can make a snowdrift in North Dakota look like the frozen tear of God. Or, no, perhaps it was the light, the emerging clarity of the equatorial sun, illuminating a tumble of ravines and coarse, ragged cliffs; a vegetation that seemed to change its composition the higher one looked; a lush jungle cacophony below, and then as you gazed higher, up to the lofty, eminent peaks of jagged mountains, where a few clouds swirled around saw-toothed summits, a sharp, barren greenness, the crests of newborn mountains. It was like some strange fusion of island types, a hybrid of the tropical combined with something rougher, more temperamental and moody, like the isles one sees off distant coasts in the higher and lower latitudes, recalling some scene from *Where the Wild Things Are*.

Turning my eyes to the water, I immediately noticed an extraordinary surf break, a long right-breaking wave just below a steep precipice, the breaker curving around the headland. Anywhere else in the world and there'd be a dozen or more surfers on this point break, all pummeling each other as they jostled for position. This wave, I thought, would be worth big bucks on other islands. Some chiefly landlord would claim it, a backpacker's resort would pop open, and surfers from around the world would flock here for the chance to experience a few barrels. But not here. There wasn't a soul on the water. There are just six hundred people living on Fatu Hiva, divided between two villages. There are no hotels. The island lacks a runway, so there aren't any prop planes ferrying visitors from Papeete. It is a difficult place to reach. The only way is by sea.

As for tourists? That would be us. As I gazed upon the sandals and dark socks combo that European men of a certain age inexplicably favor, and the wide-brimmed sun hats nestled upon stacks of gray hair, and listened to the whir of cameras, I thought it unlikely that any besides myself was jonesing for a chance to shred a few waves. What I'd give, I thought, for a boogie board and a local to point out the jagged rocks that I sensed were lurking below the surface, ready to slice apart a femoral artery. Such was the allure of this wave.

As the crew unloaded cargo onto a barge, we arranged ourselves into steel-hulled launches and roared toward the island like invading marines. I felt awkward, as I always did when in the company of some kind of group-travel excursion. To see the world, I thought, one should be quiet, stealthy, like James Bond. We were not James Bond. We were Gérard Depardieu and the cast of *Murder, She Wrote*. Lovely people, but I was feeling a disconnect between the remoteness of the locale and the familiarity of my shipmates. They, the native Fatu Hivans, however, were ready for us. They'd seen this show before, the monthly attack of well-traveled European pensioners, and even from a distance I could already discern the commercial gleam in their eyes. Much as I enjoyed the company of my fellow shipmates, I knew I'd have to leave them if I was to ever garner some kind of authentic Marquesan experience. It's why I liked traveling solo. The world presents itself unfiltered in all its mess and glory. This, I thought, as I beheld the scene that awaited us, was stagecraft, a well-rehearsed play. *See native handicrafts. See native dancing.* And so, as we landed, where we were soon gathered around a few local women for the Tapa-Making Demonstration, I figured I'd simply enjoy the scenery and find some way to work up a sweat. The last thing my home needed was another knickknack from the South Pacific, and I wandered away from the group, the guides, and the local ladies turning bark into a coarse paper, and walked on, whereupon I soon found myself in a long tin-roofed shed, bargaining over handicrafts.

What can I say? The reason I live in a home full of Pacific art is because I'm kind of a sucker for really well-crafted indigenous handiwork. Some people like oil paintings and ceramic cats. I like bark etchings and carved shells and scary masks made out of moss. As soon as I wandered into the shed, I could tell that this was a village that paid some serious attention to the making of art, in particular the tapa, which is crafted from the bark of mulberry, breadfruit, or giant banyan trees, upon which they painted figures and elaborate designs based on the tattoos that Marquesans traditionally inscribed upon their bodies, transforming their physical appearance into living canvases. They displayed their work on long adjoining tables, and as soon as I wandered in, the lone foreigner in their midst, they had but one urgent question for me: *"Est-ce qu'il y a des Américains sur le bateau?"*

Really, I thought, does the presence of Americans still bring such a tingle of wanton joy? Like the Japanese, Americans have a reputation for wildly overpaying for things when in foreign places. Lacking a bargaining culture of our own, the rest of the world sees us as walking ATM machines, and whenever a merchant encounters a Yankee accent, they quiver in anticipation. But those days are gone, I thought. I wanted to explain that times had changed. Whereas once the dollar had been king, it was now an enfeebled currency. The world, inexplicably, had become expensive. In the nineties, when I lived in Eastern Europe, I managed just fine on about a hundred dollars a month. Today, that covers perhaps two middling meals in a restaurant in Papeete. Even third-rate hip-hop stars today, when they do those videos displaying their affinity for booty and mullah, now prance about with wads of Euros and Swiss francs. And as for your average middle-class American, I wanted to explain to the handicraft sellers hovering around me, we have this weird retirement scheme where we are more or less obliged to hand over our savings to this place called Wall Street, which is kind of like entrusting your future to a leech, and as you watch it engorge itself with your blood, you simply hope that someday in the future, the leech will give it back. Most of us—especially those under the age of forty-five—don't have pensions like those Commie Europeans. And because leeches are not to be trusted, I wanted to add, Americans are now tightwads. Shocking, but true. It's like our whole national character has undergone some kind of seismic change, and you, dear foreign merchant, should be made aware. But instead, I said that regrettably there were no Americans on board. I could do this because I am a chameleon when it comes to nationality, and in this instance, it would do me no favors to be an American. Reputations die hard.

So I explained that, sadly, this was a boat of French, Germans, Swiss, and a couple of elderly New Zealanders, and I fear that I pretty much ruined their day. Cheapskates all, nationality-wise. I myself, today, would be Dutch, the cheapest, most penny-pinching, scrooge-like traveler on the planet, and so when I saw an extraordinary tapa made of darkened banyan cloth—perhaps five feet long and three feet wide—upon which a moving image of a dancing, tattooed Marquesan warrior had been painted, I felt I was well positioned, bargaining-wise.

"Twenty-five thousand," said my interlocutor, a cherubic woman with a friendly, albeit all-business, demeanor, who wore a hibiscus flower in her hair and whose skin glistened with coconut oil.

Well, that settled it. I didn't have 25,000 Polynesian francs, roughly the equivalent of 230 US dollars. And this was a cash-only island. I showed her exactly how much money I had in my wallet, because that's the kind of savvy negotiator that I am, and she quickly decided that all 20,000 francs in my possession would be adequate. But don't tell anyone, she whispered confidentially, and don't show your money. This, of course, was no longer a problem since she now had all of it. She assured me that, not to worry, she'd make sure the tapa would make its way back to the boat, and so I left it with her, because that's the kind of flinty-eyed judge of character that I am. As I departed, I could hear her talking to her compatriots, noting with delight this strange Dutchman, an apparition who shopped like one of those legendary Americans.

Pleased to have contributed my part to the local economy, and thrilled to have such a beautiful tapa, I walked onward through the sparsely inhabited village—a scattering of modest tin-roofed bungalows arranged around a white-steeple church—and found a dirt path leading deeper into the bush, toward the hills of the high country. It's a small island—a mere thirty-one square miles—but everywhere I turned my gaze it was like encountering a new land. Near the village, the fruit trees were enormous. Massive banana trees with giant clumps of green fruit; *pamplemousse*, or grapefruit the size of melons; there were trees bursting with ripe mangoes and, of course, breadfruit that hung from branches like Chinese lanterns. Even the noni, a foul-smelling fruit used throughout the Pacific for medicinal purposes, was gigantic, at least double the egg-size specimens I'd been familiar with. What was this place, I wondered? Jurassic Park? Even the pigs were gargantuan. I half expected to see some colossal pterodactyl circling above the valley, in the shadow of a verdant bowl of 3,500-foot mountains, hungering for a stray mammal ambling in the open on a sun-drenched path, looking for prey that was feeling mildly lost and befuddled.

But I walked with purpose. I immediately felt a greater affinity for Heyerdahl. He'd chosen his island well. It would be so easy, I knew, to live off the island's offerings. This was no grim, drought-stricken atoll. It was a veritable Eden. There were copious sources of food; the sea was aswarm with fish; every mountain beheld a freshwater stream. And while mosquitoes were a burden, the island lacked no-nos, the microscopic bloodsuckers and egg layers that bedevil so much of the Marquesas. If your inclination was to renounce Western civilization, you could do far worse than to set forth for Fatu Hiva. But of course, even in Heyerdahl's day, the world he sought to escape had already inflicted a heavy toll on Fatu Hiva.

The first Westerner to spot the island was the Spanish explorer Álvaro de Mendaña, who named the islands after his benefactor, the viceroy Las Marquesas de Mendoza, in 1595. Luckily for the Fatu Hivans he never made it to shore, which was most fortunate, because in the northern Marquesas, he had a habit of shooting locals on sight, while spending his downtime infecting hundreds of women with syphilis, and marking the occasion of his visit to what he thought was the fabled gold-laden kingdom of Solomon with three enormous crosses on the island of Tahuata. It wasn't until 1825 that the first Westerner set foot on Fatu Hiva, and it would take another fifty years until missionaries succeeded in converting the locals to Catholicism. By then, of course, the decimation of the population had begun in earnest, and the surviving remnants, mostly young adults—the diseases had carried away the small and the old—abandoned their hillside villages to settle into the two remaining coastal hamlets. Today, deep in the forests of Fatu Hiva and the other Marquesan islands, hundreds of ancient villages lie dormant and undisturbed, reclaimed by nature, hovered over by ghosts.

I was searching for one such remnant of the old Marquesas, a petroglyph that Heyerdahl examined, of which he waxed poetic, conjecturing about its resemblance to similar carvings in South America. I expected a longish trek, but found it after a half-hour amble up a grassy sidetrack surrounded by a canvas of coconut trees. It was up a small hillside, where I was startled by the bleating of a goat. I found a cluster of boulders, and casting my eyes deeper into the forest, the faint outlines of what I thought might be *maraes*, flat and terraced ceremonial clearings, now overgrown with bush-tumble and trees. Walking around the huge rocks, I found the petroglyph. Some say it is of a bonita, but to my untrained eyes it looked like a whale. It didn't have a little fishy mouth, but rather the lush-lipped open-mouthed cavern of a feeding whale, and if those leviathans were as rare then in these seas as they are now, it is no wonder that some Marquesan of yore had chosen to mark his encounter in stone. As I used my finger to trace its lengthy outline, I heard the rustling of palm fronds and felt the first stirrings of a morning breeze—some strange meteorological change was afoot. I felt a sudden chill in the warm, humidity-sodden air, and because my brain was no longer dull and foggy, and instead prone to wild imaginative leaps, I immediately thought of ghosts and the curse of the *tiki*, possibly because I watched far too much *Gilligan's Island* during my formative years, and I decided to hightail it out of there pronto. I'm telling you, this is a strange, magical island, a place, I thought, much more accommodating of the paranormal than Roswell. You *sense* things here.

I retraced my steps, or rather, galloped back to the village just in time to join the trekkers. We had been forewarned about this hike—a seventeen-kilometer tramp to the village of Hana-vave, the other hamlet located on what was once known as the fabled Bay of Penises, said to be the most beautiful in the South Pacific—the bay that is. We'd hike up to a summit of about 2,500 feet, followed by a knee-shattering descent to the village. Those with heart conditions, arrhythmia, high blood pressure, wobbly joints, and enormous beer bellies were strongly discouraged to attempt the hike—there would be no defibrillators brought on this journey—and they were soon whisked back to the boat, which would sail onward to Hanavave as soon as it had finished unloading its goods in Omoa. I checked out the remaining hikers. It seemed somehow important to be the first to summit, no matter how modest the peak. No way was I going to lose to some middle-aged periodontist from Dortmund. I'm not sure why this was important to me—it betrayed a lack of serenity—but I felt it crucial to demonstrate, if only to myself, that I was fitter than a group of balding, older, gray-weaved, arthritic retirees with dubious prostates and severe bunion problems. I scanned the assembled passengers, a healthy lot, all things considered, but detected no rival until my eyes met the steely gaze of the hard-bodied Swiss woman I'd encountered in the gym. She had a glint in her eye, and it suddenly occurred to me that she was probably some world-class alpinist for whom a 2,500 vertical climb was but a mere warm-up for a free ascent up the north wall of the Eiger. We had already established that we had no common language. She spoke neither English nor French, and my German—such as it is—found the Swiss dialect incomprehensible. I did, however, note that during meal times with her husband/partner her wineglass remained as empty as mine, which could mean nothing, or that we shared a particular commonality.

As we headed up a steep bush trail, I fell in step with Mareile, the archeologist on board. I told her about the petroglyph and the remnants of the *marae* platforms that I'd seen in the bush-tangle.

"They're everywhere on these islands. It makes me very sad to see them. Most have never been examined or excavated."

"Why not?" I wondered.

"Many are taboo. And even when we do receive permission, it is often rescinded the moment we find a skull or artifact. And sometimes bad things just happen. On the north coast of Hiva Oa, we'd begun excavations in caves full of petroglyphs and rock art. Unfortunately, while we were working, the chief's son fell out of the back of a pickup truck and smashed his head. When he died, the whole valley was declared taboo."

I reflected on this for a moment. It seemed evident to me

that the Marquesans actually *cared* about their heritage, which may seem obvious—what culture doesn't—but these islanders had become nearly as extinct as the dodo bird, and what they'd found when the onslaught of disease and contagion had finally run its course, leaving but a bare sliver of survivors, was a new regime of French functionaries and stern missionaries, determined to exterminate the last vestiges of the old ways.

"Yes," Mareile agreed. "And remember, it was only the young adults who'd survived, and they'd largely been unschooled in the ways of their ancestors. It was a lost people with no memory of the old ways. They were now taught French, instead of Marquesan. Church was mandatory. And they'd lost their connection to their forbearers."

Well, all that seemed depressing as hell. Usually, it takes the allure of television and the Internet to snuff out a culture, but not here. A little pestilence and plague, a few fire-and-brimstone preachers, and a sprinkling of French bureaucrats were enough for the Marquesan culture to be brought to the brink of doom.

"But these days, the Marquesas are such an optimistic place," Mareile added brightly.

Say what?

"Since the eighties, beginning in Hawaii, there's been a revival in Polynesian culture. And ever since the nineties, the Marquesans too have begun to search deep into their roots. They may not remember the legends or all the medicinal uses of plants found here, but they have reclaimed the old dances. They now teach Marquesan in the schools. And did you notice the woodcarvings and the tapas?"

"Yes," I said, "I even bought a large tapa—against my will—because my house already looks like the home of the Swiss Family Robinson."

She laughed at this. "You bought it, I suspect, because it was the most beautiful artwork you'd seen in the Pacific, right?"

I couldn't argue with that. The image on the tapa I'd bought—the dancing warrior—managed to be both joyful and melancholic, as if it were the portrait of some aged relative, now infirm and feeble, but for a brief moment, long ago, a camera had captured him with eyes full of vigor and dreams, the inevitable misfortune and disasters yet to befall him, and as he gazed into the lens with a warm, determined face, the shadows of life still seemed so distant, as it always does for the young, for whom hope and fate had yet to diverge.

"And how much did you pay for it, if you don't mind me asking?"

"Every franc I had. About twenty thousand."

"That's not so bad, you know. A couple of years ago an American paid more than two thousand dollars for a similar tapa."

"Ah," I said. Explains much, that.

"And have you seen the tattoos?" Mareile continued.

They were hard to miss. No tramp stamps here; nor the barbed-wire circling deflating biceps; and not a smidgen of inscrutable Chinese calligraphy found anywhere, ankles and shoulders included. This was the real deal, and as far as I could tell, every Marquesan over the age of eighteen was elaborately bedecked in the distinct, swirling designs of the islands, men and women alike. My favorite happened to be the ship's crane operator, who'd gone for the full-skull mask, a fearsome-looking man who was often bedecked with a flower tucked behind an ear pierced with a thick golden loop. On a smoke break, he'd told me of his desire to one day visit America. "But with this face," he'd said in French, "I don't think they'll let me in." And then he laughed like he couldn't care less.

"But what about kava? Do the Marquesans drink it today?" I inquired of Mareile, suddenly unsure whether this was a question asked with sincere curiosity, or whether this was a remnant of my lizard brain, searching for the local, traditional mind-altering brew. Stevenson, I remembered, wrote about kava, mentioning the narcotic effect the foul-tasting mud-water, which is made from the shredded remains of a particular pepper plant that grows high in the hills of Polynesia and Melanesia, had on a local chief. Kava was an important part of the traditional culture in the Marquesas. Had this too been reclaimed?

"No," Mareile noted. "It was among the first things the missionaries forbade. These days people prefer alcohol."

A poor trade in my opinion. Missionaries in the nineteenth century, with some notable exceptions—like Father Damien, who tended to the lepers exiled on the island of Molokai in Hawaii—could be such narrow-minded, overbearing half-wits. In fact, it was probably part of the job description. I was the kind of drunk who in the end preferred to simply amble up to the attic of my own mind, shut the shades, and tune out the world for a good, long while. Others—many, many others, apparently—get all riled up and agro after belting a few shots of whiskey. They cause problems, which is why drunkards have such a bad name. But no one causes trouble after a few shells of kava. They don't do anything, frankly, except from time to time look up at all the pretty stars and the lush glow of the moon and then they fall asleep and have weird and lively dreams. But kava was foreign, different, exotic, and unfamiliar for dogmatic evangelizers, and therefore it was banished by the narrow-minded clerical numb-skulls that seemed to make up the vast majority of the nineteenth-century missionary corps, whether French Catholics, English Episcopalians, or American Methodists. I think I can state with some certainty that the introduction of alcohol on the islands left a trail of carnage far deeper and wider than any that could reasonably be attributed to kava. I may have a little bias here, but if there happens to be a Marquesan reading this, go on, toss out the bottle of Pernod, go back to the old ways, and get yourself a nice bowl of kava. The Mrs. will thank you for it.

Mareile was obliged to wait for the huffing German-speaking contingent of hikers, and I hiked onward, soon encountering my old friend. "*Ça va bien, Edgar?*"

"*C'est extraordinaire, n'est-ce pas?*" my roommate said, wheezing, but with a bright twinkle in his eye. He was wearing his GOOD BUSH BAD BUSH T-shirt, upon which there was an image of our former president—that would be the bad Bush—next to a photo of a more feminine bush. Honestly, I don't make this stuff up. Go to the Marquesas, and eventually you'll see some tiny long-haired seventy-five-year-old French guy wearing a shirt with an image of the president next to the female pudendum. I have no explanation for this.

We were standing on a high ridge. To the left of us, steep cliffs cascaded a thousand feet and more to the darkened blue of a deep-water ocean, the white outline of the *Aranui* toy-like and fragile as it made its way around the headlands to the next village. Across from us, on the right, was a deep, lush valley and a wall of mountains, the Tauauoho range, which rose to a respectable 3,600 feet. Up here, the landscape had changed dramatically. It was more pastoral, with cragged pandanus trees bravely leaning over the ridgeline, and a topography that rolled and wobbled, like a green storm-tossed sea.

We stood there, admiring the scenery, until our eyes gazed across the valley and up the formidable wall of mountains, where we noticed a peculiar white oval-shaped *something*. Edgar thought it might be a satellite dish. This seemed highly improbable to me, and I asked if I could borrow his camera, whereupon I zoomed in. *"Non,"* I said, and then explained that it was a hole in the mountain, and if you looked closely, you could see a narrow, perilous cliff-side trail leading toward the opening. I recalled what I'd read in Heyerdahl's book. In the old days, Marquesan men, in the weeks preceding their marriage, were sent high up these cliffs and through this narrow porthole, which opened to the wild and forbidding eastern coast of Fatu Hiva, where they were expected to survive on their own, to become men, to prepare for their roles as husbands and fathers and village leaders.

This, I explained to Edgar, contrasts with my own particular culture, and since he appeared, judging from his T-shirt, to have certain preconceived notions about the United States, I felt it important to illustrate some of our own traditions. In my country, I explained, in the weeks preceding a marriage, men are expected to travel with a posse of their closest friends to a place in the desert, far away from their known world and all who know them. We call this place Las Vegas. And here too the men are expected to survive on their own, which they do by drinking copious amounts of liquor while carousing with strippers and gambling away their savings on games of chance. Afterward, they make a solemn oath to never tell another soul about their experience in this desert. What happens in Vegas, they say, stays in Vegas. Edgar said that he very much preferred the American tradition, and this pleased me because so many people these days have less than positive feelings about the United States, and so I try to do what I can, because what are we as travelers but ambassadors for our own countries?

I left Edgar to contemplate the mysteries of the American bachelor party and picked up my tempo. The trail led higher again and I walked past a few remaining hikers, nodding to them with a friendly *Bonjour* or *Guten Tag*, until I reached a series of steep switchbacks, shaded by a thick growth of trees, where the air suddenly felt cooler and misty. *Aha*, I thought, as I saw a familiar form, the Swiss woman from the gym, hiking alone with a determined pace, three switchbacks above me in the haze of a passing cloud. The competition. I realized, of course, that trying to beat a forty-ish woman to the top of a modest peak during a vacation cruise to the Marquesas was perhaps not the noblest or most uplifting of ambitions, that in fact it was kind of pathetic and small-minded, but having scraped across several bottoms and endured a few significant losses, I sought victory and triumph wherever I could. I climbed faster. I could feel a satisfying burn in my thighs and noted the increased rate of my pulse. Two switchbacks. Now one. And then she sensed my presence.

And she sped up! I could feel her thinking—no way was she going to let some forty-ish American beat her, a Swiss citizen, a woman of the mountains, to the summit. I increased my pace again. So did she. Unbelievable. There can't be more than two people on the planet who behave like this, and here we both were. I contemplated running. Should I do that? Just sprint past her with a *whoosh* and a cold, eat-my-dust, beady-eyed glance. I wanted to. But then what? I did a brief mental inventory. That would be really childish, wouldn't it? But not in a good way. And yet, I would then be first—like Edmund Hillary on Everest—and that would be a victory, a proud moment, an accomplishment to be celebrated for all time, a sweet memory for when I become old and feeble. But then she was out of my sight, and I rounded a corner, swiftly, the rubber burning off my shoes, and found her sitting on a picnic table. This was the mighty peak, the summit where we'd been told to wait for the others. She gave me a satisfied smile, cat-like. I smiled back, nobly, I thought, all relaxed, like I wasn't really trying to finish ahead of her or anything.

"*Grosser Gott*," I said, the only Alpine German I know, a common greeting heard in the mountains of Bavaria.

"*Grosser Gott*," she said with an arched eyebrow. God is great, indeed. And then she reached into her rucksack and pulled out a pack of Marlboro Reds, offering me one. Yes, I thought, we are definitely of the same tribe, and we sat quietly smoking, and though we had no more words to speak, it only takes two of our kind to call it a meeting. And this pleased me and I felt good and soon I was lifted from the crushing sting of defeat.

Oh, these missionaries. What have they wrought?

And I say this as a God-loving man, a churchgoer, a Roman Catholic, for Christ's sake. I didn't actually intend to become a Roman Catholic, of course, even though I'd been loosely raised as one. No, I'd wanted to become a Buddhist and study the Four Noble Truths and follow the Noble Eightfold Path as I learned of the Four Immeasurables while making my way through the Three Marks of Existence. And so when it was time for me to look into this Higher Power business, Buddhism had been my go-to religion. I spent time in monasteries in Tibet. I visited the sacred tree near Varanasi, India, where the Buddha, Mr. Siddhartha Gautama, delivered his first sermon. These Buddhists, I thought, seemed cheerful and jolly, happily pursuing the Middle Way, and I wanted whatever it was they had. But, as I soon learned, Buddhism isn't actually a religion with a Higher Power. It's a tool, a method for living, and though compassion is stressed, its precepts—at least to my eyes— involved enormous amounts of self-absorption and, frankly, the last thing I needed was to spend more time inside my head, though I did pick up, cafeteria-style, the habit of at least trying to meditate.

So I moved on, dragging my family—wife willing; kids not so much—from church to temple, trying to find a spiritual home that felt comfy and snug. We'd tried the Unitarians— nice people, Prius drivers, earnest bumper stickers—but there didn't seem to be much of a *there* there, and as we watched the congregation's youth club perform their interpretation of a Higher Power—the girls performing a skit in which they worshipped Justin Bieber; the boys a superhero robot—we said *adios*. We tried the Episcopalian Church, which was just as WASPy as we'd feared, and then, when we heard them sing, we covered our ears and fled. I'm sorry. It has to be said: Episcopalians sing like bleating goats. What to do? Should we become Jews? Many of our friends were Jewish. And Saturdays worked for us. But this conversion business? So much trouble, what with all the circumcisions, the Bar Mitzvahs, the learning of Hebrew. What else was there? I told my wife that I thought she'd look pretty fetching in a burka. Very mysterious. But that conversation went nowhere.

Finally, we shrugged and with no great hope, we wandered into a local Catholic Church. My wife too had been raised as a Catholic, and like so many had wandered onward. We had no great love for the Vatican. But then, inside the church, we heard the music, the singing, and it was spine tingling. And the sermon? It was about social justice. So we began to learn a little more about this particular church. It was gay friendly. Weekends were filled helping the homeless. There was a constant stream of volunteers and aid money being sent to Haiti. There was a Zen Buddhist meditation group that met in the church every Saturday. And others for single parents and the unemployed. *Whoa*, we thought. Was Rome aware of this parish?

We'd stumbled upon some rebellious outpost of the Church, where the priests were approachable and thoughtful, and always up for a good argument. They empathized with the phenomenon of doubt, valued and cultivated intellect and reason. They were—and I think I need to keep this quiet, lest some ambitious monsignor in Rome hears about it and files a report, but they belonged to an order with a long history of independent thinking—the Jesuits. We were happy here, and I even began to sing during Mass, which, because I sing like an Episcopalian, is an excellent way to embarrass your children.

So I'm no Church hater, no enemy of Christendom. But these early missionaries? They irk me. I've always had a suspicion that no matter which religion I choose to adhere to, I'll be wrong. Die, and the next you know you're face-to-face with the elephant god Ganesh. I figure it'll be no big deal, because after all, it's the effort that counts, and I like to think that the Supreme Being thinks likewise. In the meantime, it's nice to have choices. The more the better, I say. And this is what bothers me about missionaries. Imagine the world in say the year AD 1400—the astonishing diversity in beliefs and customs, all the extraordinary manifestations of spirituality, humans in every corner of the world finding their own way to the Big Questions, seeking to satiate some primal instinct to connect with the Cosmos. What a great menu of religion that would have been, and imagine that instead of greedy conquistadors and militant Wahhabists and prim Puritans, people would have been left free to choose their own way, guided by their own conscience and wandering curiosity. I'll tell you what that would be like: We'd still have the Bay of Penises in Fatu Hiva.

The descent from the summit was swift and punishing. Unlike the ascent, parts of the way down were paved. From time to time four-wheel-drive vehicles needed to make the journey from Omoa to Hanavave, and given the pitch of the mountain, it'd be impassable without this narrow sliver of cement. And it was bone-crushing, every step an act of gravity-defiance. But the views were stupendous. With every small movement of the sun, the palette of colors on Fatu Hiva changed and mutated, like an eternal kaleidoscope, lending to the island different moods, an ever-varying temperament. One moment you sense something serene and halcyon, and then as you turn a corner and come across some steep, cascading green rampart in the shadow of a passing cloud, you feel something intimidating and colossal, some force that was not to be trifled with. Lower down, I walked past a small shrine to the Virgin Mary, carved into the cliff and surrounded by stones and flowers, a foreshadowing of a certain name change.

Soon, I was down in the valley, back among the fruit trees and the swaying of coconut palm fronds. I heard the soft neighing of a horse tied to a tree and then the ever-present *whoosh* of the ocean, the sound of waves washing ashore. Hanavave is located in a narrow basin, surrounded by astonishing black basalt cliffs, many shaped like conical towers, which loom above the village. As I walked through the small settlement, there was nary a person to be seen, until I reached the rocky shore, where the men were loading bags full of noni to be transported back to Tahiti, while the women, all dressed in red lavalavas, waited for us visitors to arrive. *See native dancing.*

I headed straight to the water, took off my shoes and shirt, emptied my pockets, and dove in, swimming past the kids playing in the surf, and headed farther out, toward the deep water. I wanted to get a proper look at this bay, the full panorama, and I kept swimming, figuring that if there were little ones playing in the water, then there was unlikely to be a shark problem. It is the telltale sign in the South Pacific. Are the children in the water? If so, then it's all good. Or do they not dare play in the ocean? That's your cue right there that here lurk Tigers and Bulls and

Hammerheads, and therefore you do not swim, no matter how alluring the warm, lapping, azure sea. So I felt confident, safe, pleased to feel the grime of the hike wash off of me, and I swam until I was some distance out and finally I turned to take in the splendor of what many—or at least those few who have made it to Fatu Hiva—call the most beautiful bay in the world.

It is indeed striking and glorious and worthy of its reputation as one of the finest visual tableaus in the Pacific. The play of the late-afternoon light lent a soft radiance to this spectacle of cliffs and palms and a gentle curving shoreline above which rough, phallic-shaped towers of rock extended their shadows. It is obvious why, for so long, this place was known as the *Baie des Verges*, the Bay of Penises, a noble name, and also funny, which may be why I'm attached to it, since—as I've been told—for the addict/alcoholic, their emotional and intellectual development becomes stunted right around the moment of their first using, which would bring me exactly to the age when I'd think the phrase *Bay of Penises* guffaw-inducing hilarious. And perhaps that is why I felt so saddened that the missionaries deemed this description entirely unacceptable, and therefore they'd inserted a discreet *i*, a semantic fig leaf, so that it became the *Baie des Vierges*, the Bay of Virgins. As I treaded water and beheld the massive citadels, I didn't think that any actual virgins would take solace in the name change—those basalt towers are an intimidating sight.

But then my mind moved into an entirely different direction. I heard a splash nearby. And then another. Heavy splashes. My senses were now hyperaware. Tuna? No, they're a pelagic fish. They wouldn't be this close to shore. Wahoo? Barracuda? No, whatever it was was heavier, bigger. And then, not twenty yards distant I saw a fin. Oh no, really? This is how it ends? I finally clean up only to be eaten by a fucking shark. My heart was going *thump-thump-thump*. Then I saw another fin, three, six, more. And then I saw them leap and twist and dance in the air. Spinner dolphins. A whole pod of them, feeling footloose and acrobatic, and as I watched them swim by I thought it didn't really matter what you called this bay, and that Stevenson was right—as usual—when he said that your first island in the Marquesas will always, at the very least, touch a virginity of sense.

Chapter Six

On day six of this voyage on board the *Aranui III*, while docked in a small bay protruding deep into the island of Tahuatu, I discovered that I was wrong, apparently, about the correlation between children playing in the water and the presence of carnivorous sharks. The morning had begun promisingly enough with the sighting of a large manta ray swimming—no, flying, hovering, gliding—right next to the portside railing of the ship, where I had stood, breathless, in stunned wonder, for it had long been a dream of mine to actually see one of these wonders of the deep. Oh, oh, oh, I said over and over again, a manta ray, a manta ray. This was a lone wanderer, with perhaps a twelve-foot wingspan, and it moved with a gasp-inducing grace, silently flying near the surface, appraising the ship.

I immediately barreled my way toward the gangplank, stopping briefly to pick up snorkeling gear, and soon found myself on a cement jetty, where I scanned the shoreline for a suitable entry point into water colored a milky aquamarine. Swimming with manta rays was right up there on my Top 100 Things to Do Before I Croak list, and now was the time to seize the moment.

Fifty yards ahead of me I saw a small ramp, a boat launch, where a dozen kids cavorted and swam. A narrow seawall extended a short distance into the bay, creating a protected cove of calm water. The boat launch, I noticed, was slick and mossy green, and a few of the crazier kids took running starts and glided down the incline like tropical snowboarders before splashdown. I'm going to shatter my tailbone, I thought, if I'm not careful, but I figured the indignity of sliding down the ramp on my butt was worth the payoff of getting up close and personal with a manta ray. I marched onward with flippers dangling from my hands and a mask and snorkel jammed on my forehead. Three Marquesan women in repose, their forms shaded by trees from the morning glare, offered an indifferent *Bonjour*. I scanned the water, searching for the telltale shadows of surfacing manta rays, when right there in front of my nose, deep into this sheltered cove aswarm with precious little people, the water rippled as a dorsal fin emerged from the depths.

My head did a cartoon wobble, like it was trying to shake off the effects of a recent impact with a sledgehammer, just to make sure that my eyes were not lying. Not only was there a dorsal fin but it was immediately evident that it was attached to a not-insubstantial shark. There were no markings on the fin. This was not a white- or black-tipped reef shark. Maybe a grey. Or God forbid, a tiger. Or a bull. It kept swimming closer, languorously, methodically, until I saw its full shape. Six footer.

Eyes darted from shark to children. The adrenaline kicked in, and now I galloped like Roy Scheider on a Nantucket beach, trotting back and forth along the jetty. Shark. What should I do? The kids were oblivious. They needed to be warned. Think. I whirled toward the three Marquesan ladies. *"Excusez-moi,"* I said. *"Mais il y a un . . ."* What the hell was the French word for shark? *Re . . . "Mais il y a un requin là."* My mask had dislodged and was now burrowing into my left eye. I pointed a flipper toward the water.

The ladies glanced up. *"Oui,"* said one. *"C'est un requin."*

Yes, well, shouldn't we be doing something. Like blow a whistle. I turned to look at the shark. The water was so clear I could see every gill, the wet sheen of its dorsal fin reflecting sunlight, the death-stare of its eyes. It was just ten yards from the nearest kids, coldly stalking them.

"Il y a beaucoup de requins ici," said the same woman with a mirthful glint to her eyes. Might not be my place to say, but is it good parenting to let your kids play where there are *beaucoup de requins? "C'est pas dangereux,"* she said, reading my mind. Only in the South Pacific is a man-size torpedo-shaped fish with three rows of prehistoric teeth and a cantankerous disposition not regarded as dangerous.

I turned back toward the water. The shark was now gone, as stealthy in its disappearance as in its arrival. If this were the United States, there'd be mass pandemonium. Beaches would be shut down. Signs would be posted. A dozen lifeguards would spend their days toting binoculars, searching for shadows and ominous dorsal fins. But we were not in the United States. This was the Marquesas. I stood there for a moment pondering the situation and concluded that I needed to man up. Surely, the ladies were right. Reef sharks are not dangerous. Yes? And somewhere out there was a curious manta ray. I watched a couple of boys swoosh down the ramp like it was made out of frozen ice. That, I thought, is dangerous. Let's maintain perspective.

So I approached the ramp, sat on my bottom, and scooted toward the water. Apparently, the sight of a foreign man with a mask and snorkel resting askew on his head, sliding down a boat ramp like a toddler on a slide, is regarded as funny in the Marquesan culture. The kids hooted and laughed and pointed and basically collapsed in a pile of mirth. Yes, well, I thought, you know what would be really funny? My falling on my ass. But I denied them that joy and inched my way down.

The commotion interested the three ladies and they peered over the jetty to see what all the hubbub was about. I reached the water and was busy putting on my flippers when they asked where, exactly, was I planning on going snorkeling. I pointed toward the deep water beyond the seawall and said that I was heading yonder. "*Je cherche pour une* manta ray," I said. The women nodded. "*Ce n'est pas dangereux? N'est-ce pas?*" If the kids are in the water, then the water is safe. This has always been my guiding principle when swimming in this part of the world. Sure, there might be a few reef sharks but as long as you hadn't nicked yourself shaving then it was fine, right?

The women wrinkled their noses. "*Non, c'est pas très dangereux.*" Was that a qualifier, that *très* there? Not very dangerous. What did she mean with *not very dangerous*? "*Mais faites attention aux requins-marteaux.*" Pay attention to a what now?

"*C'est quoi ça?*" I asked with great hesitation.

The women all tried to explain just what, precisely, a *requin-marteau* was. It sounded like a really high-end cognac, and like cognac, I gathered that this was something I should seek to avoid. But still, I had not an inkling of which particular species of shark we were discussing until a boy used his finger to sketch its distinctive shape on the mossy surface of the boat ramp. It looked like a menacing whale that had swallowed an anvil.

"Hammerhead?"

Oui they all said in unison. "Ammer-ead."

Evidently few things are more entertaining for Marquesans than the spectacle of some foreigner attempting to crawl up a moss-sodden cement boat ramp upon learning of the presence of *requins-marteaux*. Really, I don't think we need to draw this out, but as I wandered back to the ship, listening to the guffaws and twittering of the locals, I saw the winged shadow of a manta ray languorously swimming in the middle of the bay, serenely gliding above swarms of hammerhead sharks. That's how they roll, you know—in packs of dozens, with a few twenty-foot alpha sharks leading the hunt. Swimming with manta rays was on my list of things to do; swimming with hammerheads not so much; and here, apparently, you have to choose. For me, the only choice was to walk away. Were I to create a list of 100 Things Not to Do Before I Croak, swimming with sharks, particularly known man-eaters like the hammerhead (currently holding the number eight spot on the International Shark Attack File) would definitely crack the top ten, and since I could already cross off at least seven items on that checklist (falling off a waterfall, getting shot at, ending up in rehab, etc.), I was happy to stay dry. This was a list where I needed to keep a few openings.

Chapter Seven

Q*u'est-ce que tu fais?"*
       This would be Yvonne, standing next to me in our
narrow galley bathroom as I stood in front of the mirror, shirtless, performing my morning ablutions. I was pleased to hear
the familiar *tu*. I guess it's inevitable when you share a bed-
room. Eventually, all formality disappears, even among the
French. But I had no answer for her. I searched hard in my
francophone brain, but I could not find the word for *nipple*.

How to explain, I wondered, the phenomenon of chaffing?
I'd been preparing for a run that day and knew the tropical sun
well enough to realize that going shirtless would be madness.
It would be hot and sunny, and no matter how much SPF 500
sunscreen I slathered on, it would soon dissipate with my sweat,
and I'd finish the day looking like an overcooked lobster, spending my remaining time in the Marquesas moving about like a
shedding robot, grimacing in pain, as I'd leave a serpentine trail
of peeling skin in my wake. Obviously, I should wear a shirt,
which would get sodden with sweat, and then it would scrub
against my nips, over and over again, mile after mile, and that
would hurt, and while I'm okay with a certain amount of agony

and misery, I draw the line at bleeding nipples. My solution was Vaseline. Few things are more discomforting than a post-run shower with nipples that feel like they'd been voraciously consumed by twins with emerging vampire fangs. I'll say this about the long-distance male runner: To breastfeeding moms, we understand now.

And so, as I slathered on the Vaseline, I tried to explain that I was going to run from Vaipaee to Hane, the two villages on the island of Ua Huka. I guestimated that it was about a ten-mile run, which normally wouldn't be a problem, but I had no idea what kind of hills I'd face. Like all the islands in the Marquesas, Ua Huku had emerged from a cataclysmic volcanic eruption, rising to a lofty 2,800 feet. A flat island this was not. There were a mere 480 people living on this dry, crescent-shaped island, outnumbered by wild horses that'd been brought over from Chile more than a century ago. And so I prepared for the worst—Vaseline, of course, sunscreen, a baseball cap, and a large bottle of water, wishing now that I had brought a camel-back, because I hated running with the rhythm-impinging feel of a water bottle in my hands.

Yvonne was an engineer by trade, and she understood the problem immediately. Also, she was a woman. *"Tu es fou,"* she declared. You have no idea, I wanted to add. But this, I thought, as I put on my shirt and laced my running shoes, was what kept me sane.

I'd been reading Haruki Murakami, the Japanese author, on my Kindle. He'd written a treatise called *What I Talk About When I Talk About Running.* I admired him for his discipline. He'd declared his intent to become a serious runner, which for him consisted of a baseline of 36 miles a week, or 6 miles a day for six days a week, for a total of 156 miles a month. After some time at that distance, he increased it to 186 miles a month, and soon he was habitually running marathons in under three and a half hours. I envied his systematic approach. I, on the other hand, ran according to whim. Once I had attained a certain ability for distance running, I ran however far my soul dictated. Some days, when it didn't feel right, particularly while I was destroying my Achilles tendons, I pulled up after four miles. On others, when all I intended to do was a six-mile jog, I would feel so good or I'd be so deep in thought that eighteen miles would pass before I called it a satisfying workout.

Murakami wrote of running as a kind of meditative event. I'd tried the meditative run, but since I'd learned how to meditate by focusing on my breathing, stilling the monkey mind by concentrating on the simple inhalation and expulsion of air, I found it completely counterproductive when running. During a good meditative session, when stillness was crucial, the breathing would eventually lead to a kind of emptiness, and I could feel—kooky as it sounds—some kind of dreamy, floating sensation, as if I were hovering not so much above the universe, but within it, like I'd been atomized and disassembled and now just existed, connected to the same life force that created the Crab Nebula or a single-cell organism. This rarely happened, however. I've got tribes of monkeys living in my head.

But concentrating on my breathing while running just left me feeling winded. Breathe in, breathe out, would soon turn to gasp in, gasp out, and all I'd focus on was my air intake, and how it seemed insufficient, and wouldn't it be preferable to stop right here and now, and sit down, maybe have a sandwich, and think of something else, like how good a bar of Toblerone would taste. For me, running alternated between the plodding, let's go forward, one step at a time, and just move on kind of running; or alternatively, I'd find myself so deep in thought that every step, every mile, seemed to pass accidently, thoughtlessly, without effort, and soon I'd find myself in another state.

Unless pain was involved.

"Pain is inevitable," Murakami had written. "Suffering is optional."

This struck me as a very Buddhist sentiment. I had chosen the Catholic team, of course. We're all about suffering.

We had tied up the ship . . . No, let me rephrase that. At the crack of dawn, four psychotic members of the crew—divided into two teams—grabbed the heavy, water-sodden ropes and set forth in small boats to secure the lines to shore. And I am using the word *shore* very loosely here. This was a narrow anchorage, a channel wedged between steep cliffs that in the morning sunlight looked like a mesa found in the American Southwest. The ocean waves rose and fell as they funneled through a daunting hourglass of dizzying precipices into a shallow cove, forcing the rope guys to time their leaps perfectly as they jumped—while carrying ropes as thick as your thigh—onto a narrow sliver of wet, crumbling rock, which they did with considerable aplomb as Edgar led the early-bird passengers through a rousing cheer.

Once again, we boarded our landing craft and approached the island with all the subtlety of the 2nd Battalion 3rd Marines and proceeded to lay siege. I believe the itinerary for the day included handicrafts, horseback riding, a visit to an arboretum, followed by artillery practice, marching drills, latrine digging, and a nice Polynesian buffet. I, however, had decided to desert and it wasn't long before ditchdigging seemed like a dreamy alternative to the foolishness I had committed myself to.

Did I mention that there are hills in the Marquesas? Well, there are. Big ones. Where I come from hills are finite and manageable. They tend to roll. If they ever get steep, it's usually just for a couple of blocks and then they even out and you resume your nice, leisurely run. Not so on these islands. While the other passengers were busy perusing the handicraft skills of Vaipaee's artisans, I set out to see what it's like to have a cardiac event nine hundred miles from the nearest emergency room. It began right from the get-go, as I followed a narrow road that rose precipitously just outside the village, switchback after switchback on a dry, sun-drenched hillside. No breeze reached these canyons, and it wasn't long before I felt the grinding, unrelenting heat. Typically, I didn't mind running in sultry weather. Sure, you may collapse of heat stroke but at least your muscles are nice and limber. Nothing had quite prepared me though for mile after mile of torturous uphill running under an unrelenting sun. It seemed to go on forever and soon my thighs were burning, my pulse was thumping, and every breath was painful. Only a couple of miles in, and already this had turned into one of those really snotty runs, where the inhalation and expulsion of air becomes violent and explosive. Just as I was beginning to flag, a jeep passed me carrying a French television crew, who were here filming a documentary about the *Aranui* and the Marquesas. *Allez, allez, allez*, they yelled as I choked on their dust. Okay, I thought, I shall *allez* a little farther before I collapse and die, and when this seemed imminent, an entire caravan of passengers rolled past me, all loaded into jeeps, like they were heading toward the Battle of Inchon. Again with the *allez, allez, allez*. No wonder all those guys on the Tour de France are doped up. If that was the only word I heard for three weeks, I'd resort to drugs too.

Fortunately, I'm not a drug addict, just an alcoholic, and now all the skills and habits I had learned as a lush served me well. The single-minded fealty to a goal irrespective of costs. The grim acceptance of misery, and the Jedi mind trick that tells you that it's not so bad. The conviction, false or otherwise, that says, any minute now, this is going to feel good. The enthusiastic acceptance of your abnormality: Normal people do not run up hills with a 10 percent grade in ninety-five degree weather; but you are not normal, and therefore it's okay. The determination to keep going even if it means an early death.

This was a mind-set that felt familiar to me. *Embrace the suffering*. If you can drink a liter of vodka, you have what it takes to become an Ironman. It's true. It takes years of steadfast devotion, untold months of anguish, an unwavering commitment to solitude, a fondness for taking things to the edge, and a constitution that embraces pain for you to succeed at either endeavor. You never start out believing that you can down a bottle of vodka but with enough practice and diligence you find that it becomes second nature. The important thing is persistence. And so it is with running. A year earlier, if you had told me that one day I'd be running mile after mile up a steep-sided slope in withering heat on a faraway island—for the fun of it, no less—I would have looked at my wobbling gut and snorted with laughter. Not bloody likely. Which goes to show you how unpredictable life can be. You can do it, I told myself, even as my legs and lungs were telling me otherwise. Keep going. Don't stop. And I didn't, and as I crested the summit, there before me lay a sweeping vista, a cascade of mountain ridges and grassy valleys, and the shimmering blue ocean.

I could see a lonesome runway, but otherwise the entire panorama betrayed not even a hint of human activity, except, of course, the road, which I was pleased to see now followed the contours of the island, a long downhill glide and then a few trifling bumps until it curved into the next bay, where I presumed I'd find the tiny hamlet of Hane. I drank what remained of my water and ran onward. There's an air of striking desolation on Ua Huka, an austerity that suggests little rain ever falls here. Every island in the Marquesas appeared to have its own microclimate, from lavishly green Fatu Hiva to the dry severity of Ua Huka. Despite the lack of trees and shade, heat exhaustion was staved off by a constant breeze that flowed uninterrupted from the ocean, and as I made my way to Hane it occurred to me that running is different from drinking in at least one fundamental way—you never regret it when you're done.

And so I ran happily onward, until I reached a little village of tin-roofed bungalows at the mouth of a sterling bay. Here too all activity seemed to have been suspended as the inhabitants gathered near the shore in front of a small museum, where they nodded and dozed in a listless heat, awaiting the arrival of the cavalcade of jeeps that would deposit the *Aranui* passengers. One look at me and it was apparent that I was unlikely to do anything uplifting for the local economy. Clearly, anyone foolish enough to run across the island would also be the kind of thoughtless moron to spend all his cash on the first handicraft he saw on the first island he visited, which is too bad because the good citizens of Ua Huka are veritable master carvers and sculptors. I spent a few minutes perusing tikis and bowls made out of rosewood and coconut wood, and soon joined the French television crew, who were sitting on a stoop, seeking a shady respite from the heat. We got to chatting and it wasn't long before I nixed the neuroscientist option for the next life. What I really wanted to be now, should we get to do this again, is a TV sound guy.

Seriously. There were three of them, all roughly in their thirties, and they spent their time traveling the world, putting together documentaries about the earth's wonders. The on-screen talent, I learned, did indeed write his own scripts, and came off as the Boss Man for the trio. He was the one with all the responsibilities—deciding on shots, dealing with the Home Office, periodically having to shave, etc. The camera guy did all the heavy lifting and was always one hernia or one dropped camera away from ruin. And the sound guy? He just stands there holding a lightweight microphone and a headset. Then *ka-ching*, paycheck, and he trots off to the Andes. It sounded ideal to me, a lazy traveler's ideal profession. No thinking. No lifting of heavy objects. Just keep the mike out of the camera's view and know what a woofer is. Easy-peasy. Then they asked me what I did.

"*Je suis un écrivain*," I said, suddenly feeling very pompous. When speaking in English, if you say that you are a writer people tend to look at you fondly, and then they'll tell you exactly what they wanted to be when they were little—a fireman, a bunny doctor, a Power Ranger—before they grew up and became responsible adults. From then on, whenever they introduce you to others, their eyes get a little misty when they mention, with a conspiratorial wink, *He's a writer*, as if they were announcing the discovery of the neighborhood hobbit. Or they look at you blankly, waiting for you to finish the sentence: "I mean, that's what I do in between shifts at Denny's."

Say that you are a writer in French, however, and people just assume that you've already won the Nobel Prize in Literature—twice. You are immediately regarded as some kind of formidable intellectual in possession of a golden tongue and a devastating wit. You may look like an unwashed, overweight accountant in desperate need of a haircut, but you will now be regarded as roguishly sexy. How else to explain the existence of Bernard-Henri Lévy, France's most famous writer, a comically affected old geezer who traipses around the world in immaculate white shirts that he wears unbuttoned to the navel as he defends the privileged male's *droit de seigneur*? This would never happen in America, where writers are regarded as affectionate pets, whimsical Peter Pans always two steps removed from adulthood, until they become bitter and old and take up tenure in the nation's college English departments. It's no wonder, really, that so many American writers speak so fondly of France. All you have to say is *je suis un écrivain* and people stand up as if in the presence of greatness.

Which is exactly what this television crew now did as they shuffled to their feet. They appeared to be under the assumption that I lived in Los Angeles, possibly because they had seen me running, which is something only vain, body-conscious people did, ergo L.A. Also, the on-screen talent and I wore the exact same kind of sunglasses, which made this a perceptive assumption, since I did indeed buy my shades at the duty-free in LAX, shortly after I'd slapped my forehead with a big *d'oh* when I'd realized I'd forgotten to pack a pair. It hadn't occurred to me that in the depths of an East Coast winter that it might be sunny in the South Pacific. Naturally, they put two and two together—writer plus Los Angeles equals screenwriter—and they asked me what films I'd written. Tempted as I was to take credit for *Gigli*, I explained that I was just a regular old writer, the kind who calls a tweet a good, productive day.

"*Ah,*" the cameraman said. "*Comme Hemingway ou Hunter Thompson?*"

Do you see what I mean? Immediately, there is this presumption that because you are *un écrivain* you are comparable to two of the titans of twentieth-century American literature. Words again failed me as I searched for the French equivalent of *hack*, so I described myself as a travel writer, which is pretty much the same thing. Immediately, they wanted to know what I thought of the Marquesas.

How to explain the magnificence of the islands? How to convey the majesty, the ethereal beauty, the haunting history of the Marquesas? I thought for a moment. "*C'est très . . . jolie.*"

Yes, they agreed. It is very pretty. And we stood there for a long moment soaking in all this prettiness. But why, the on-screen talent wanted to know as he took a deep drag off a cigarette, did I decide to run up that monstrous hill. Oh, I don't know, I thought. Maybe because I don't want to end my days fellating a shotgun like those pill-popping alcoholics Ernest Hemingway and Hunter Thompson. But this seemed too complicated for me to express in French. I filched a cigarette and thought of what Papa might have said.

"Because," I said in French, exhaling a plume of smoke, "it was there." And then I turned my gaze to the mountains, to my conquest, squinting with grim delight. I had triumphed over Nature's cruelties. I was a Man. And I was *un écrivain*. The world submits before me.

They nodded reverentially at the deep sagacity of it all, and I thought, you know, I really need to move to France. I could get used to this.

Chapter Eight

I wasn't feeling particularly happy with this smoking business, however. I knew, of course, that there is a strong correlation between nicotine addiction and alcoholism. Almost no one in the developed world smokes anymore except for the lushes. Eighty percent of all alkies smoke. As for the other 20 percent—the health-conscious drunks and pill poppers who only eat organic foods and manage to stay the onset of the inevitable booze gut through a rigorous devotion to Pilates and daily runs as they shovel fistfuls of Vicodin down their gullets followed by three bottles of red wine (red because it's *heart smart*)? They pick up smoking once they get to rehab.

It's true. At my particular institution of choice, we were allowed just one phone call a week. No Internet. No e-mail. Just one call. The first words out of my mouth were *Send a carton of smokes now.* They say that for the alcoholic giving up the drink, a yawning void suddenly opens up and it needs to be filled pronto. In rehab, it's filled with nicotine. This is a dumb thing to do, of course, but people going through withdrawal aren't exactly feeling like the sharpest tools in the shed. Conventional wisdom says that you should only deal with one addiction at a time. This, of course, is the equivalent of telling an alcoholic that now would be a good time to take up a two-pack-a-day habit, maybe hit the casinos in Atlantic City, and develop a nice little sugar addiction. Science, however, tells us that it's best to dispense with all the vices at the same time. If you're going to suffer, might as well be efficient about it. Neurological tests done six months after treatment show that alcoholics who also refrained from smoking demonstrated far higher rates of brain repair than those who continued to smoke. So I'd quit again not long after I was discharged and assumed a health-conscious lifestyle. If life was going to suck for a while, best to get it done and over with.

And so I felt guilty as I danced with the nicotine devil again. I was the worst kind of smoker now—the moocher, the sort of person that refused to buy a pack of their own, thinking that it didn't really count as long as I refrained from purchasing smokes myself. But smoking here satisfied some primal impulse. It was illicit, which in my way of thinking equated something good. It felt foolish and reckless—also a plus in my book. And it replicated what drinking did for me at the end—a brief rush, followed by dizziness, nausea, a skull-shattering headache, and waves of remorse. It was a perfect substitute. And, I reasoned, of the two addictions nicotine was far preferable to alcohol. Both will kill you, but only alcohol will turn you into a self-absorbed asshole.

If there is one island where we can do a little compare-and-contrast of the two addictions it is Hiva Oa. There are two celebrities buried in the Calvary Cemetery in Atuona, a surprisingly substantial town of 1,500 (a lot for the Marquesas) that lies in the shadow of a 4,000-foot eminence called Mount Temetiu, a striking prominence with a steep, verdant crest around which, on an otherwise sunny day, a swirl of puffy white clouds elicited a dramatic windswept plume, as if God's hair dryer was now focused on its slopes. It was here that Jacques Brel lived his remaining years.

You know, of course, who Jacques Brel is, right? Neither did I. But he is, apparently, a legend in the francophone world. If I were to summarize, I'd call him the male Edith Piaf, a singer of chansons about loss, obsession, death, and all sorts of other cheery subjects. He was Belgian, so maybe that explains it. Have you ever met a happy Belgian? Exactly. But Brel was wildly successful, selling a gazillion albums and appearing in more than ten films in the fifties and sixties. And then he learned that he had a tumor on his lung. So what did he do? He bought a sixty-foot ketch and sailed off to the South Pacific.

I liked him immediately. When confronted with death, do you look it in the eye? No, you run away. He had planned on a three-month circumnavigation of the world, but perhaps summoning the spirit of Robert Louis Stevenson, he elected to stay in the South Seas, and after a fifty-nine-day sail across the Pacific he found himself on Hiva Oa, which he would come to know as home. But why this island?

Legend has it that upon arrival, Brel encountered a few teenage boys strumming a guitar. Casually mentioning that from time to time he liked to carry a tune as well, the boys lent him their instrument, whereupon he sang a couple of his hits in his deep, lugubrious voice. When he finished, the boys regarded him silently, and then informed him that he can't sing worth *merde*, and proceeded to demonstrate what a good Marquesan song sounded like. Brel enjoyed the response so much, and the implied promise of anonymity, that he elected to stay.

He took to a modest cottage in the hills above town and proceeded to pursue all sorts of ennobling endeavors. He built the first cinema in the Marquesas. He took up flying, soon buying a plane of his own, which he called *Jojo*, and used it as an air ambulance, ferrying the sick and the wounded to distant Papeete. Today, you can find Jacques Brel's plane, a Beechcraft D50C Twin Bonanza, in a small museum in Atuona, a lovingly crafted space devoted to his memory. It reminded me of one of those small-town museums that display an assortment of curios and artifacts, all gathered by townsfolk with a great affection for the place and a determination that no one forget their little corner of earth. Jacques Brel was not long for this world, alas. He died of lung cancer at the age of forty-nine, and now lies in a simple, well-tended grave, surrounded by flowers and ferns, and stacks of stones where visitors deposit their prayers and remembrances. He was a smoker, obviously, but more importantly he was a good, noble, altruistic person, so score one for the smokers.

Now let's consider the active alcoholic/addict. A few yards from Brel's final resting place lies another grave. It's unusual in that above it, on the hillside, are acres of white crosses, the tombs of priests and nuns and devoted Catholics, whereas this one is made of red volcanic rocks, and instead of a cross or headstone, it is lorded over by a statue of a wild man, a paean to *La Vie Sauvage*. At its base is a simple, white, hand-painted inscription—PAUL GAUGUIN 1903.

As I stood before it, I found myself next to Mareile. Many of the passengers had elected to board a bus for the short journey from the pier to the cemetery, and we had walked together, stopping first at a black sand beach, and departing moments later after we were enveloped in a blizzard of no-nos, which are the planet's most irritating insects, and reason enough to bring back DDT (I jest. Mostly). As we'd walked, we'd discussed Gauguin. Yes, he made nice pictures, and, yes, his impact upon the art world was enormously influential, but I was more interested in the man himself. As we approached his grave, I asked Mareile about what was known about Gauguin's vices—what did he consume and how much? This was the sort of minutia I was interested in.

"In 2003," she said, "we excavated a pit next to his home, where we found bottles of wine, absinthe, and morphine. Matching it to store records, we estimated that on a typical day, Gauguin drank a bottle of wine, a few draughts of absinthe, followed by some morphine. So you see, it wasn't so much."

So scratch moving back to Europe. Obviously, I can't live there again. In much of Europe you're not considered an alcoholic until you wake up underneath a highway overpass and begin your morning with a shot of antifreeze and a gulp of perfume, followed by a lunch of vanilla extract and a pint of mouthwash, and then you tumble through the remainder of your day, waving at your neighbors who merely regard you as a devilish bon vivant. Knowing a little something about how an alcoholic operates and the extraordinary acts of subterfuge involved in covering one's tracks, I suspected that Gauguin imbibed a trifle more than that—you need only read his writing to realize that he was a seriously fucked-up individual—but let's say for the sake of argument that a bottle of wine, an unknown amount of absinthe, and a few shots of morphine constituted his daily intake. It would kill a normal man.

Let's ignore the wine altogether. Thomas Jefferson drank a bottle a day. Lots of people do. If I'd been able to maintain that level of drinking, it's unlikely that I would have ever given it up. But absinthe? The old-school 150-proof green nectar, the spirit known for its hallucinogenic qualities, the firewater that by 1915 was banned throughout Europe and the United States? Mixed with morphine, the most powerful opiate ever created? That shit will mess you up. In fact, the two sedatives will conspire with your brain and tell it, hey, let's not bother with this breathing business. Let's just . . . drift off. Did you get that, kids? Do not mix opiates with alcohol. You'll pass out and the next thing you know you're face-to-face with Ganesh.

Obviously, it takes years to acquire that kind of tolerance. If you do a trajectory of Gauguin's life, you can match the progression of the disease with the ever-flourishing degree of asshole-dom that he exhibited. Born in Paris in 1848, Gauguin moved to Peru as a wee lad, getting an early jump on the itinerant life that he would pursue until his death. He returned to France, spent some time in the navy and the merchant marine, and began a career as a stockbroker. He'd married and soon found himself the proud papa of five children. Paul Gauguin, at this moment in time, is Mr. Bourgeois himself. And then he took up painting.

It is here where your opinion of him all comes down to your perception, your disposition, your values. For many, this is all that matters: A gifted man found his calling and in the years to come filled canvas after canvas with brilliant, inspired strokes, enriching the cultural heritage of the world. Let the art speak for itself, most will say. The foibles and personal failures of the artist have no relevance. Art for art's sake.

Then there are the romanticists, the ones who see in Gauguin a noble, burning vision, a brave willingness to unshackle himself from the pedestrian, suffocating mores of the day, the savage aflame with the pursuit of art. Gauguin abandoned his family in Denmark, where he'd gone to pursue a business that went sour. No matter, the dream beckoned and he wandered first to Brittany and then Provence, where he spent his time painting, carousing, acquiring syphilis, and hanging out with Vincent van Gogh, who had two ears at the start of their friendship, but just one at the end. Make of that what you will. But here Gauguin acquired his extraordinary palette of colors, the breakthrough style that somehow took the best of impressionism, symbolism, and naturalism, and created a new visual language, one that spoke to Cézanne and Matisse and Picasso and generations of artists to follow. He yearned for simplicity, the primal, the savage, and in its pursuit he moved onward to Martinique, to Tahiti, and finally to the Marquesas, to Hiva Oa, where he died in penury, because our silly, narrow-minded world could not fathom his brilliance. He was dazzling, misunderstood, and an inspiration for those willing to sacrifice everything for the immortality of beauty.

Or you could put on your schoolmarm's glasses and simply regard Paul Gauguin as an alcoholic/addict doing what is called the geographic, the ceaseless moving to escape his own asshole self. I know: Pot meet kettle. I have considerable expertise in asshole-dom, it's true. I know of what I speak. Leave the kids at home alone late at night as I go out and search for one more bottle. Passing out midday and forgetting to pick up these very same children from school. The endless lies. The going off on weekends so I could quote work unquote and drink myself into oblivion. And these are the people I love more dearly than life itself, and yet, in the throes of addiction, that was what I was reduced to—an asshole. It's why in meetings, I think we need to change our standard greeting. It should be: Hi, I'm Maarten. And I'm an assoholic. The recent advances in the neuroscience of addiction are all well and good, but for the afflicted, in order to move on, it's best to acknowledge what, exactly, we truly are when we imbibe—incorrigible assholes.

Which is why Paul Gauguin interests me so much. It's not his paintings, wood carvings, and sculptures, though I do admire them and think they rightfully belong in the pantheon of the greats. No, what rings my bell is the sheer depravity of his asshole-ness. We don't even need to look to outside sources for confirmation of his loathsomeness. Just pick up *Noa Noa*, his little book about his time in Tahiti. Right there on page fourteen, after encountering "young women and young girls, tranquil of eye, pure Tahitians," he goes on to describe their inner lives: "All, indeed, wish to be taken, literally, brutally taken without a single word. All have the secret desire for violence." In this way, he continues, "she has not given her consent for the beginning of a permanent love . . . it has a savage sort of charm."

Now, I grant you, I never read *Fifty Shades of Grey*, so what do I know? But I'm going to guess that being mauled by a goateed, pot-bellied Frenchman with a Pinocchio nose, reeking of liquor and with the dead-eyed stare of the morphine-addict, probably doesn't figure very prominently in the fantasy lives of women, young or old, islander or continental. But Gauguin wasn't really interested in grown women. He was a pedophile, a syphilitic sexual tourist who in between painting and getting plastered abused girls and young women by the score, leaving a trail of infections and unwanted children in his wake. He claimed to yearn for freedom from civilization and artifice, to live unmoored by rules and custom, so that he could pursue a higher, truer existence, the life of the savage, a term he fetishized. It was his reasoning, his justification for the life that he led, which was sordid and unhappy. Reading *Noa Noa* is like reading the mawkish notes of the criminal rationalizing the crime. Tahiti left him "brutally disappointed." It was too civilized for him, and he departed for farther shores, to Hiva Oa. He too has a museum here, and you could tell right away that it was an official, government-sanctioned kind of Cultural Center with sterile videologues, sanctimonious descriptions about his life and work, and a re-creation of his *Maison du Jouir*, or House of Pleasure, complete with a fishing pole dangling from the second-story open window, which Gauguin used to fetch his bottles from his well. This, I think, was meant to convey something charming and rascally about Gauguin. Of course, what I saw was the ingenious solution to that most intractable of problems confronting the addict/alcoholic—stairs. They are a fucking nightmare when you're fucked-up. You think it's a coincidence that most of us end up in a double-wide trailer instead of a fifth-floor walk-up? No, that's what passes for forethought among junkies and drunks.

There is no original art remaining in the museum, just desultory reproductions. His years on Hiva Oa must have been miserable ones. He did not have long to live as his body was ravaged by advanced alcoholism and syphilis. Or perhaps it was a fatal dose of morphine that finally did him in. More telling, is the stunning absence of friends or companions during his last days on Hiva Oa.

Standing before his tomb, which, I noted, carried far fewer prayer stones than Jacques Brel's plot, I turned to Mareile.

"He's not really there, is he?" I said, pointing to the grave.

"Probably not," she acknowledged.

"So, we're just standing here looking at a pile of rocks."

"Most likely."

"And, any idea where his bones might lie?"

"Well, they could be in a mass grave in the old, overgrown cemetery. More likely, he was buried in the bush somewhere. He was just regarded as another poor, dissolute foreigner on the island. He wasn't the only one. And when they died they just disposed of the bodies as they saw fit."

See, alcoholism/drug addiction bad. Smoking okay. No one misses Paul Gauguin. We're not even sure where he is. Sure, we like his work, though knowing a little more about him, I can't quite figure out why his paintings command the big bucks.

They seem so idyllic, so natural, so innocent, and yet, if you know anything about their creator, you realize that they are morally fraudulent. These are no celebrations of the primitive, the pure, the uncorrupted. They now seem cloying and sentimental to me, except for his self-portraits, which are unsparing and painted with a gimlet eye chronicling the wreckage of the passing years.

As I walked through the town—there really isn't much to see, frankly—I found a tourist office, which surprised me, because as far as I could tell there weren't any tourists, save for ourselves, and we'd just be lingering for a couple of hours, perusing the lives of a couple of dead men. I walked in, met a friendly young Marquesan woman, and asked in French whether she happened to have a lot of visitors to Hiva Oa these days. *"Non."* She smiled, shrugging her shoulders. And then she thought about it for a moment. *"Quelques Chinois."*

I swear you cannot go anywhere in this world without running into the Chinese. Which is good, and bodes well for the future. Travel is the great mediator between cultures. Also, I lived in hope that mainland Chinese tourists would descend en masse on the world's so-called Chinese restaurants and give the owners a stern talking-to. What is this Won Ton Soup? And Sweet and Sour Chicken? And who the hell is General Tso? How about some *real* Chinese food? The people, they are a-yearning.

But I digress. I asked if she happened to know whether any of Gauguin's descendants could still be found on Hiva Oa. Yes, she said. They lived on the north coast, in the village of Puama'u. Excellent, I thought. And did they take after their illustrious ancestor?

They have his nose, she informed me with a giggle. And a few are artists working with paint or charcoal.

And by chance might they be known for their fondness for drink.

"Ah oui, monsieur. Ils boivent beaucoup."

Twelve cases of Heineken. Thirty-six cases of Hinano. Three cases of Orangina. One case each of Sprite and Fanta. Three cases of water. And one refrigerator.

Yes, I counted. This was what was off-loaded from the *Aranui* as we anchored off Puama'u. It's a strange sort of village for the South Pacific. Elsewhere, people tend to live in a fairly compact area. The homes are near to each other and you'd rarely need to raise your voice to speak to a neighbor. Not so in Puama'u, which was an elongated sliver of a village, a mere three hundred people living as far away from each other as they could while remaining in the same jurisdiction.

We had come not for the town, however, but for the nearby Me'ae Lipona, perhaps the most important archeological site in the Marquesas, and home to an impressive eight-foot tiki, the largest outside of Easter Island. It is located in the shadow of a steep cliff, which back in the day was used as a defensive fortification and as an excellent place to bury skulls. It seemed like such a lofty and grand place, safe and sound, surrounded by the comforting skulls of your ancestors. As long as you weren't squeamish about bones, it looked like a fine hangout, a place of contemplation, like a monastery on a hill. Heyerdahl had come here too, and of course, in his eyes every stone-gray statue was further evidence yet of the Marquesans' Incan origins. There is, for instance, the "Flying Tiki," which appears to be of a woman giving birth to a god, but has a kind of bas-relief upon which many see the image of a llama, which would be most unusual because there aren't any llamas in the South Pacific. But where do we find llamas? In South America, of course. Some say that it's actually an image of a dog, though many, speaking in a dark whisper, say that Heyerdahl intentionally defaced the tiki to make it appear that right here in the middle of the Marquesan jungle there just happens to be a South American llama. And over there, that stone tiki with the bulbous eyes? That could only be a Peruvian frog. It's like beer goggles for archeologists. Put them on and you can see anything you want.

The entire site was well tended and cleared of brush, and as a consequence it made it more difficult to *see*, to feel the pulse of the place. I much preferred the glimpses of old settlements that I'd seen in the jungle, half buried under a new growth of trees and ferns, where you have to listen, to be still, to open your imagination to what once was. The Me'ae Lipona, in contrast, had been scrubbed and polished and now, for me, felt as lifeless as a museum exhibition. I like a building with soot on it. I prefer my medieval paintings stained with the smoke of incense and a thousand candles. And I like my tikis mossy and hidden amidst a tangle of banyan trees and ferns. Sometimes you need to see less to see more.

I walked back down to the village, which was fronted by a golden-sand beach, a rarity in the Marquesas. I took note of the waves, which were big and frothy, and dove in for a swim. Soon I was joined by the rest of the contingent of *Aranui* passengers and now the real carnage began. You could tell right away who was a coastal dweller and who lived far inland, where waves and oceans were about as familiar as unicorns and leprechauns. The former always beheld the water, its movements, the sudden onset of a particularly gnarly set of dumpers, and dove and bobbed accordingly. The landlubbers waded in waist-high, right into the break zone, turned to look at the shore, perhaps to smile for a picture, as a wall of water rose above them, peaked, curled, and broke upon them, smashing them underwater, the poor souls emerging with bathing suits askew and startled faces and battered bodies. And no matter how often you yelled *Attendez* it would happen over and over again, causing me to doubt in the healing powers of neuroplasticity, because here, very clearly, was some novel stimuli that demanded a swift adaptation in behavior, and yet it never came. Again and again it happened to the very same people. Just turn the fuck around, I felt like yelling, as I cringed every time they were smashed and held under and swept forth in the collapsing froth. Man, I thought, how is it that some of you are still in the gene pool?

And just when the impeding catastrophes could not get any worse, they did. Three local boys had now joined us, mounted on steeds, and proceeded to run their horses through the clumps of visitors, whether in the shallows of the sea or on the beach itself. They'd wait until they could sneak up on them and then send their horses into a gallop, missing the pensioners by inches. I could only endure this for so long before I yelled, *Arrêtez. C'est dangereux*, you dim-witted punk-ass sons of bitches. But then I noticed their big noses and figured that here were a bunch of little Gauguins. These apples, clearly, didn't fall far from the tree.

Finally, I gave up and just watched the mayhem unfold from a log in the shade, where I was soon joined by Marc, a Frenchman, who spent his time between the Marquesas and Patagonia in Chile. He'd lived between the two for twenty years now. Clearly, this was a man ready for the apocalypse. To which he readily agreed, beginning a long exposition on the grim madness of our global economic system, its glorification of consumption as the end-all-be-all measurement of human progress, the surge of inequality, the perfidy of the bankers, the utter insanity of polluting our atmosphere to the point of irreversible climate change, the instability and suffering that will be unleashed for the generations to come, the tragic shortsightedness of inflicting such pain on our planet for the sake of a few dollars more for a very few, the inability of our political systems to address the globe's problems, the prevailing sense that we were on the cusp of some catastrophic, unstoppable change that would alter the face of the earth and all who reside upon it.

Wow, I thought. I always figured I was bad at small talk. But I found myself nodding, uh-huh, exactly, as he articulated my own inchoate sense of the world. But this was why I loved these serendipitous encounters on the road. Sometimes you need to travel far to see your own thoughts articulated into words. Marc had lived in the Marquesas long enough to have known Gauguin's daughter, who had died at the age of eighty-one. "She was a slim Polynesian woman with long gray hair and Gauguin's nose. Her mother had her at the age of thirteen, the same year Gauguin died. The family didn't think much of Gauguin. If anything, they harbor a sense of shame. They felt that he was a drunken pervert, no different really from so many other foreigners who washed up here during that time. Their perspective is very much framed by the Catholic Church. The Church despised Gauguin. He was always trying to prevent people from working on roads or schools or churches. He wanted his *vie sauvage*."

We watched the men unload the cases of Heineken and Hinano, as the boys on their horses continued to terrorize the pensioners, while still others continued with their ocean battering. And I thought, it's funny how after a while, a skull-strewn redoubt on a quiet clifftop deep in the jungle can seem like the most placid spot on the planet. Sometimes, when searching for serenity, it's best to be among the dead. They don't drink; they no longer abuse the living; their sense of humor has presumably evolved (and no longer consists of terror-izing the old with charging horses); they are wise to nature and unlikely to get battered by a wave; they just lie there, body-less, with empty sockets staring into the void. Sure, their craniums may have been bashed in by a war club, but they seem to have accepted it now, and moved on, staring blankly at infinity—and God knows what resides there—and I resolved to find a skull or two when I got home. Nothing quite preaches perspective like the wide-eyed stare of another's scalp. So I was grateful to be here in the Marquesas. I'd found something else to look into. Next time I'm in a flea market and I see a skull, that thing is mine.

Chapter Nine

Let's step back for a moment and consider our hero, Robert Louis Stevenson. The first thing one gleans is that he does not mess around—no hemming and hawing for him, no dithering, no extended multichapter clearing of the throat. Open up *In the South Seas* and by paragraph three he's making landfall. In a mere two paragraphs he's told us that his health was sketchy, that a voyage to the South Seas was recommended, and accordingly, he'd chartered a two-masted schooner of seventy-four tons.

In June 1888, he departed San Francisco and set forth for what he termed the *eastern islands*—what we now call French Polynesia. Early the following year, he found himself in Honolulu. Unwilling "to return to my old life of the house and sickroom" he sought passage on a trading schooner and spent the subsequent four months adrift in the equatorial Pacific, roaming among the low-lying atolls of the Gilbert Group, until he reached Samoa in the winter of 1889. "By that time gratitude and habit were beginning to attach me to the islands; I had gained a competency of strength; I had made friends; I had learned new interests; the time of my voyages had passed like days in a fairyland; and I decided to remain." He wrote, "At this very moment the axes of my black boys are already clearing the foundations of my future house; and I must learn to address readers from the uttermost parts of the sea."

Whew. We're just going to let "the axes of my black boys" reference slide for now—the lingo of the day can clang from time to time. What follows is this: "The first experience can never be repeated. The first love, the first sunrise, the first South Seas Island . . ." And now we're off, the book unspooling as a record of observations and experiences made as he voyaged among the luminous islands of the South Pacific, each island like a self-contained planet, orbited by history and legends, islands that were now in flux as the old manners encountered the ways and predilections of foreigners who'd arrived upon their shores, eyes aflame with possibilities. But who was this masked crusader at the center of it all?

Stevenson was a sickly boy, growing up among a modest family of lighthouse engineers. Life, every waking minute of it, was precious. Perusing through the index of my favorite biography of RLS—*Louis: A Life of Robert Louis Stevenson* by Philip Callow—I noted that after "Writing" and "Letters," the lengthiest entry was for "Illness," a half page that takes us from "Australia" through "bronchial diseases," "California journey," "France," "hemorrhages" (163, 176–177, 185–186, 200, 244, 277, 304), "Morbidity about," "Pacific Islands," "sciatica," all the way to "Youth." Very helpfully, this last entry was followed by See also "Depression." Which I now also did—"Depression," 32–33, 108, 124, 138, 302–304, 310, and just as I was feeling pumped that we managed to go from page 138 to page 302—the Pacific Island chapters incidentally—without any black moods whatsoever, I was being guided to See also "Death"; "Morbidity," and really, I don't think we need any more.

In short, childhood was rough. He spent much of it in a state of recuperation under the care of a nurse he'd come to know as Cunny, who read him biblical tales and attended to his bronchial coughing and hemorrhaging. He was accepted to the University of Edinburgh, where he followed his father's wishes and studied engineering, and predictably found it miserable. In childhood, he'd spent so much time alone, swimming in his head, creating fantasies and penning prose, and now he was doing battle with quadratic equations, linear algebra, applied physics, and civic engineering. He did what he could, but mostly he drifted into the Bohemian orbit, growing his hair long as he assumed a wardrobe of velvet jackets fastened with snake buckles, topping it all off with a jaunty Tyrolean hat. Like a Brooklyn hipster, he experimented with creative facial hair—an etching from the era shows him with a prison-style handlebar and a soul patch. Also, he was wearing a hat, not Alpine, more like a Turkish fez. In any event, he had it going on.

He picked up the pen and soon was participating in the literary salons of the day, contributing essays and stories, engaging in literary spats, joining cliques and departing them in acrimony. Some biographers claim that he was a denizen among the whorehouses in old Edinburgh, though proof is scant. Maybe he did. Maybe he just wanted to talk. His sexuality—and really, this is just based on my own amateur sleuthing into his life, and not sourced on anything particular, more of a sum-of-its-parts kind of thing, so please don't go on Wikipedia and write, "RLS may also have been gay"—remained curiously ambiguous. Eventually he dropped out of his engineering studies and pursued a degree in law. He would never practice a day in his life.

From time to time, whether due to sickness or anxiety, he sought relief in laudanum, a tincture of opium and morphine.

Whenever I hear someone describe the wonders of modern medicine, I think with a quiet sigh of what you would have found in your average nineteenth-century corner drugstore—cocaine, opium, morphine, heroin, all available without a prescription, and all advertised, whether as "Mrs. Winslow's Soothing Syrup" or "Dover's Powder," as a cure for anything from coughing to consumption. Even the pope at the time, Leo XIII, was a daily consumer of Vin Mariani, a mixture of red Bordeaux and a generous serving of coca leaves. Being a gin-consuming lush was generally frowned upon during this genteel age, but nodding out on heroin was considered healthy and ingesting cocaine was regarded as a satisfying means to sharpen the mind—see, for instance, Sherlock Holmes or Sigmund Freud.

Laudanum was, predictably, a very popular drug among writers and poets, including Lord Byron and Percy Shelley, as well as for the working class and certain women chasing the look of the day, which, interestingly enough, corresponded very closely to the heroin-chic faze of the mid-1990s—pale, skinny, and androgynous, with dark raccoon circles under the eyes. Evidently, during the Victorian era, Kate Moss would have been considered quite the hottie.

Stevenson, however, would never become an addict. He was more prone to worrying that, one day, he'd become one of those sad souls swimming in the bottle, like those he sometimes encountered in the taverns of Edinburgh. On board the *Casco*, in a reflective mood, he wrote of his youth: "How I feared I should make a mere shipwreck, and yet timidly hoped not; how I feared I should never have a friend, far less a wife, and yet passionately hoped I might; how I hoped (if I did not take to drink) I should possibly write one little book, etc. etc."

His relations with his parents were largely good, though

they came to an impasse when his father, Thomas, a Tory to his bones, suspected his son of atheism, a devastating charge. This was also the age of Darwin, when science and faith began to diverge, leading to a kind of generational schism, like in the sixties, except RLS dressed way cooler than the bell-bottomed hippies. But with time, the stern Mr. Stevenson would loosen the checkbook and dispatch funds to his struggling son, who'd set out to pursue a literary career, then as now a remarkably stupid way to make a living. It was a tension that would pervade his life—the urge to be the Bohemian roustabout, unmoored by custom or bourgeois expectation, while attaining the success, prestige, and income that afforded him grand hotel suites and a long correspondence with Henry James.

He wrote a couple of travel books, *An Inland Voyage* and *Travels with a Donkey in Cevennes*, which were modestly successful, though neither has aged well. Bruce Chatwin, a travel writer with many uncanny similarities to Robert Louis Stevenson, dismissed *Travels* as "the prototype of the incompetent undergraduate voyage." Other books followed: Once he moved to the United States, pursuing the American divorcée Fanny Osbourne, he penned *The Amateur Emigrant* and *The Silverado Squatters*, both works of nonfiction.

In the first, he wrote of America as "a sort of promised land" as he'd joined the hordes of emigrants—Jews, Scots, Italians decamping from their old, troubled countries with their hungers and pogroms—and settled among them in steerage class. "We were a shipful of failures, the broken of England." He'd see the best and worst of humanity on board the ship, the men so sick they slept on pools of vomit, the Scot who played a sonorous fiddle for the frightened women, the soot-stained children running amuck, creating games and levity wherever their spirits took them. On board, he was known as "Shakespeare," the lone passenger to carve out a space to write. He'd lose another fourteen pounds on the voyage.

New York greeted him with sheets of rain. He slept on the floor of a boardinghouse and soon joined the stampede to the trains in New Jersey. Lost children wailed but no one paid them any heed as hopeful passengers rushed to westward trains. He was drenched for days, acquired scabies, and was delirious with hunger. In a letter, he marveled at the simplicity of suicide. In Chicago, he switched trains and again in Council Bluffs, Iowa, where he was sorted according to compartments—families in one car, single men in another, and Chinese coolies in the last. He was struck by the "uncivil kindness" of Americans. He itched ferociously. He no longer slept. Hunger was his companion. "My illness is a subject of great mirth," he wrote in a letter, "and I smile rather sickly at their jests." He envied the Chinese for their superior hygiene, and began to despise his fellow compatriots for mocking and jeering the Native Americans who stood alongside the stations. The train followed tracks across a barren desert and soon began the ascent up the Sierras, and here finally Stevenson could feel the imminence of relief. The air turned cooler, cleaner, and soon they were descending through forests and rivers and mountains, into the clarity of the California sun and the first scent of the ocean. He departed in Oakland, crossed a San Francisco Bay as smooth as a pane of glass.

He'd come for Fanny. Read enough biographies about Robert Louis Stevenson and you discover that Fanny, what you make of her, is like a Rorschach test. Many found her moody, impulsive, prone to the vicissitudes of extreme emotions, a woman who accepted Stevenson as a hen would an errant chick, a nitpicker who inhibited Stevenson's claim to greatness. Others were more kind, recognizing that few women, then or now, could long endure Stevenson, the swirl of drama he created wherever he went, the extreme impulsivity, the long demands for silence as he worked, and the never-ending sickness, the "Bluidy Jack" as Stevenson referred to it, which required ceaseless nursing. His prospects, as a writer, were poor. His life span questionable. No great catch he.

They'd first met in France, where Fanny had fled to escape a philandering husband with her two children: Lloyd, who'd come to be a constant presence in her life with Stevenson, and Belle, who'd marry a ne'er-do-well alcoholic named Joe Strong, who floated from Hawaii to Australia, claiming to be an artist but eventually surviving as a parasite on the author's generosity. From France, Fanny returned to the United States and Stevenson, as was his wont, followed in pursuit, despite protestations from family and friends who all counseled that she was an inappropriate match—she was forty, a decade older than RLS; had kids (always a complicating factor); uncertain finances of her own; and was known to be temperamental. It was this trip that was the source material for *The Amateur Emigrant*.

But what did he see in her? In photographs, Fanny has a strong, lively face with expressive eyes that seem, even in a photographer's studio, a moment away from expressing mirth or a malevolent glare. She does not seem like the docile, accommodating type. Here was a woman of opinions, firmly stated, which made her, in these corseted Victorian times, an anomaly. Perhaps, then, this was what Stevenson was looking for: a strong woman who would take no guff, a woman who, when needed, could mother him through sickness and black moods, a woman who when reading a draft of his prose would call it like it is—sentimental gibberish—and who, perhaps most importantly, felt as untethered from the conventions of the day as Stevenson did.

His arrival in Monterey, where Fanny resided, was unwelcome. Her divorce had yet to come through and she could not afford the appearance of impropriety. And of course, when Stevenson entered the doorway, cosseted in rags and fleas, and looking like Skeletor after a really bad night, he hardly set Fanny's heart aflutter. Dejected, he walked eighteen miles into the hills beyond Carmel, and were it not for the frontiersmen who found him delirious and hallucinating, it is likely that there his cross would lie. Fanny had meanwhile moved on to Oakland, while Stevenson remained in Monterey, which he'd found agreeable, going on long walks along the bluffs, awestruck at the pounding waves, and settling into a town that remained largely Mexican in character. He made friends—as was his gift—and wrote freelance articles for the *Monterey Californian* for two dollars a week as he healed from malaria and pleurisy. And still, he got sicker. He'd cough and rooms would tremble. His lungs bled; blood seeped from his mouth.

It was Fanny, dismissing the inevitable gossip, who swooped down and finally rescued him, moving him into her cottage in Oakland as doctors hastened for the death knells. He recovered—he miraculously always did—and they moved on to San Francisco, where he received astonishing news. His father, aghast at the stories of penury and misery that had befallen his son, sent word that Stevenson could count on an annual stipend of 250 pounds, and even more remarkably, this woman would be welcomed into the family. Fanny's long-sought divorce had finally come through.

The marriage occurred in 1880, in a vicar's garden, with the solemn exchange of silver rings, and they decamped for Napa, settling for their honeymoon in a squalid abandoned silver mine, spending their time hammering and chiseling, seeking to create a homespun hearth before abandoning it to its inevitable ruin. Then they made haste for Scotland and the

British Isles. They'd settle for a spell here, and a spell there—they were always moving somewhere, elsewhere—and in the meantime Stevenson's work began to find an audience. His essays appeared in the more illustrious journals. His stories found readers. And yet he remained poor as a church rat, surviving largely through the grace of his father's allowance.

It had begun with a map. It would be Stevenson's first novel, something that had long eluded him, despite numerous attempts. "It is the length that kills," he'd written. Few endeavors require the depth of concentration and imagination that a novel requires. (Even Jonathan Franzen, I'd bet, spends a month on the couch, a bag of pork rinds next to him, his hand on the remote as he lies in a catatonic stupor, watching a marathon session of *South Park* as he recuperates from a just-written novel. No wonder it takes him a decade.) Stevenson, for a long while, would look "upon every three-volume novel with a sort of veneration." And then he'd shuffle off, dejected, back to penning his little essays.

It was the appearance of children in his home life that would serve as a catalyst for his great adventure yarn. With Lloyd at his side, he sketched the contours of his island, mapping the coves, inserting the treasure chest, his febrile imagination conjuring young Jim Hawkins and a one-legged pirate named Long John Silver. The book was all action and suspense. "If this don't fetch the kids, why they have gone rotten in my day," he noted. Every night, he read chapters to his family. His literary friends—you know the kind, the ones with the MFAs, the ones working on experimental fiction, where the words *story* and *character* are dismissed as the affections of the lowbrow—were dismissive and snooty. But Stevenson had seized on something. He could tell a rousing, good yarn.

And yet, he still felt abashed. He had ambitions of being the

Dickens of his age, and now here he was, crafting a boy's tale, playing pirate with his father and stepson, and submitting the tale to a magazine called *Young Folks*, which serialized *Treasure Island* while Stevenson hid behind a pen name, Captain George North. No matter. Stevenson was now, at the very least, a solvent writer. To his critics: "I will swallow no more of that gruel. Let them write their masterpieces for themselves and let me alone."

In the meantime, Stevenson's sickness would ebb and flow. He quarreled with Fanny. He fell into a funk. He continued to write, including a collaboration with his wife that almost sank the marriage. Fanny, as she wrote to her mother-in-law, had resented being "treated like a comma." And yet, as always he worked, dancing among projects and half-finished stories.

One night, he had a dream, a nightmare presumably, from which he dared not wake. When he did, he ate a brief lunch, and retired to his room, took a large draft of laudanum, and, presumably high as a kite, spent the next three days and nights penning what would become *The Strange Case of Dr. Jekyll and Mr. Hyde*, finishing it in a state of exhausted triumph.

Here, the author—this one, me—would like to interject. Sixty thousand words in three days! Good God. Where, exactly, does one procure this laudanum? It sounds like a downer, and yet . . . did I read that cocaine was involved? So it's an upper, mellowed by morphine? Can it be synthesized? Is it smokeable? Injected? Why aren't we making this stuff now?

. . . Ahem. What's really remarkable is what happened afterward. Stevenson gathered Fanny and Lloyd around him and proceeded to read his tale about the duality of human nature, the transfiguration of good into evil, the intoxication of living without moral constraints and its toll on the soul.

Lloyd sat enthralled. "I don't believe there was ever such a literary feat before as the writing of *Dr. Jekyll*," he later recalled. Fanny, however, insisted that Stevenson had missed the mark entirely, that he'd failed to see the essential allegory of the tale. Furious, Stevenson tossed the manuscript into the fireplace. He raged at her myopic imbecility. They had a colossal argument, and then, pointing to the ashes of his work, he conceded that, well, perhaps on second thought, she'd been right after all, and he returned to his room, to his laudanum, and wrote a new draft, again in three days.

I have a special affection for *Dr. Jekyll*, of course. I think anyone who has engaged in a course of action that violated their moral code, and did so not with remorse but rather great enthusiasm, will empathize with the tale. That it was written during the height of the Victorian era, with its buoyant belief in the inevitability of progress and rectitude, makes it all the more remarkable. Stevenson, clearly, had a dark side, and perhaps this too explains his wandering ways. The contented stay put. The disaffected always have one foot out the door.

Stevenson's father died in 1887, and now, suddenly, the last bridge that compelled him to stay in the British Isles crumbled. He was left an inheritance, his books were generating a tidy cash flow, he'd married an American, and much to everyone's surprise, his mother, Maggie, was soon too afflicted with the wandering impulse. They set sail again for America, this time on a ship of animals—apes, baboons, cows, horses—a veritable Noah's Ark, all setting forth for the New Land, where, to his astonishment, he was now received as a star. He found it all rather bizarre—the reporters, the fawning attention. "If Jesus Christ came they would make less fuss." And yet, as always, the Everyman pose had a discordant note. He liked the grand hotels. And his ego was now honed and chiseled. "[Rudyard]

Kipling is by far the most promising young man to have appeared since—ahem—I appeared," he'd write.

They intended to move to Colorado, but it was deemed too far, too high up for Stevenson's lungs, and so they settled in a cottage in the Adirondacks, the rustic simplicity as appealing to the author as a suite at the Ritz. Soon, of course, the harsh winter descended. The snowshoes were brought out, so too the earmuffs, the fur coats, and layers of mittens. And still they froze. It was into this wintery scene that Sam McClure, a fellow Scotsman and publisher of the *New York World*, appeared. They got to chatting. The South Pacific was mentioned. Hmm . . . What if . . . ? Finally McClure declared: "If you get a yacht and take long sea voyages and write about them, stories of adventure and so forth, I'll pay all expenses." Not long thereafter, Fanny found her way to California. Soon, a telegram was sent: "Can secure splendid sea-going schooner yacht for seven hundred and fifty a month with most comfortable accommodation for six aft and six forward. Can be ready for sea in ten days. Reply immediately. Fanny."

"Blessed girl," Stevenson wrote back, "take the yacht and expect us in ten days."

Let's ponder this for a moment . . . Are you done? Would you get on that boat? We're talking six–seven months minimum. No Coast Guard, of course. No GPS, no radios, no studly dudes dropping out of helicopters to save your ass during a force-ten gale. We're looking at a month, perhaps two of straight blue-water sailing—storms, cyclones, sharks, unrelenting sun, the tedium of the doldrums—and nothing between you and the vast, desolate depths except a sliver of timber. And your destination? An island where there are still many who know what you taste like—and I don't mean that in a sexy way. Think femur bones. Cannibalism. Long Pig. The Special Menu.

Would you go?

What if you had an upper respiratory system that from time to time hacked up great globs of blood? And let's say recent illnesses had left you the proverbial ninety-eight-pound weakling? Would you still go? If you are Robert Louis Stevenson you don't betray even a hint of hesitation. Of course, it's unclear what he'd have done if he'd had the option of flying, while being attended to by Hotette, but I imagine he'd still have chosen the schooner for the adventure, the romance, the accomplishment, and the peculiar adrenaline rush that accompanies crossing an ocean slowly. Few things, of course, stir the imagination quite like a cruise to the South Pacific—the swaying palm fronds, the warm ocean dappled with sunlight, the steep crests of volcanic islands, the friendly chitchats with maneaters. Of course you go.

It was an odd party that'd boarded the *Casco*: There was Stevenson, of course; his wife, Fanny; his mother too; his stepson, Lloyd; and a maid, Valentine. Among the crew was a Russian, a Finn, two Swedes, and a Chinese cook who preferred to be thought of as Japanese. The boat was captained by A. H. Otis, who'd read *Treasure Island* and thought little of Stevenson's knowledge of seafaring ways. He also didn't think it likely that the author, thin and emaciated as usual, would survive the voyage, and accordingly he'd stowed what he'd need to bury him at sea. And this business of bringing his elderly mother along? Pure madness. When asked what he'd do if Maggie, who had more than a passing resemblance to Queen Victoria, should also find herself deceased, as seemed probable, the captain said he'd "put it in the log."

But he was wrong. He'd misread his passengers. The Stevenson clan was born for the sea. This, after all, was a family of lighthouse builders. They knew of the elements, its dangers and furies. Prim, proper, delicate Maggie Stevenson—she would, a few months hence, write: "It is a strange, irresponsible, half-savage life & I sometimes wonder if we shall ever be able to return to civilized habits again." They were mutating chameleons, adapting and assimilating no matter the environment, whether a Paris salon or a storm-tossed sea.

Stevenson claimed a large stateroom for himself. Young Lloyd was berthed in a small compartment, while Fanny and the other two women shared a cabin with a skylight. (See? Kind of odd, no?) He'd read and write, but mostly he'd spend his time on deck, barefoot, his health and mind aglow at this wonderful change in circumstances. They tumbled down the latitudes, celebrated each sunset, and soon the cold waters of the north Pacific gave way to the temperate South Seas.

Fanny was a mess, however. She'd never adjust to the sea. And you can hardly blame her. They skirted the edges of a hurricane, endured sudden squalls, the boat heeling to such an extent that water flooded the cockpit and the cabins. It is no wonder that Fanny spent many of her days hurling over the side. The captain, who didn't exactly exude sunshine and butterflies, was often irritated with her. For once, it was Louis who was the hale and hardy one.

For more than a month they sailed. Land was becoming but a distant memory, their only company the occasional seabird seeking a handout, until early one morning, on July 20, 1888, Stevenson arose in the predawn darkness, awaiting the sunrise and its promise of an island. "The interval was passed on deck in the silence of expectation, the customary thrill of landfall heightened by the strangeness of the shores that we were then approaching." And then, as the sun crested the horizon, there lay the Marquesas: "like the pinnacles of some ornate and monstrous church, they stood there, in the sparkling brightness of the morning, the fit sign-board of a world of wonders."

And this, of course, is why we always get on the boat.

Chapter Ten

And yet, as I watched the *Aranui* sail past the headlands of Nuku Hiva, its familiar, comforting shape tumbling over the horizon, I couldn't help but feel happy to be back on terra firma, even upon a small island in the vast remoteness of the Pacific. I had jumped ship, deserted, and like a runaway from a naval vessel of yore, I had leapt in a quest for freedom. I was never very good with itineraries. I have nothing to say about the passenger fashion show. I could set my watch to the smoky waft of the Swiss banker's Cohiba. The rhythm of life at sea had begun to be set in stone. But I liked to move according to my own clock. And now I was free. But to do what? What hills were there to climb? What roads to run? What valleys to explore? What ruins to investigate? And how would I get along with the inhabitants of Nuku Hiva?

Whenever I read contemporary travel accounts of the Marquesas, I find that the locals are often described as aloof, guarded, and unfriendly. I'm not sure why this is so. Just how warm and accommodating are New Yorkers to their visitors from Japan? Or can you imagine what it might be like for a Mexican tourist traveling through the great state of Alabama? Do Parisians get all warm and fuzzy with the hordes of Americans trampling about the Eiffel Tower in August? Is Moscow a nice place for visiting Nigerians? And if your name is Abdul or Emir or Muhammad, is there a border agent anywhere outside of the Middle East that greets you with a smile? For the most part, visitors to our own countries are invisible. For some, they're a nuisance. Rare are the locals who go out of their way to ingratiate themselves with the befuddled visitor from overseas.

Which is why I was so pleased to meet Moke. He was a big dude, six four at least and perhaps a wobbling 260 pounds, who informed me, right off the bat, that he was a wild-pig hunter. I'd seen pig hunters in action on Malekula, an outer island in Vanuatu, and knew enough about boars to know that they are surprisingly vicious creatures when cornered and do not like to be trifled with. They will gore you in an instant. Say that you are a pig hunter in the United States and you will mostly be regarded as one of those gun nuts on game farms just looking for something to satiate your blood lust. Say it on an island in the South Seas, where you clamber over perilous ridges in a dense rain forest, armed only with a spear as you hunt for your family dinner, and you are a manly man to whom I tip my hat.

And Moke was full of helpful information. We stood on the shoreline, in the village of Taiohae, in front of a glass-smooth bay that was a flooded volcanic crater that opened to the sea. Two small islands guarded the entrance. There was a ceremonial platform, the Temehau Tohua, that contained a few modern tikis, and nearby a monument to Herman Melville, who also jumped ship, in 1842, an experience he'd used in his celebrated story *Typee*. Everyone somehow ends up on Nuku Hiva—Melville, Robert Louis Stevenson, Jack London, Jeff Probst and the cast of *Survivor*. I didn't know why that was so. I mean have you seen where Nuku Hiva is on a map? Jamaica this is not. But I was willing, more than eager, to explore the allure of the island and its hold on writers and travelers.

Moke saw me looking out to sea, and without me even prompting informed me that I shouldn't even think about swimming here. A tiger shark had mauled a local woman just two weeks prior, lacerating her leg and arm. Her hand, he told me, was now limp and useless. The predators follow the fishing boats in and seize what they can from the catch, whether hooked or discarded. Unsatiated, they cruise the bay and hunt, looking for errant swimmers. If that wasn't enough, Moke informed me that not a week earlier another woman was killed by a falling coconut, so *fais attention* with the trees. Also, recently, a local Marquesan took a visiting German yachtie, Stefan Ramin, into the hills to hunt for goats and murdered him, whereupon he burned the corpse and ate what remained of the charred remains. The attacker hid in the mountains for fifty-two days until he was apprehended. Now this caught my attention. Nowhere in my guidebook did it say, from time to time, a local might regard you as Jeffrey Dahmer once did the contents of his refrigerator.

So you see? Who says that the Marquesans aren't helpful? This was exactly the sort of information that as a visitor I found useful. Don't swim with the tiger sharks. Beware of coconut trees. Decline all offers for goat hunting. And know that some might regard me as a meal. Thank you, my friend, now would you happen to know where I could rent a room for a while? Clearly, Moke was a fount of useful information, and he pointed me to a small, two-story building on the hillside and bade me a good day.

Excellent, I thought, as I slung my backpack onto my shoulders and walked on. Sharks and coconut trees I knew to be wary of. I once owned a pickup truck in Kiribati that after a few short months looked like the cratered remains of the moon. But can-

nibals? Today? Really? But I'd been reading so much early literature on the South Seas that the presence of active man-eaters lent
an air of unexpected authenticity to the Nuku Hiva experience.
I thought it would be hard to replicate Robert Louis Stevenson's
adventures on the island—he has a nice description of meeting
"an incurable cannibal grandee" whose "favorite morsel was the
human hand, of which he speaks to-day with an ill-favored lustfulness"—but now I felt a sudden burst of confidence.

It's what I liked about traveling. You never know what to
expect. It keeps you on your toes. I found the building Moke had
pointed to, surrounded by a large, overgrown garden, and was
immediately shown to a small room on the second story, which
contained a balcony that I shared with the neighboring room.
These were the only two rooms that appeared to be occupied,
but in Pacific culture they go to great lengths to avoid any semblance of loneliness, which is regarded as either tragic or suspect.
I stepped out onto the balcony and immediately encountered a
couple speaking Hebrew. The man, a young, voluble, balding
fellow with a nervous disposition, turned to me and, assuming I
was French, spoke at a rapid clip *en français*, while his female
companion, an olive-skinned beauty with a mane of curly black
hair, painted her toes. He told me, as best as I could follow, that
he was a medical scientist on a quest to find a rare medicinal
plant that he felt confident could be used to repair broken spines.
And then he told me that he was an American and that . . .

"Hang on," I said. "You're an American. Whazzup? It's
been weeks since I've spoken to an American. Where are you
from? Where do you live?"

. . . and he didn't speak English. Nor did his companion,
who, did I mention, was smoking hot? Not that I notice these
things. I'm just including it here for descriptive purposes. And
with that the conversation was over and they returned to their

room, closed the sliding glass door with a click of the lock, and shut the shades, whereupon I heard soft, urgent whisperings in guttural Hebrew.

Really, could things get any more intriguing? In a mere one hour on the island there was already so much to be weirded out by. Rogue tiger sharks, malevolent coconut trees, murderous cannibals, and mysterious Israeli botanists. No wonder writers flocked to Nuku Hiva. Within five hundred yards of my balcony was a world of mayhem and wonder. I looked toward the bay, where a dozen yachts were anchored, riding out the cyclone season. There was the usual mix one sees in ports like Savusavu in Fiji or Port Vila in Vanuatu—a beautiful Hallberg-Rassy; a few French production boats, Beneteaus mostly, a sleek Jeanneau; a Hans Christian, one of my favorite sailboats, with its upturned rolling bow and its celebration of teak; and an assortment of really weathered sailboats that looked like they'd survived a typhoon or two, hit a reef or twelve, and lay heavy in the water, their bottoms weighed down by rust and barnacles; and each of these cruisers were top-heavy with gear and solar panels. I gnawed at my fingers in envy.

It was late in the afternoon and I headed out for a run. It was my sundown relief, my libation. I calculated that from one end of town to the other, following the curve of the bay, was about a mile, a straight run hemmed in by mighty headlands and a three-thousand-foot ridge of mountains. I set out to do six laps. It's a great way to introduce your presence to the islanders. It was again stiflingly hot, and the locals stopped and stared and laughed as I ran past, sweating freely, but I was pleased to find a flat run, one that didn't undulate or offer steep, thigh-crushing inclines. I could run like this forever, provided I lay off the smokes. I saw a few children scampering on the roadside. In the Pacific, kids are usually healthy, slim, and distinct looking. They play—I saw a group of girls in school uniforms busily engaged in a game of handball at the local school, and the boys, well, they do what preadolescent boys do everywhere. Aflame with energy, they run and tackle and chase each other, climb trees, hike hills, scamper up rocks, and burn off all that energy that schools the world over feel the need to bottle and subsume. By the end of the of the day, the typical schoolboy is an exploding supernova. So they're all fit. You hardly see a fat kid on the islands.

But then something happens around the age of seventeen. It's strange, like some wizard goes SHAZZAM and they inflate like parade floats, and by middle age they waddle through the air like sexless cartoons, indistinguishable from each other as they graze out of cans of corned beef and Pringles. Normally this would be sad, but I had cannibalism on my mind, and figured that being skinny and lean was a good defense for any psychotic man-eater afoot. I'm about six foot, and Drunk Me weighed 195. Sober Me hits the scale at 165. I always told my wife that should I hit the scales at 170–175, it probably means I'm lifting weights with a little more vigor than usual. At 180 and I'm drinking again. At 190 plus, it's time for another stint in rehab, or the park bench, depending. But now, one look at me, and like an underweight pig or cow, I'd be fit for nothing more than the grinder—like *Fargo*—which, I believed, would be more trouble than it's worth. So I was good. When you look at a piece of meat, it's the marbled fat that screams here comes something tasty. Now should a bloated William Shatner ever reach these shores, well, all I can say is don't boldly go goat hunting.

When I was finished, I took a quick shower and wandered back to the waterfront, near the small port, where a few fishing boats were tied and a slew of dinghies were roped to a pier. This was the yachtie ghetto, where sailors could access their e-mail, buy a few supplies, and gather around long tables, choosing from a few rustic mom-and-pop cafés or partaking of one of the food trucks that parked nearby. Long-term cruisers the world over are notorious cheapskates, and nowhere more so than in French Polynesia. You had to be, of course. A basic bag of groceries will set you back a hundred bucks. A simple jar of peanuts costs eight dollars. Want to stay on a resort on Tahiti or one of the other more-visited islands? Four hundred dollars. The only thing that appeared to be subsidized was French wine, the fuckers. I don't claim to be any kind of travel-guide writer, but I can't for the life of me figure why a typical tourist on a budget would head for French Polynesia. Why, when you have the beauty of Hawaii, the beaches of the Caribbean, the culture of Vanuatu, and the deals in Fiji? This was a place for hedge fund managers and the sort of people that travel by private jet, like the one I saw when I arrived in Papeete, which carried the logo of the Miami Dolphins. No, you had to be as diligent as a backpacker and find the cheap pensiones, shop for basic provisions at the corner store, and when you see a food truck, park yourself in front of one of its folding tables and eat as the locals or the yachties do. Restaurants were for spend-thrift chumps and European pensioners.

Crepes? Why not crepes for dinner? I approached the small van, ordered a banana crepe, found another shop that sold fresh young coconuts and mangoes, and felt pleased to have regained a semblance of sanity to my budget, which had been bludgeoned on the *Aranui*. I settled at a table and was soon joined by groups of affable cruisers. The families were the sanest of the lot, couples with adolescent children who had set forth to give their clan the experience of a lifetime, sailing the seven seas from one exotic port to another, every day a new adventure. Then there were the older couples, crusty and familiar as only those living in a confined space get after a number of years at sea, rarely sailing now as they inhabited agreeable ports for a season or three at a time. And then there were the solo sailors, always men, in my experience, who were without exception lacking any discernible sanity and clearly off their meds.

I met one such lunatic, a short, stout Frenchman with a US Navy cap. He'd crossed two oceans alone—the Atlantic and the Pacific. He was supposed to have sailed with his son, but inconveniently, the son lay dying in a hospital of cancer, so he set off on his own, wrecking one boat in the Mediterranean and another in the Caribbean—pesky reefs. He'd bought his next boat in Seattle. Just $37,000, he said, a very good price for a boat rigged for extended blue water sailing, though it needed a few repairs and new sails. He spoke of the men who tried to rob him in Panama at knifepoint. And then he asked me to stand up and he demonstrated how he punched them in the throat *comme ça*, swinging his knobby arm. And then he kicked them and beat them, and after that no more problems in Panama as he blew out his chest like one of those dead puffer fishes one sometimes sees on the beach. But now, alas, monsieur, he is in hiding from the French authorities. He had bought his boat in America. Duties needed to be paid. So he was laying low for now, *tu comprends*.

These tough little men were always a wonder to me. But I liked his spirit. He asked me if I'd come by *bateau*. Yes, I'd said, the *Aranui*, but I'd left and now found myself here, in that small building up the hill.

"*Avec les Juifs?*" he said. "*Ils sont ici pour l'or*," he informed me with a confidential whisper. And then he explained how they went from village to village, from household to household, offering to buy up anyone's gold.

Psshaw, I said. The French and their anti-Semitism. It's baffling, really. Perhaps the Jews weren't here for gold at all.

Maybe they'd come to collect a few Christians to bake into matzo balls. I explained that my good neighbor was some kind of medical scientist, a botanist searching for a plant to help the unfortunate souls with broken backs. The Frenchman laughed so hard tears streamed from his eyes.

"*Aah, les Juifs,*" he said. "*Du vin, monsieur? Nous avons besoin de vin.*"

Now, I thought, might be a good time to go before I was inflicted with a boozy recitation of the *Protocols of the Elders of Zion*. Man, these French. You can't even be a nice Israeli medical botanist without having your motives impugned. It was nearly dark as I wandered back. The sun sets with a swift brilliance in the tropics, and this, of course, being France, there wasn't a shop open where I could buy a flashlight. I walked up the potholed road, found my hillside, and proceeded to whack my face with every low-lying branch, trip over every errant rock, lose myself in a tangle of thorny bushes, slip in mud pile after mud pile, so that by the time I returned to my room I looked like I'd belonged on the losing side of some epic battle against a violent uprising of murderous forest dwellers. But eventually I found my room, tripping over every stair until I found a light switch, and emerged onto the balcony, filthy and scarred and bleeding from a gash on my knee.

The Israeli took one look at me and without further *adieu* asked me how much I wanted for my watch. "*C'est un Tissot, n'est-ce pas?*"

Well, yes. I got it for my thirtieth birthday. It's not for sale. At least not yet. Talk to me as I leave French Polynesia.

And my ring? It's white gold, yes.

I think so. But it's my wedding ring and as of last check I was still legally entitled to wear it, though I'd had to get it re-sized when I quit drinking. Who knew how fat your fingers get when you drink a couple of bottles of wine a day? Also not for sale, though it's yours should I relapse again.

Did I have anything else?

No. What did I look like? P. Diddy? But I seem to be encrusted with all sorts of plant material? Perhaps that might interest you.

My Israeli friend excused himself and said that he wasn't really a botanist. He was traveling the islands, going from village to village, and trying to get the locals to depart with their gold. You can buy it here for about two or three hundred dollars an ounce. In Tel Aviv, you can sell it for twelve hundred or more an ounce. It's incredible. It's like picking fruit. He was becoming rich, he said. These poor villagers, they knew the value of nothing. Do you know what the spot price for gold was? You have to be a fool not to take advantage of these stupid villagers. This was the chance of a lifetime. Meanwhile, his partner was painting the toes on her other foot. Really, I thought. Why don't we discuss the Torah instead? But he wouldn't let it go, his eyes aflame with gold, no different from a conquistador of yore, but without even the illusion of something beyond the purely mercantile.

This conversation was becoming both boring and disturbing, and so I bade them good night and settled down with my Kindle, browsing though the Sober Lit I'd downloaded. *Infinite Jest* was my go-to book for when I was craving hard. I'd just need to read a few pages about Don Gately, during the Year of the Depend Adult Undergarment, as he attended to his commitments at Boston-area AA meetings. No one writes about the gawping maw, the horror, of addiction and the pain-in-the-ass, life-or-death struggle of early sobriety like David Foster Wallace. Or sometimes I'd read Mary Karr's *Lit*, but would soon have to close the book whenever I read too many pages because I'd find myself with a deep and abiding crush on the author, which, apparently is not unusual. David Foster Wallace had her name tattooed on his arm, which was subsequently crossed out with, of course, an inked footnote when he'd moved on to other loves. Or I'd read Caroline Knapp's *Drinking: A Love Story*, but then my mind would wander as I'd try to recollect where exactly did I meet her. Though she was older than I, we were both in Boston at the same time and her face seemed strikingly familiar, yet I could never quite place her and this bothered me. Or I'd try, again, to trudge through Pete Hamill's *A Drinking Life: A Memoir*, but it must be a generational thing. I have a hard time reading through the Big Swaggering Dicks of the fifties and sixties—the Mailers, the Updikes, and the like, who write of their virility like a fourteen-year-old braggart holding forth in the boy's locker room, describing the feel of Mary Jane's yielding bosom. And Hamill's book is 90 percent about drinking and traveling and newspapering, and then one day he quits with the boozing and everything's peachy. Not my experience at all. So I scrolled down to my rock star bios. Duff McKagan's *It's So Easy: And Other Lies* is a good, tight read, but what I really enjoyed were the pictures; the pale, sickly, bloated, miserable-looking rock star onstage with Guns N' Roses, followed by pics taken ten years later, him aglow and fit and surrounded by an adoring family. Finally, I settled on *The Heroin Diaries*. There's nothing redemptive about Nikki Sixx's memoir of the worst year of his life. It is merely a recounting of the horrible trap of addiction; the loathing of the partaking, followed by the inability to stop. I put it down after reading about the author snorting a beach ball's worth of coke while fucking a stripper, turned off the light, and said a small prayer.

Thank you God for helping me stay sober today. And thank you for providing me with material so that one day I may be able to justify the cost of this trip to French Polynesia, which has been hideous and crippling. But an anti-Semitic Frenchman? An Israeli Jew with a lust for gold? Really? This is what You send me? You know that as a Gentile, I can't touch that. What's next? Will I be encountering a black man eating a watermelon tomorrow? A Chinese guy doing kung fu? A WASP in seersucker shorts? A gay man with a lisp? You, Sir, have a very twisted view of comedy. But thanks for the cannibal. Good night. Amen.

And I spent the rest of the night listening to my neighbors being all romantic-like. Seriously, God, did I mention that you have a peculiar sense of humor and a warped sense of justice?

I awoke with the sun and headed to the beach to do some yoga, what I called Bikram-lite, starting with the Standing Deep Breathing and moving on to the Half-Moon Pose, the Awkward Pose, the Eagle Pose, a wobbling Head to Knee Pose, and onward through the Balancing Tree and the Triangle Pose, bypassing entirely the Toe Stand Pose (it defeats me), followed by a little Wind Removing, a nice, stretchy Cobra and a Full Locust, leading into the Bow Pose, and a blood-releasing Fixed Firm Pose, a relaxing Half Tortoise, an excruciating Camel Pose, a little Spine Twisting, and then the welcome relief of the Dead Man Pose, where I lingered for a good long while, feeling the warm water lapping at my feet as the tide came in. And then I opened my eyes and wondered where the hell everybody was.

Typically at dawn, the Pacific is a bustle of activity. It is what passes for rush hour on an island. Homes are swept; the boys are in the trees gathering toddy; the fishermen are out on their boats; the kids are marching to school, but here . . . nothing, just the quiet movement of the sea and the slow ascent of a golden sun. Maybe if I'd drank *vin* and had sex all night, I'd still be slumbering too, but I traveled as a monk—early to bed and early to rise—and now I was bereft. Clearly, even out here, they kept French hours, so I headed back to my room and opened Robert Louis Stevenson's *In the South Seas.*

Coming from the north, Stevenson and the *Casco* first arrived at Anaho Bay, on the other side of the island, where there was once a sizeable village. They anchored and were soon surrounded by canoes, and their ship was suddenly aswarm with islanders "tattooed from head to foot in awful patterns; some barbarous and knived . . . I knew nothing of my guests beyond the fact that they were cannibals." His visitors, however, were hardly barbarians. They had come to trade and to admire the fine lines of his ship. The women too clambered on board, declaring it finer than any church. "I have seen one lady," Stevenson wrote, "strip up her dress, and, with cries of wonder and delight, rub herself bare-breeched upon the velvet cushions."

This gave me pause. I took a glance around my room. This seemed unlikely to be replicated. The furniture, for instance, was made of cane and not conducive to any bare-breeched delight. I read on. Stevenson's account, to say the least, is confusing for the uninformed reader. He moves, helter-skelter, from Anaho to Taiohae, where Fanny Stevenson, very thoughtfully, teaches the local queen how to roll her own cigarettes (count me a fan of her), with side trips to Hiva Oa, a few digressions about Kiribati and Samoa, and seemingly random expositions on depopulation, missionaries, ghosts, the treatment of children, death, French colonizers, chiefs and *tapus*, and all seemingly based on five minutes of observation, followed by ten pages of discursive explanation, which makes him the father of long-form journalism, I guess. This didn't really bother me since I was more interested in the creator than the creation. Most of his best work on the Pacific lies in his fiction—*The Wrecker* and *The Ebb-Tide*, in particular. But I was looking for some experience, some adventure that I could follow, so that I could see and feel what Stevenson discerned as he explored the islands. He has a nice take on cannibalism, observing: "We consume the carcasses of creatures of like appetites, passions, and organs with ourselves; we feed them on babes, though not our own; and the slaughter-house resounds daily with screams of pain and fear." He goes on to express the torture the pig endures as he is led to slaughter. "Ladies will faint at the recital of one tithe of what they daily expect of their butchers."

But of the island's cannibals? "They were not cruel; apart from this custom, they are a race of the most kindly; rightly speaking, to eat a man's flesh after he is dead is far less hateful than to oppress him whilst he lives, and even the victims of their appetite were gently used in life and suddenly and painlessly dispatched at last." The German yachtie killed and consumed in the hills above Taiohae would probably dispute this, but I liked Stevenson for his fresh perspective, his easy willingness to discard the conventional wisdom of his day, and his open-eyed humanism. In his mind, cannibalism was largely the inevitable result of overpopulation and famine on finite islands, where the opportunity for other food sources was limited. That it was ritualized was just human nature. And yet, of course, the eating of another's flesh makes an impression. Even Stevenson, tolerant, understanding, culturally sensitive, given the times, ends a chapter in the Marquesas with a recounting of a cannibal chief holding the hand of Mrs. Stevenson: "His favorite morsel was the human hand, of which he speaks today with an ill-favored lustfulness. And when he said good-bye to Mrs. Stevenson, holding her hand, viewing her with tearful eyes, and chanting his farewell improvisation in the falsetto of Marquesan society, he wrote upon her a sentimental impression which I try in vain to share." So gifted with the tongue, Stevenson was rendered speechless. Seeing a cannibal holding the delicate morsel of your wife's hand will do that to you.

Stevenson was often sick in the Marquesas, but he did manage to go horseback riding high in the hills above Hiva Oa, where he encountered "a woman naked to the waist, of an aged countenance, but with hair still copious and black, and breasts still erect and beautiful." She offered him "two crimson flowers." I was no longer on Hiva Oa, but I figured this—a horse into the high hills of the Marquesas—was something I could do, and if I encountered a woman with "breasts still erect and beautiful," well, bonus points for me.

Hungry now, I found a café nearby, and was soon greeted by a friendly, heavily tattooed Marquesan woman and her husband, a white man, also tattooed in Polynesian script and built like a Mack truck. The Marquesas clearly were no place for small people, local and foreigner alike. He took my order—coffee, fresh juice, fruit, yogurt—and I watched him lumber toward the kitchen. I knew who he was. The yachties had spoken of him. He was, apparently, a former French Foreign Legionnaire, a German. The French station a regiment of Legionnaires in Tahiti. They don't fuck around, these French, with asserting their authority in their colonies. I made it my mission to learn his story, which would be difficult I knew. Foreign Legionnaires aren't exactly known for their chattiness.

"So," I said, as he brought me a pot of coffee, which was excellent by the way, "I gather you're German." He looked at me blankly. His eyes could only be described as cruel, as if they'd seen much that a normal man could not even begin to fathom. "I spent a lot of time in Germany," I said, barreling on. "My father used to live in Nuremberg." Again, not even a hint of some kind of conversational give-and-take. Maybe it was wrong to mention Nuremberg with its Nazi associations. These Legionnaires, I suspected, trended to the right. "So where are you from in Germany? Bavaria? Lower Saxony? Berlin? The east?" I asked, mildly, just making chitchat.

"Just Germany," he said. And then there was a long, uncomfortable pause. "I haven't been back in many years."

Yeah, probably because you have a criminal record and numerous outstanding warrants, I thought. Isn't that the typical Foreign Legionnaire's story? A young man involved in petty crime, seeing no outlet, until he hears the siren song of the French Foreign Legion. Sign up, gain a new identity—including a name and passport—submit to a few years of brutality and a seven-year stint in France's disposable legion, and walk away free, should you live. It beats prison, presumably. And the hoodlum's life on the streets.

But I had known some former French Legionaries and admired them, sort of. The idea of honor seems so antiquated in our day, though with a Legionnaire it's hard to know where noble distinction starts and violent bloodlust ends.

"I spent a lot of time in Eastern Europe back in the day," I said, sipping my coffee. "In Bosnia. During the war." This was true, but only because I was an idiot. "I was in Mostar."

The German looked upon me with some interest now. "And what were you doing in Mostar?" he asked.

Oh, I don't know. I was twenty-three. I was freaking out. Pissing my pants. Getting shot at. Crying for my mommy. Nearly getting blown up. Whimpering. That sort of thing.

But instead I said I was a journalist. I had attached myself to the Bosnian Army, which was then getting annihilated by both the Serbs and the Bosnian Croats. The Bosnian commander assigned me to a bunk with the "international volunteers," the ex–French Foreign Legionnaires, a half-dozen Brits, Scots, and Canadians. On my first night, as soon as I heard the shelling, I cowered underneath my bunk. An Englishman spoke: "Those are outgoing shells, you know." Oh, swell then. Shall make a note of it. And then I removed an assault weapon from my bunk—surprisingly heavy, these things—and tried to get some sleep, whereupon the outgoing barrage was met by incoming shells. "Might want to move away from the windows now and stay next to the sandbags," I was told. It took me a couple of days until I could distinguish between incoming and outgoing mortars, but really, it made no difference. I saw the grim explosive cracks of sniper bullets pinging off nearby walls and felt the concussive waves of bombs landing next to what remained of the Stari Most, the old bridge that would soon be sunk by a Croat's shell. And everywhere I wandered there were the makeshift graves of those who had fallen, most notably in Mostar's busiest roundabout.

It's not the sort of thing I like to think about. Much easier to write about the gutter of alcoholism than the grim reality of that war. But this was my introduction to French Foreign Legionnaires. Of course they weren't "official" soldiers then. Others would call them mercenaries. But this implied that they were fighting for money, of which there wasn't any in Bosnia at that time. In the evenings I'd smoke weed, which grew wild in the mine-infested hills around Mostar and drink slivovitz with the ex–Foreign Legionnaires as shells and sniper fire rained upon the town. They'd tell me of the Bosnian civilians they saw nailed and crucified on the door of a mosque, and the Chetniks—the bearded Bosnian Serbs—that they beheaded as the radio squawked with the taunts of the Serbian soldiers in the hills. Pass the slivovitz, I'd said, and could that joint make its way back to me now, please? What these soldiers loved, more than anything, was "action"—that was the word they used. To be in action was to kill or to be killed. It was the ultimate adrenaline rush, and whenever they discussed the day's events on the front, their eyes would glaze over in orgasmic delight. They were the ultimate adrenaline junkies, and even the regular Bosnian soldiers kept a wary distance from them.

But I mentioned nothing of this to the German. He simply asked me when, exactly, was I in Mostar.

"March/April, 1993."

He nodded. He knew his history. "I was never in Bosnia," he said. "But I spent a lot of time with you Americans."

No surprise there. Nearly every battlefield over the past decade has been occupied by Americans.

"I spent some time training at your Fort Bragg."

"With Delta Force?" I blurted. It was their home base, and I figured that's where international special forces went to mingle. Of course elite American Special Forces were encouraged to survive, whereas the Foreign Legionnaires were meant to be France's cannon fodder, the expendables.

And now he looked upon me hard. "Who are you, exactly?"

What could I say? "I'm just a traveler, curious about the people I meet."

"I spent most of my time in North Africa," he said. "And I think that's enough about me. Now, would you like some more coffee?"

I didn't. I'm a jittery mess when hyper-caffeinated. The nature of this conversation had clearly come to an end and I spent a few minutes tapping my fingers until I remembered the raison d'être for my being here. "Hey," I said. "I'm hoping to do some horseback riding up in the hills. Would you happen to know of someone who could help me out?"

"Yes," he said, his eyes suddenly alive. "I'll send you to Celine. You'll like her. She's a real man-killer."

And with that, his wife punched him hard in the gut.

Chapter Eleven

Celine was a Marquesan woman with an indeterminately aged countenance, but with hair still copious and black, and breasts still erect and beautiful. I know this because she didn't bother with a bra underneath her white T-shirt. Her shoes also didn't match. Nor her socks. This was a woman who marched to her own drum, unpretentious and direct, and I liked her immediately. I admire a person comfortable in their own shoes, and if they're mismatched so be it. Know thyself and be true. We drove off in a battered red pickup truck and spent much of the morning visiting her entire family, which is to say every residence and shop in the greater Taiohae area. "I have ten brothers and sisters," she said in French, as I prepared for another day of brain-frying linguistic exertion.

As a kid, I'd gone to a school in Canada in which half of all my lessons were taught in French, but that was a long time ago now, and I still felt the crushing disappointment of discovering that my neighbor here in Nuku Hiva was not, in fact, an American. How I'd been looking forward to speaking a language where I didn't have to think twice about verb conjugations. It'd been nearly a month now since I'd spoken more than a few sentences in my natural tongue, and pleased though I was that I could still recall my schoolboy French—why is it so easy to recall what you learned thirty years ago, and brow-crushingly difficult to remember what happened last week?—I yearned to be able to speak thoughtlessly, which is my de facto conversational modus operandi. But perhaps it was best that here, at least, there was some kind of pause between thought and spoken word as I searched for just the right *bon mot*. First thought wrong, I was told in rehab. So true.

"I have ten brothers and sisters," Celine said, and I believe I met each and every one of them, as well as cousins, uncles, nieces, and nephews, as we moved from shops to homes and waved at every soul we encountered along the roadside. Celine's family appeared to be single-handedly repopulating the Marquesas.

"Yes," she said with a laugh. "But that's why young people can't marry anyone from this island. We're too close. So they find husbands and wives from other islands—Hiva Oa, Fatu Hiva, Tahiti, or France."

Wherever we stopped, the conversation slipped into Marquesan, followed by hoots of laughter, and I stood quietly alongside, until Celine explained that they were mocking my gold-craving neighbor. "There's no gold here," she said with a delighted cackle. "Look at us. We are a simple people, and this man, he comes to our houses thinking we have treasure chests buried in the sand. *Il est fou.*"

Pretty much my feelings exactly.

"But come. Let us to go to my horses. They are my love."

We stopped first at her brother's home, the like of which I have never seen before or since. It was painted a cheery turquoise with simple window slats and a tin roof and walls bedecked with the skulls of horned boars, cows, the long sun-bleached snouts of horses, and satanic-looking goats. It was like stumbling across some backwoods shack straight out of *Deliverance* and I kept a wary eye out for banjo players.

Celine picked up a couple of saddles and as we drove off we were happily chased by a couple of dogs. She stopped and let them hop into the bed of the truck as we drove higher into the hills of Nuku Hiva. This, easily, was the most mountainous of the Marquesas, with a high alpine plateau where cattle grazed among evergreens, surrounded by a formidable range of four-thousand-foot peaks. Here too, every corner of the island was like its own microenvironment. The north coast was dry and rocky, the south wet and verdant, and the middle felt like Switzerland with its pine forests and cows. The Marquesas were unique, unlike any island group I'd ever seen, a dream landscape for both poets and scientists.

Celine unlocked a gate, and we soon found ourselves next to her horses. "You know how to ride, *oui*?"

Yeah, I was born on the saddle, a veritable cowboy, a *gaucho* of the high plains. The last time I rode a horse was in the Dominican Republic where I'd let my stallion wander too close to the mare in front, which irritated her, whereupon she kicked out her hind leg, hard and fast, missing the stallion but shattering my kneecap, causing me to limp painfully for weeks thereafter. But since then, I figured, I'd ridden camels and elephants, and I assumed that if my seven-year-old son could ride a horse, well, how hard could it be?

"*Bon*," she said. "You take this one," she said, saddling an agitated, neighing horse that stood approximately eighteen feet tall. "*Non, monsieur. Comme ça,*" she said. Apparently you're supposed to use stirrups when climbing upon a horse. Just leaping upon the beast and crawling over its back is *just not done*. Okay, I thought, settling in as Celine directed my flip-flops into the stirrups. *Giddy up.*

Fortunately, my horse was a follower, not a leader, and taking after Celine's confident horsemanship, we spent a few hours following a narrow trail, the dogs trailing underfoot, happy and frisky, as we ambled into an ever-shifting landscape, heading higher, from shadow to sunlight, as Celine explained and expounded upon every tree or bush we encountered. She was at home here, at peace with her island and her place therein, and proud. We plucked guavas from the trees and fed them to both the horses and to ourselves. It is the only place I have ever seen an apple tree grow next to a flowering banana tree. The view changed with each corner, with every rise in elevation, and the panorama was striking to behold. Below us was the Taipivai Valley, where Herman Melville gathered the material for his popular novel *Typee*—and a novel it was, not the autobiography many assume. He spent three weeks there, after escaping from a whaling ship, though his story takes place over four months, wherein he recounts the usual clichés of the Polynesian sexpot. He wasn't the first Westerner to find himself agog by the women of the Marquesas, of course. Here is Charles Porter, an American naval commander who visited in 1813, who was taken not only by the women's easy delights but by the reaction of their male relatives: "It was astonishing to us to see with what indifference fathers, husbands, and brothers would see their daughters, wives, and sisters fly from the embrace of one lover to that of another, and change from man to man as they could find purchasers. Far from seeming to consider it an offense against modesty, they seemed to view it only as an accommodation to strangers who had claims on their hospitality."

The Taipivai Valley is largely devoid of people now. All that is left is a small village. We could see its few tin roofs and the narrow curve of a dirt road and a large swath of coconut palms. Amorous adventure, alas, cost the Marquesans dearly, and the world described by Melville and Porter—its easy love and carnal hospitality—is now for the history books. What's really interesting is reading the accounts written a mere fifty years later—how casually dismissive of death the letters now were, as if it were the natural order, God's due, that Marquesans die. Irritating that, and we can only hope that these same letter writers were one day afflicted with leprosy and the pox.

The path we followed was muddy and slippery, and from time to time my horse would lose its purchase and there'd be a brief moment when I could feel my heart lurch. This was but a foreshadowing of what was to come. The path steepened again, and now I stood high in my stirrups as the horse galloped up the inclines, slipping here and there, its hooves crumbling momentarily, saved only by the momentum of its movement. Every instinct told me to hold the reins fast, to slow the beast down, to take it easy. Nice and slow, I thought. Let's just inch our way up. No way did I want to end up as a cushion for a collapsing twelve-hundred-pound horse.

"*Non!*" Celine yelled. "Let him run. Otherwise he will fall."

Isn't there a beginner's course around here? A pony park? Did I misrepresent myself? Sure, I'll wear a Stetson. I'll drive a pickup truck. But I'm an urban cowboy, lady. If you want to line dance, I'm your guy. But barreling up muddy, rocky, slippery, steep slopes on massive horses, beasts that I sensed were ready to topple at any moment, well, let's just say that it left me a trifle uncomfortable. But I did as suggested and gave the horse free rein, urging him on, as we surged up a vertiginous peak, and now, suddenly, I could see why the effort was entirely worth it.

We dismounted and took a gander at the view. Below us was a plummeting precipice, a couple of thousand feet at least, cascading down into a valley so serene and lovely and breathtaking that if God ever made a cathedral of His own, it would be here, and this would be it. In the distance was a plunging thirteen-hundred-foot waterfall. The mountains were ornately lush, a green vertigo that began with the coconut palms in the valley, a few towering banyans, and then a rising crescendo of trees and brush, desperately holding on to the tenuous grip of rising cliffs.

"This is a very special place," Celine said, as she let the horses wander free. "You are the first foreigner to be here."

Take that, Herman Melville.

"Look, do you see? Those blue birds. They are lorikeets. And there? The white bird with the long body. It only lives here in the mountains. And high in the mountains is a kind of eagle that lives off fruit. And there, do you see that bird with the long black wings? It also only lives here in those hills. But the problem is the rats. They climb into their nests."

Celine continued to speak of the beauty of her island as she hand-rolled a cigarette. "This place is not like Tahiti with its crowds and pollution. Tahiti is finished. Here, it is like it always was."

Minus the people, of course. There are about 2,500 people living on Nuka Hiva now, a small fraction of what once was. But I told her how much I admired how the culture was returning. She nodded and agreed, but when I mentioned the Marquesan Festival, a once-every-four-years gathering of dancers and artists from throughout the islands, she frowned and disagreed.

"It's not good," she said. "The tourists come then. So people dance for money. That's all they see, the money. Me, I am a dancer and I don't dance for money. I dance for free." And now she began to sway her hips and dance, finding a song in her own mind.

"But there aren't any tourists here," I countered as she swayed and sashayed. "There can't be more than forty rooms on this island."

"There are enough. They started to come in 1979 when they built the runway."

"But no one flies to the Marquesas," I noted.

"There is the *Aranui*."

Okay. Guilty. "But that only comes once a month."

"And the *bateaux*."

"There are twelve in the harbor."

"It is enough."

And she asked me to hold her cigarette as she danced on as the birds soared on updrafts and the horses ate contentedly on the tall grass. The dogs rested, watching her, attuned to her moods. I wasn't sure what the German Legionnaire meant when he referred to her as a man-killer. Try to translate a thought through three languages and you never quite know what results. Was she quick with the knife or slow with the heartbreak? Eventually, her hips stopped swaying, and we walked the horses down the steepest part of the mountain, moving them in zigzags so that they'd keep their footing, and as we hopped back on to our mounts—I used the stirrups this time, like John Wayne—Celine rolled another cigarette.

"Hey, Celine," I said. "Tell me how good that cigarette is."

She laughed. "When people tell me not to smoke, you know what I tell them. I say shut up." And without prompting she took out her pouch of tobacco and papers and rolled one for me.

"Menthol," I said. "I can't ride a horse smoking a menthol."

"Yes, you can."

The weather had turned over the next couple of days. Wind swept the island. The bay was foaming with streaming froth. The sailboats bobbed and weaved as their sheets and rigging clanged against the masts. Rain swept the island in sudden squalls. Wet, misty clouds swirled around the mountains, shrouding them. A tropical island awash in rain, the coconut trees straining in the wind, is a depressing place, and I twiddled my thumbs waiting for brief bursts of sunshine, whereupon I laced my shoes and ran through sloppy, muddy puddles, killing time until I could explore the island further. Finally, sensing no break in the weather, I gave up and, seeing a path rising above the town and over a low ridge, I followed it in the drizzle, hiking around the headland and through an open gate, the trail bordered by a thick growth of trees, and I wandered through the bush, sopping wet now, for about a mile until I came to a lonely beach.

Hey, I thought, looking around. This looks familiar. Wasn't this . . . Yeah. It had to be—the beach used in *Survivor: Marquesas*, the reality television show that . . . Sorry, I used the word *reality* there. I'd found myself on a few *Survivor* locales by now and they're never more than a mile or two from a town, a comfortable hotel, and a slew of bars and restaurants. The contestants might go hungry, but not the crew. I'd watched the very first *Survivor* years ago, when the conniving wickedness of contestants was still fresh and interesting, but it had been a long time since I'd tuned in to subsequent shows. But because I'm very diligent about researching the places I visit, I'd watched what I could of *Survivor: Marquesas* on YouTube, and felt very pleased to now be in the exact same spot where a contestant, who'd somehow managed to impale his hand on a sea urchin, had desperately pleaded for someone to urinate on his hand—for medicinal reasons, of course—and was soon obliged by a helpful female contestant. It really is the little things in life that make it worthwhile.

Now, however, there was just the weathered remains of a homespun lean-to and a bleak desolation to the beach, and I did not linger long, hiking back to town in the driving rain, where I was soon met by a rolling red pickup truck, the windows down, as Celine yelled, *Qu'est-ce que tu fais?* as she invited me into the cab of her truck. I hopped in and told her I'd been to the beach on the other side of the hills, where *Survivor* had been filmed, and she just rolled her eyes. "It was like an invasion," she said. "For two months, it was like we were an occupied island."

"But it's all good," I said. "The world learned a little something of the Marquesas, *n'est-ce pas?*"

Here, I believe, I encountered a really expressive display of emphatic cussing. It's sad, really, that I learned my French in Catholic school, because to this day I still don't know how to swear creatively in French, though if I'd chosen, at this moment, I'm sure I could have learned the schoolyard grammar I was so lacking.

"But see," I said. "On this show America was introduced to the tribal communities of the Marquesas, and how they were ruled by a stern yet benevolent chief named Jeff."

"^%F#@#F%&*%Fmerde."

Okay, I probably didn't translate that accurately. Am putting learning all the naughty words in French on my list of things to do, right next to acquiring skulls.

"Do you have some time?" Celine asked.

Oh, I don't know. I'm on an island in the middle of nowhere, without an ongoing ticket or a way off, amusing myself by going on desultory hikes to the set of *Survivor: Marquesas* in the drenching rain. Yeah, I think I've got a couple of minutes to spare.

"Come," she said. "I'll show you the old Marquesas."

We took a high road that clung to the lofty side of Mount Muake, which looms above Taiohae, as the weather finally started to clear, offering grand views of the town and the turtle-shaped bay. Clearly, Celine was a proud Marquesan, so I asked her why on earth were the islands still French? Didn't that seem kind of odd to her, to be a citizen of a country on the other side of the planet, one where she'd never set foot? Wouldn't it be better to be independent?

"*Non,*" she said. "The Marquesas are very expensive and we are poor. The French give us money."

Yes, I said. But French Polynesia is expensive because the French themselves have completely warped the local economy. The independent Pacific isn't nearly so pricey.

She agreed, and said things were simpler here in French Polynesia until they began with the nuclear testing. Then all this infrastructure was built, runways were constructed, and now there were hordes of French *fonctionnaires* gallivanting around the islands, their pockets flush with Western paychecks, which caused all the prices to rise.

Well, just kick them out then, I said. Everyone eventually casts off their colonizers, *non*? Live free or die.

She laughed at this. *Vous, les Américains!* But without France, she said, we would be ruled by Tahiti and that would be unacceptable. France gives us money; Tahiti wouldn't give us a franc.

And that settled it for her. Better to be ruled by a faraway, middling continental power that sends a check from time to time than the conniving Tahitians. Try as I did to ferment revolt, she would have nothing to do with it. "It is best the way it is," she said. She would never vote for independence. You can't trust a Tahitian, you know.

We drove through the Taipivai Valley, a mix of wild forest growth and cultivated coconut palms, as Celine pointed toward the remnants of old stone platforms, the site of yet another abandoned village. "Here is where your Herman Melville stayed. They were very kind to him, but he writes about them like they were all cannibals."

Um, weren't they?

She smiled. "Well, okay, a little bit. But you'd think all we did was kill people and eat them every day. We eat fruit and fish too, you know. Eating people was for special occasions, like your holiday. What do you call it? Thanksgiving."

Oh, right. I could just envision that meal. Mashed potatoes, cranberry sauce, sweet potatoes, pumpkin pie, and a roasted corpse with a nice black truffle butter and white wine gravy. The stuffing would be tricky, though. Welcome to Chez Hannibal Lecter. Would you like some fava beans and a nice Chianti?

"Okay, here is your cannibal village," she said, parking the truck near Kamuihei, an ancient settlement restored for the Marquesan Festival some years back. Throughout the islands of the Marquesas there are numerous stone *paepaes*, nearly all overgrown by the ever-encroaching forest. Most building material in the Marquesas, of course, was made of wood and thatch and has long since decomposed, leaving only the carefully arranged stones and boulders as the last remaining vestiges of what were once full and lively villages. In Kamuihei, however, a few dwellings, done in the manner of the Marquesas of bygone days, now occupied the *paepaes*, which together with the tikis and petroglyphs, allowed you to visualize how the islanders once lived. But what was really striking about the site was an enormous, six-hundred-year-old banyan tree that soared over the village and the surrounding forest. It made me think of *Avatar* for some reason, a giant tree of life and mystery.

"Here's where we killed the victims," Celine said.

Okay, so maybe it wasn't the tree of life.

"We called this the knot of power. The victims would be hanged on hooks, see, like the long pig. They would be beaten by a war club. But we didn't eat the whole man. Just a little bit."

"Just a little bit? Seems like such a waste, don't you think?"

She smirked at me. "The man was eaten for his *mana*, that is the invisible power that resides in the head."

"And who, exactly, were these unfortunate meals?"

"Antisocial people."

Antisocial people? That sounds like every teenager I've ever known.

"It was the people who broke the taboos. Or sometimes they would raid another tribe. There were five main tribes on Nuku Hiva then. But usually they would just take one or two people. It wasn't like they went off to kill the whole village. It was for the ritual. And then they would throw the bones here, you see?" Celine said, pointing to a pit in the recesses of the banyan tree. "And in this pit," she said, pointing to the one next to it, "is where they held the victims."

I couldn't even begin to fathom what it must have been like to find yourself in the pit of doom, next to a pile of bones, as a crowd gathers like . . . Thanksgiving.

"But then the white men came," Celine continued. "And you know what happened to us, *oui*?"

I nodded, feeling contrite and guilty. Bad white people.

"Many ships used to come to the Marquesas. In 1813 alone, there were more than sixty *bateaux* here. And they brought the diseases. And now there was hunger. So instead of eating a little bit of the man for his *mana*, now people began to eat the whole body. It isn't our culture to do that, but when a person is hungry . . ." She shrugged and wandered off. "Do not step on the red stones," she said as I followed. "They are sacred. But look, the sun has come back. I will show you more of beautiful Nuku Hiva. You see how friendly we are?" And then she chomped her teeth and smiled, with malice or mischief I'm not sure.

There is a prominent isthmus that divides Anaho Bay from Hatiheu, and we parked the truck and hiked between the two.

Anaho Bay, of course, is where Stevenson first anchored, and it is no wonder that he so quickly felt the appeal of the Marquesas. It is the proverbial postcard image of the South Seas, a long curving sandy shore with a fringing reef, framed by coconut palms and embraced by "rude and bare hills," as Stevenson described the scene, "enclosed to the landward by a bulk of shattered mountains," where he soon beheld "the scent of the land and of a hundred fruits or flowers." Sounds intriguing, no? And it is. It's the kind of place where you can imagine lingering for a good long while. There is the reef, for instance, a rarity in the Marquesas, and a warm, inviting turquoise sea alive with fishy critters, little *Nemos* and longnose emperors. But that beach is hell on earth, a place where the no-nos, blizzards of them, will feast upon you until all that remains is the sun-baked carcass of your bones. "It is for this reason that very few people live here anymore," Celine noted, as we hightailed it back up into the hills, hiking onward to Hatiheu.

"Still beautiful," Celine observed. "And no more no-nos," as we wandered through a sleepy village toward a black-sand beach with smooth, water-sculpted stones, surrounded by steep and eroded basalt cliffs. It was more lush here, primeval, and alive. The clouds and rain had completely dissipated now. I spent a few minutes just standing, still and alert, and when no insects bothered me I figured I could live here, contentedly, happily, tending to a garden and doing a little fishing. This too was one of Stevenson's favorite locales in the Marquesas, though he was irritated to no end by the Catholic school that once lay here, educating what remained of the island's youthful boys, who had been plucked by the government and sent here to a boarding school, learning little more than the tedium of Scripture, separated by the width of the island from the girls' school in Taiohae. "Prayers, and reading and writing, prayers again and arithmetic, and more prayers to conclude: such appeared to be the dreary nature of the course." And the boys? "They sit and yawn." Perhaps Stevenson would be pleased to know that nothing remains of the school. It was destroyed by a tsunami on April Fool's Day, 1946.

"Look," Celine said, pointing high toward one of the towering cliffs. "You see the statue? It is of the Virgin Mary. So you see, we are very civilized now."

"Ha," I said. "Do you know who Robert Louis Stevenson is?"

"*Non*," she replied.

"Well, he visited your island back in 1889, and he too noticed the statue of the Virgin on the mount. Do you know how he described it? 'A poor lost doll, forgotten there by a giant child.'"

"*Oui*." She laughed. "She is a lost doll."

"And do you know what else he thought? He said that eating a man, *c'est pas un problème*, it's how you treat him while he lives that matters."

"*C'est vrai*. I like your Robert Louis Stevenson."

And now we looked out to the ocean, which had calmed and was smooth, and there we could see the great shell of a green turtle, swimming contentedly beyond the break zone.

"The turtle is very special in our culture," Celine observed, as we watched it swim languidly by. I liked turtles. No, really, I mean that. Like penguins, they are clumsy and comic on land. In the water, they are like thespians on the stage, acrobatic and confident. You think they'd choose one or the other—land or sea—but they live betwixt and between, voyagers among worlds. They are earthbound astronauts. "We believe turtles travel freely between our world and the spirit world. It is a sacred creature."

"So the Marquesans wouldn't eat a turtle, right?"

"Only on special occasions. Like the man."

Chapter Twelve

One of the really strange things that happens to you when you spend a significant amount of time in the Marquesas is this irresistible impulse to get a tattoo. It must be something in the air. Until now, I'd managed to lead an ink-free life, which is remarkable really. I'm not sure if I've mentioned it, but I've been known to have a drink or twenty, and not once did I feel any compulsion to have anyone stick a needle into my body and unload a syringe of ink. Not in my teens, or twenties, or thirties. And now here I was, sober, over the age of forty, feeling the need to be stained for life. I can't explain it. All I knew is that for the first time ever, I wanted a tat. Now. Here. A big one.

It's unsurprising, really. Consider the early Westerners to wash upon these shores. When Krusenstern, the Russian explorer, arrived in the Marquesas in 1804, he was startled to discover the presence of one Jean-Baptiste Cabri, a Frenchman from Bordeaux, who had sailed with an English whaling vessel that wrecked, and as the apparent lone survivor, found his way to Nuku Hiva. He'd lived there for untold years by the time the Russian commander encountered him, so long, apparently, that he had all but forgotten his native language, and in the words of one historian, "had so much lost the manners and habits of civilized life, that little difference was to be discerned between him and the natives, with regard to his habits and mode of living." Naturally, having assimilated: "His whole figure, not excepting his face was tattooed." When finally he was rescued, he spent his remaining years being exhibited throughout Europe like a circus freak, a monkey in the cage.

Nowadays, of course, it's rare to see anyone in the Pacific, long-term Westerners included, without a tattoo. And yet, despite having spent years on the islands myself, I'd never had any particular urge to use my body as a canvas, as a forum for self-expression, a means for conveying something essential about my character. It wasn't the needles. I have no fear of them. I know; good call not trying heroin. Nor was it the pain. Throughout my childhood, rare was the year when I didn't end up in an emergency room for stitches. I've fractured vertebrae, broken bones, dealt with concussions, shattered my feet in a fall, pinched a few nerves, torn some tendons, had a few teeth pulled, etc. etc. And never once did I finish a bottle of prescription pain meds. Weird that, but lucky. When it comes to catastrophes in my life, I'm focused.

Nor was I ever bothered by the permanence of a tattoo. These words, for instance, if you're reading them, will be around forever. I've regretted a few sentences, but I can't take them back. They're out there, published somewhere and hovering in Internet-land. It's something we all deal with now. Someone posts a picture of you upchucking on Bourbon Street, tags it, and there you go, a proud moment that for generations to come will be available for comment and celebration. "Wow, Grandpa, look, your puke is purple like my stuffed dinosaur." It's why I never understood the cult of futurology around the Internet. To me it seems like some great tool of archeology, every moment now frozen in the embers of time, an entire life embedded on planet Google. On this planet, you never escape high school.

No, what dissuaded me from ever getting a tattoo in the South Pacific was—how to say this politely?—Caucasians with tribal tattoos from the Pacific look like dweebs. Yeah, The Rock can get away with it. So too all those Samoan NFL football players. But have you ever seen an alabaster-skinned, long-haired, redheaded man with a beer belly in a shiny-white swimsuit with a full-body suit of Polynesian swirls and symbols? I have, and it gives me nightmares to this day. The dissonance was overwhelming. Or a twenty-three-year-old Canadian with traditional Maori facial tattoos? I'm not talking about a prison teardrop—and good luck getting a job with those things on your face—but the full monty, a face drenched green with curls and swooshes, like he'd had a violent encounter with a bucket of paint and lost? An ink-stained face on a crusty Marquesan seaman can look cool; on a hollow-chested white boy from the 'burbs and all I foresee is years of therapy.

And yet . . .

I saw a newspaper, one of the local French Polynesian papers, and I spent a while reading about François Hollande, the president of France, and his tax proposals, and then moved on to the Sports section—FC Lorient beat Rennes; Olympique de Marseille defeated OGC Nice; and shockingly Paris Saint-Germain lost to Toulouse FC. It still continued to baffle me, the *Frenchness* of the islands, the same white noise one would find in Provence. I spent a while casually perusing the paper, and then noticed the date.

Well, hey there. It was my sobriety anniversary. Exactly a year earlier, I'd found myself deposited curbside at rehab, where I had my photograph taken, signed some papers—and God knows what they were; if I ever have another child, I'm sorry, but it appears I may have sold you to an Albanian circus—checked in with the nurse's station, where I was informed that 156/98 was not a particularly good number when it comes to blood pressure, that I was already in the throes of some nasty alcohol withdrawal symptoms, including a pulse rate that was boom-boom-booming at ninety-five beats a minute, and that it would soon get worse, potentially much worse. Thus the need for meds. I was shown to the detox room, which I shared with another alcoholic who snored like Thor with a bad cold, a shivering heroin addict, and a tweaked-out wild-eyed pill popper, and so began a week of hell, two of regret and befuddlement, followed by a week of sanity and health, which I very much hoped to continue, knowing right from the get-go that the odds were not good.

And now here I was, exactly a year later, on the far side of the world, still befuddled, somewhat sane, reasonably healthy I hoped, but at the very least alive, and I suddenly felt the need to commemorate the occasion. Typically, at meetings of like-minded souls, it's done with cupcakes. There's hugging and clapping and cheers and sweets. A year is a big deal. Of course, I can't even begin to count all the times I've heard of people with three, seven, ten, even twenty years of sobriety *going back out*, only to return untold months or years later—if they're lucky and don't die—sheepishly, a little embarrassed, describing how that little glass of cabernet quickly descended into a gallon of vodka and a pint of NyQuil a day, but now, thanks to a six-month stint at the local Department of Corrections, they've dried out, and they've decided to *come back in* and *take it one day at a time*. I hate those stories. But I'm enthralled by them too. Tell me more about how bad it was, I want to say. So really, one itsy-bitsy glass of wine and the next thing you remember is hurtling through the windshield of a car? In Argentina? It really is a day-by-day thing, and so it will remain for all time. And yet, put together 365 days of continuous sobriety and, well, you want a fucking cupcake.

But there are no cupcakes on Nuku Hiva. There are, however, tattoos, so I decided to get one of those instead. It made perfect sense in my world.

I knew what I wanted, design-wise, more or less. The only question was how should I go about finding a tattoo artist on Nuku Hiva? My South Pacific island instincts had kicked in by now, and I knew that were I to ask a Marquesan they would invariably lead me to their brother or nephew or cousin, and I'd find myself confronted by some seventeen-year-old kid wielding a needle and a sketchbook of drawings. That's just how it works. The family takes care of its own out here, and if some foreigner drops out of the sky with a hankering for a tattoo and you've got an unemployed cousin with a creative disposition who could use a few francs, custom dictates that you bring these two people together. Everyone wins; the family earns some income, and the foreigner has his traditional Marquesan tattoo. Sure, he may have asked for a small dolphin on his back, but your cousin doesn't really know how to do dolphins, but he does this really neat jellyfish with gnarly tentacles, so he gives him that instead. They're both sea creatures right, so what's the problem? And if there is one, well, the foreigner eventually goes away and so too the problem.

Fortunately, I knew of a certain German expat on the island, and he, marked as he was with the distinctive geometric arches and symbols that are unique to the Marquesas, did not look like a dweeb. Of course, as an ex–Foreign Legionnaire, you could tattoo a kitten on his forehead and he'd still manage to look fearsome and ill-tempered and not the sort of person you'd casually call a pussy. But I figured he'd be a good go-to guy for some objective advice on finding a tattooist who wouldn't leave me weeping in regret or dying of hepatitis C.

"Yes, of course. I know of someone," he said when I spoke with him. "You want a traditional Marquesan tattoo, *oui*?" I nodded. "Okay, just don't get a turtle or dolphin, *tu comprends*? That's what every *étranger* gets." And then he flexed the warrior tats that ran up and down his arms, his body language conveying the distinct impression that no matter how I decided to get inked, I would still only be a smidgen of the man he was. These arms, he seemed to suggest, have killed men. That's fine, I thought. To each their own. I was getting a tattoo because I hadn't killed anyone.

We made arrangements and when the appointed time came I met the Legionnaire, and together with his wife and extended family—essentially half of Taiohae—wandered to the shoreline, to what appeared to be a thatch-roofed boathouse, near where a few large outrigger canoes were stored on the beach. And here I met my tattooist, who appeared to be . . . a seventeen-year-old kid wielding a needle and a sketchbook of drawings.

You are joking, I thought. I had expected to encounter some island elder, a keeper of the old ways, a traditionalist, sure in his knowledge and practiced in his skills. I turned to the German and gave him an arched-eyebrow WTF look. "He is very good," he informed me. "He is my nephew." And then he wandered off with a cheery wave, leaving me behind with his Marquesan family, who stood by with eager anticipation, curious to see how this *étranger* would deal with the pain.

Now how did this happen? This is French Polynesia. No effort is spared to change these little South Pacific islands into outposts of Europe. It's all France all the time out here. You can buy a fresh baked baguette, enjoy it with a café au lait while reading the newspaper, catch up on Ligue 1 scores and the lat-est fashion news from Paris, and then go home and watch a Gérard Depardieu movie on television. There is nothing here forcing you to assimilate, and as far as I could tell, none of the other expats here had, preferring to maintain the rhythm of continental life in an island setting. It's why I had asked a for-eigner for his recommendation and not a Marquesan, specifi-cally for their impartiality, their ability to convey advice or aesthetic judgment that was not colored by the whirl of family obligations. And now here I was, confronted with a *nephew* and a needle.

"*Et* . . . ," I said, trying not to sound alarmed. "Um . . . so how long have you been doing this?" I asked, in French, trying to ascertain his age.

"*Huit ans*," he said. Eight years. They let nine-year-olds stab ink-stained needles into people around here? Perhaps he just looked younger. Maybe he did have some experience? Or he was some kind of prodigy in the world of tattoos. We sat on the beach and flipped through his catalogue of designs, but what I wanted to see was some real-world display of his work. Surgeons, after all, practice on cadavers and dead pigs before they're sent into the operating room. Young tattooists in the Marquesas practice on what, exactly? The only thing I could think of was foreigners who eventually go away.

His name was Felix, and he dipped into his bag of gear and pulled out a small notebook computer and I soon found myself enthralled by the pictures he'd taken of his work. Jesus, that looks painful, I thought, as he showed me photos of a local woman he'd tattooed. The tattoos followed the length of her spine and then fanned out across her shoulder blades. There were photos of ankles, arms, legs, necks, torsos, faces, all inked in the distinctive style of the Marquesas. These were all taken moments after the work was completed, when the flesh still looks raw and abused, and they reminded me of what one might find in a police coroner's report. *The deceased has several identifying marks, including geometric tattoos on the left buttocks . . .*

"*Vous avez choisi?*" Felix asked, as we moved inside to the boathouse, which had a pool table, two chairs, a Formica desk, a stunning view of the bay, and a cement floor that appeared to be the marching grounds for several battalions of ants. I needed a moment to think. While Felix set up his tattoo kit, I stepped back outside and wandered to the edge of the water. Did I really want to do this? Haven't I seen enough people my age, at the beach, with tattoos that they'd gotten in the nineties, now faded, resting on sallow skin and flabby bodies, grim reminders of a lost weekend in the Florida Keys? Yes, I thought. Yes, I have. Did I really want to join them, the ink-stained masses of Generation X? No, I thought, though I am proud of my generation. We are the sane generation. But it is true that, for a brief spell, there was a certain regrettable overindulgence in tattoos and all things Seattle. But this was different. I was not in Seattle or the Florida Keys. Nor was I presently flabby. I was fit. I was in the Marquesas. I was sober. And I couldn't find a cupcake.

"*Bon,*" I finally said. "*Je suis prêt.*"

We spent a long while discussing the details of my tattoo— its design, size, placement—and as soon as we were in synch, he asked if I'd mind if he put some music on. He scrolled through his tunes, and soon we were listening to what I can only describe as some French Polynesian mutant variation of Throwing Muses. Perfect, I thought. Nothing like a little of that old-school Gen-X alternative sound, mixed with South Pacific sensibilities, sung in French, to accompany a forty-two-year-old getting his first tattoo in the Marquesas. The band was from the Tuamotus, and if I'd had use of my arm I would have written their name down, but Felix now had it and was focused on outlining the tattoo with a red marker.

I had decided to get a turtle. French Foreign Legionnaires, of course, are known for their prudent lifestyle decisions, but there was only so much advice and direction that I was going to take from someone who had signed up to fight another country's wars in Chad. And a turtle met my own personal Caucasian with Polynesian tattoos–dweeb test. For centuries, American and European sailors on naval ships and whalers commemorated their first equatorial crossing with a tattoo of a sea turtle. And I had crossed the equator, on a wooden sailboat no less. Admittedly, this was years ago, but I've always been a procrastinator. Now that I was getting a turtle, I looked forward to sailing across the Atlantic so that I could match it with a sea anchor on the other arm. Sail onward to China and I will have earned a dragon, and if I was feeling really ambitious, a rounding of Cape Horn will allow me to ink a fully rigged tall ship on my back. A couple of lucky accidents at sea and I'll get the peg leg and an eye patch too. I'll look exactly like *Treasure Island*'s Long John Silver. As you can see, I take my work very seriously. It is my ambition to be known as the Robert De Niro of travel literature.

A sea turtle also reminded me of a trip I had taken a few years ago, back when times were still good and I was, very briefly, flush with cash. I had taken my family to Maui, and one morning, while my wife and I had taken the boys out to do some ocean kayaking, we were joined by a large green turtle, who swam between our two boats for a good long while, enthralling us with its courtly manner and wizened visage, its eyes alert and friendly, before it plunged back into the depths. Stay sober, and I get to do cool stuff like kayak with sea turtles with my family. Drink, and lose the family. In Marquesan culture, of course, the turtle is the creature that travels freely between the temporal and the spiritual worlds, and this seemed somehow fitting for my own particular situation as I journeyed from one world to another.

Felix suddenly brought my attention to the needle he held in his hands. "It is new, you see," he said as he opened the package. And now our music was accompanied by the soft whir of his machine. A crowd had gathered, silently watching. Everyone had tattoos of their own, and yet I could see the women wince as Felix brought the needle to my arm. Really, I thought? Is it that painful? I felt the needle penetrate my skin and . . .

Okay, unbeknownst to me, I must be some kind of masochist.

"*Ça fait mal, n'est-ce pas?*" one of the women asked. Actually, no, it didn't hurt at all, more like a cat scratching against lightly sunburned skin. Getting a tattoo is not the sort of thing I'd want to do every day, but I'll take it over a visit to the dentist's office. Indeed, after a while, it began to feel vaguely pleasant and soothing, which made me think that my wiring is even more askew than even I was aware. It took the entire morning to complete. In the meantime, people would come and go and have a gander. I couldn't bear to look at the tattoo myself as it progressed. I worried that I'd have the same reaction you get when you're halfway through a bad haircut, the moment you realize that for the next two or three weeks you're going to look like someone who's just been released on furlough from the state psychiatric ward. Oh man, you think. I'm going to look like a skate-punk with a bad attitude? Really? On my wedding day? But then you get over it because hair, of course, grows back and you resolve to never again get a seven-dollar haircut, until four weeks later when, once again, you find yourself in the same one-eyed barber's chair. But at least there remains the option of one day spending upward of ten dollars on a haircut. Bad hair can be corrected. Tattoos, of course, cannot. And so I spent the hours staring at the multitude of ants that crawled along the floor. What were they after, I wondered? I saw them carry a roach like it was some kind of triumphant trophy, but that wouldn't justify the vast armies of ants that were marching up and down the cement floor. What had they found? Rotting fruit? A dead bird? Rats?

And so the hours passed, until finally Felix declared that he was *fini*. I took a look at the crowd, trying to read their faces. *C'est bon*, a few said. Others gave me the thumbs-up. Some, however, maintained inscrutable faces and wandered away, silently, without comment, and they troubled me greatly. Felix had a pocket mirror available, but I declined, preferring to study just what, precisely, I had done to myself when I got back to my room on the hill. I was told to apply coconut oil to the tattoo for the next few days. Also, I must keep it out of the sun for at least the next week. Really? Out of the sun? In the South Pacific? In this heat? It was probably just as well, I soon thought. I generally wore an athletic tank top and was developing the most ridiculous tan lines, as if I were spending my days lounging on the beach in a woman's one-piece swimsuit and shorts. A proper T-shirt will at least get me to a respectable farmer's tan.

I thanked Felix and walked back to my room and headed straight for the mirror. My first thought, upon seeing the tattoo, was that I wanted another one, on the other arm, and perhaps a couple more on my torso, and maybe my calves. I liked this tattoo. I was Island Man now. True, my tattoo was of a turtle, but it was a tough turtle, possessed of otherworldly grace and harmony and . . . did that fin not align with the other one? And why is the shading uneven? And . . . is it crooked? Was it not straight on my arm? Did it look like it was trying to swim away? For a long moment, my heart stopped beating. And then I thought, well, I'm a little crooked too, and I breathed again and continued to stare at my cupcake. It's a flawed tattoo, but it's mine, and if this past year has taught me anything, it is to be satisfied with imperfection. Also, never trust a French Foreign Legionnaire or a tattoo artist under the age of thirty.

Chapter Thirteen

Not many people would assume this, but I'm a big fan of Rick Perry, the governor of Texas. Wait, I can hear my friends say, isn't Governor Perry that politician who couldn't remember the three departments he'd cut should he become president, the guy who agitated for secession upon Obama's reelection, the one who spends more time shining his cowboy boots than reading policy papers? Yeah, that's the guy. But you know what? He runs with a laser-sighted .380 Ruger with hollow bullets holstered on to his waist. And you know, he ain't afraid to unload should some critter pester him. There are coyotes in Texas who rue the day they encountered Governor Perry on his morning jog. That is, if they were still alive. Don't fuck with him, animal world.

The cheese-eating surrender monkeys in French Polynesia, however, won't let you run with a holstered gun, which is a travesty. I found myself on Fakarava—yes, let's say it again, Fakarava—an atoll in the Tuamotus, an island group long known as the Dangerous Archipelago, a constellation of islands and poorly charted reefs, swirling currents, and a population that before the arrival of missionaries was known mostly for their ferocity toward outsiders. I'd arrived by prop plane in the late afternoon. It had been a turbulent flight, not because of storms or angry clouds, but rather due to the suffocating heat, causing warm air thermals to rise and wreak a little havoc in the sky, though this hadn't prevented the captain from turning off the seat-belt sign approximately a nanosecond after takeoff and keeping it unlit for the duration of the flight. I had gotten up to stretch my legs in the small plane just as we encountered an air bump, which resulted in me slamming my head into the overhead compartment, causing my fellow passengers to laugh with unrestrained glee. That's exactly what the I-Kiribati would do, I thought—laugh—and this pleased me. I had once again entered the world of atolls. Difficult geography makes for an easily amused people.

I'd found a guesthouse on the outskirts of Rotoava, Fakarava's lone settlement, and after depositing my backpack in a plywood *fare* that stood overlooking a luminescent lagoon, headed out for a run. It felt good to be back on an atoll, "lying coiled like a serpent, tail to mouth, in the outrageous ocean," as Stevenson described it. It had been a difficult sail for Stevenson and his party. Indeed, setting out from the Marquesas, where they left behind the Japanese cook, who had been jailed for drunkenness, replacing him with a young Chinese man, Ah Fu, who had been marooned on the islands as a child, they hadn't intended to make landfall on Fakarava at all, but rather at Takaroa, another atoll some thirty miles distant. Alas, they were hit hard by squall after squall. "We were swung and tossed together all that time like shot in a stage thunderbox. The mate was thrown down and had his head cut open. The captain was sick on deck; the cook sick in the galley. Of all the party only two sat down to dinner. I was one. I own that I felt wretchedly . . ."

The weather had caused them to become lost, no small

danger in this part of the world, with its boat-shredding reefs and shark-infested waters, and so when Fakarava was sighted, with its clear, open passage and its promise of safety, they anchored there, in the lagoon, seeking a respite from the treacherous ocean.

I could not envision a more placid scene than the one I now beheld, however. An atoll is but a sliver of elongated islets, with tufts of coconut palms and pandanus trees, and a beach that radiates like a mirage on the lagoon, and another, just a hundred yards distant, that is often tumultuous and violent, where the ocean rages ashore, leaving a scene of ragged desolation. On every atoll, life, what there is of it, is focused on the lagoon, which was now as smooth and unrippled as a mirror, reflecting a few billowy white cotton-ball clouds in the near distance, hovering in a windless sky. I ran in the direction from whence I came, toward the village and beyond to the small airport, the end of the paved road. The heat was as intense as any I'd felt, so hot that you feel strangely cold, your skin reacting to the blazing furnace much as it does to an arctic wind. There were a few people out on bicycles, the kids lazily peddling their oversize bikes in the middle of the road, unconcerned with traffic for there was none. Even in the village itself, all seemed quiet and undisturbed. What few people I saw lingered in the shade they could find. There are about eight hundred folks living on Fakarava, nearly all concentrated in Rotoava and I suspected most were lying prone underneath a slow-moving ceiling fan, inside their tidy cinderblock bungalows, some of which were fronted by graves ringed by coral stones. There was a lone church—Catholic, of course—dating from the nineteenth century, which was painted a sun-reflecting white on the outside, and inside, as I saw through the open doors, a sky blue, with an interior decorated with streamers of shells and a mother-of-pearl altar. Near the jetty were two small general stores, a handicraft shop, and another that specialized in pearls, as well as a couple of dive shops, which together seemed to make up the entirety of the island's economy.

They came out of nowhere, ferocious and unrelenting, beasts from hell, all noise and fury, snarling, barking, their ears flattened, teeth flaring, on the chase, hunting, full of malevolent intent. I stopped running immediately, the sweat steaming from my pores, my heart racing. There were three of them, heinous mongrel dogs, and they swarmed around me, a cacophony of noise and threats, lurching forward, lunging for my legs, their mouths frothing. Mad dogs and Englishmen, indeed. I walked on, slowly, but with purpose, trying not to look into their eyes, striving to maintain a quiet neutrality, silently kicking myself for not having the foresight to carry rocks. Think, I told myself. The dogs continued with their thunder, their charging, until finally one nipped me right where my shoe met my Achilles tendon, and now I was furious. But I walked on. You cannot go *mano a mano* with three agitated dogs. I could not turn back because that would establish their dominance and then they'd tear me to shreds. I could only walk forward, which I did, in the middle of the road, where otherwise all was still and silent, wilting in the heat. And then I crossed whatever invisible boundary marked their territory, where they stopped following me, the crescendo of barking died, and once again I was enveloped by silence, the lagoon still tranquil, the palm fronds unmoving.

At the edge of the village, I resumed my run, if only so that my activity would match my heart rate, which was going *boom-boom-boom*. Nothing like a wild animal attack to get the blood flowing. I ran along a lengthy causeway, seeking to pass underneath what few trees there were for their miserly shade. There was an old stone lighthouse built like a Mayan temple of yore in the distance, on the ocean side of the atoll, beyond a cluster of coconut palms, and I briefly considered a detour for a little look-see, but I was dissuaded from leaving the road and stepping foot on another's property. One dog attack was enough for the day. And so I plowed on, stewing in my bitter bile, fantasizing about violent scenes of vengeance that involved a shotgun and three dead dogs, and for the first time in my life, it occurred to me that maybe I could live in Texas.

I ran parallel to the runway, followed it to its end, where the road crumbled into a dirt track, and turned around. I could see Rotoava near the elbow of the atoll, a few sailboats anchored in its shadow, and then let my eyes follow the length of the island as it stretched toward the horizon. The total landmass of Fakarava is a mere six square miles. It is but a speck of dust on this planet, but those six miles are long and distended, and one would need to travel thirty-six miles to get from one tip to the other. The lagoon, in contrast, encompasses nearly five hundred square miles. It is immense and joined with the sky, each reflecting the other, so that looking beyond the last vestige of visible land was like gazing upon infinity. And infinity is blue, a startling, eye-piercing blue.

Serene and calm as the scene was, I didn't hesitate to pick up the largest, sharpest rocks I could find, the kind guaranteed to leave an attacking dog crippled or unconscious should I be lucky enough to hit it, and as I again approached the village, I slowed my pace to a walk, my senses acutely attuned to any canine threat. Come on, you demons from hell. I'm ready for you now. I stalked up the lone road, armed and ready to roll, almost eager in my anticipation of primal combat, which, in retrospect, was probably not ideal in terms of making a good first impression on the fine citizens of Rotoava. Who was this asshole, they probably thought, sauntering through the village, a steamy haze rising from his body? What kind of half-wit runs in this kind of heat? And why is he carrying rocks? And what's with that crazed look? And would you look at that punk-ass crooked tattoo? My seventeen-year-old nephew does a better turtle than that.

The dogs did not stir. I saw them, lying next to a dive shop, the three of them blithely snoozing now, and as I walked by, they gave me a heavy-lidded look and went back to their slumber, their job done, which was apparently to cause cardiac arrest and/or a sudden appreciation for Rick Perry, governor of Texas. But it was when I returned to the guesthouse that I realized my adventures with sharp-toothed creatures were only just beginning. There was a pier that extended about fifty yards over the lagoon, and I walked upon it to catch my breath for a moment, before going for a swim into water so alluring as to be nearly intoxicating. At the end was where the guesthouse hoisted its dive boat, near a meshed enclosure wherein a couple of dozen fish swam and did fishy things. And on the outside of this meshed enclosure? That's right. Sharks.

Being naturally predisposed to avoiding sharks and to assuming each and every one of them is capable, at the very least, of shredding a limb or two, I never really bothered to learn how to recognize all the different varieties of shark. And these two had me completely bedeviled. They were fairly big. One was a good seven feet in length, the other about five. Their tail fins were stretched and elongated and reminded me of the fins one sees on classic cars from the 1950s. The other end looked almost feline, with alert eyes and a comparably small mouth, and they busied themselves by trying to figure out a way into the fish enclosure. Just then, I was joined by the son of the owners, a friendly French-Tuamotuan couple who also operated a pearl-farming operation. I took the son to be about eighteen and was pleased to soon learn that he spoke some English.

"Are you aware that you have a shark problem?" I said.

He laughed easily. "They are nurse sharks," he informed me. "And look over there," he said pointing toward the wooden tables and chairs that he and his parents had placed in the shallows of the lagoon, near the beach. "There's a blacktip reef shark. And two more over there," he said, now pointing to the other side of the pier. "Ah, and look closely," he said, gesturing toward the clear water below us. "A stingray." And now, all around me, in an otherwise still lagoon, I saw ripples and fins, the stirrings of large creatures prowling for dinner. I looked at him, saucer-eyed, and noticed for the first time his tattoo, which covered most of his torso, from hip to shoulder. It was of a shark.

"So you're saying there are a lot of sharks around here."

"Many, many, many sharks."

I pondered this for a moment. "Look," I said, pointing toward my tattoo. "I'm a turtle guy, not a shark guy. This is not my milieu. But is it to safe swim here? Now?" Even with the dorsal fins, that water looked outrageously appealing, and I wanted nothing more than to immerse myself in it.

"Yes," Shark Boy said. "No problem. Unless you are bleeding, the sharks will leave you alone."

Okay, I thought. If you can't trust an eighteen-year-old kid with a giant shark tattooed across his body, who can you trust? I thanked him and turned to walk back down the pier, toward the beach, and the promise of a sweet postrun swim.

"*Monsieur*," Shark Boy called out.

"Yes."

"You are bleeding."

And so I was. The back of my sock, where the dog had bitten me, had reddened with blood. It's not often that you wish French Polynesia was more like Texas, but at this moment, I yearned to be able to run, free and armed, with a laser-sighted .380 Ruger holstered on my waist. I don't particularly care for guns, nor do I advocate cruelty to animals, but perhaps suffering from heat stroke, I decided that if Rick Perry ever runs for president again, there's fifty bucks coming his way.

Reading *In the South Seas* can be a bewildering experience. It weaves wildly from place to place, leaving even the most informed readers confused as to where, exactly, we are now. Stevenson might begin a chapter as a travelogue, capturing the reader with his eye for detail and his ear for the moment, and then suddenly he'll lurch on to some tangent, describing what he heard, years later, on his verandah in Samoa, or he'll fly off on a long discourse about ghosts. In one paragraph, we're in the present, in another the past, and then we're in Hiva Oa, and now, suddenly, we're deposited on Abemama, in the Gilbert Islands, and then off we go comparing the relative merits of Catholic versus Protestant missionaries. As usual, Fanny gets to the source of the problem, writing in a letter, as quoted from Neil Rennie's excellent introduction to the Penguin Classics edition of *In the South Seas*:

> Louis has the most enchanting material that anyone ever had in the whole world for his book, and I'm afraid he is going to spoil it all. He has taken into his Scotch Stevenson head, that a stern duty lies before him, and that his book must be a sort of scientific and historical impersonal thing, comparing the different languages (of which he knows nothing, really) and the different peoples . . . and the whole thing to be impersonal, leaving out all he knows of the people themselves. And I

believe there is no one living who has got so near to them, or who understands them as he does.

Later, she'll write:

If I were the public I shouldn't care a penny what Louis's theories were as to the formation of the islands, or their scientific history, or where the people came from originally—only what Louis's own experiences were.

And again:

He has always had a weakness for teaching and preaching, so here was his chance. Instead of writing about his adventures in these wild islands, he would ventilate his own theories on the vexed questions of race and language. He wasted much precious time over grammars and dictionaries, with no results, for he was able to get an insight into hardly any native tongue. Then he must study the coral business. This, I believe, would have ruined the book but for my brutality.

Now in fairness to Stevenson, the book we now call *In the South Seas* was published posthumously in 1896, so we can't be certain how, exactly, he would have structured it should he have lived longer. He certainly intended to go big or go home, writing in a letter to his friend Sidney Colvin: "My book is now practically modeled: if I can execute what is designed, there are few better books now extant on this globe; bar the epics, and the big tragedies, and histories, and the choice lyric poetics, and a novel or so—none." Stevenson did, however, soon recognize that he had a problem on his hands, describing it as one of "architecture," but he fiercely resisted the idea of writing a simple personal travel narrative, as Fanny and others encouraged him to do, with its easy rhythm, describing the where, when, and how of the narrator's adventures. He called such minutia "infantile and sucking-bottle details. If ever I put in such detail, it is because it leads into something or serves as a transition. To tell it for its own sake, never!"

Yikes.

Soon, however, he had bigger problems. There were the letters for Sam McClure, the newspaper publisher, that he was contractually obliged to write. He never quite reconciled whether these letters should, one day, be stand-alone chapters for his big book, or merely source material, or something else entirely. A letter for a mass circulation newspaper is an entirely different thing from a chapter in a tome about the culture, geology, ethnography, and history of the South Pacific. And since he was predisposed to write the latter, his dispatches from the South Seas were met with a torrent of criticism. Henry James wrote to say that he "missed the visible in them—I mean as regards people, things, objects, faces, bodies, costumes, features, gestures, manners, the introductory, the personal painter-touch." More troubling, was McClure's displeasure. Stevenson's letters, he felt, failed for "it was the moralist and not the romancer which his observations in the South Seas awoke in him, and the public found the moralist less interesting than the romancer." McClure told Stevenson that he had not fulfilled "the definition of the word 'letter,' as used in newspaper correspondence." But publish them he did.

To which I can only say, Louis, you are a lucky man you're not around in the twenty-first century. Take up the quill now, and best-case scenario you'll find that eventually you are merely a vendor for a multinational corporation, one headed by either a German accountant or Rupert Murdoch, and staffed, at the upper reaches, by a small army of MBAs and lawyers—evil people, Louis, evil people—who look upon you, green eye-shades perched upon their foreheads, as they do their ink supplier. Nothing wrong with that, of course. No reason why purveyors of words, alone among professions, should be allowed to live in an airy-fairy world far removed from the balance sheet. The marketplace sharpens the quill. But if these consiglieres of publishing come to believe that they are unlikely to get their nickel, they will look to see whether or not you have fulfilled "the definition of the word 'letter,' as used in newspaper correspondence" and they will come after you, Louis, and slit your throat.

Let's say, hypothetically, that you are a modestly successful writer, and by this I mean you only need to work part-time at Denny's to make ends meet. You sign a new contract with your longtime publisher and receive what is quaintly called an advance, but should rightly be called *a loan from people who will gouge out your eyeballs.* Of this loan, 50 percent immediately disappears in the form of taxes, agent commissions, and what we call health insurance premiums, which, because you are self-employed, supporting a family, and living in America, are onerous and absurd. Another substantial percentage is devoted to research, which, because you are an idiot who never really thinks about the costs involved in producing a book, include a couple of lengthy trips to, let's say, oh, I don't know, India. Now let's say, hypothetically, that while you are riding the rails the length and breadth of India, a neutron bomb explodes at your publishing house. The consiglieres will call this a *reorganization.* They will use the word *synergy.* And now everyone you have worked with over the past eight years has disappeared. *Poof.* Gone. Reorganized and synergized. And you find that your little book project has now been assigned to a different imprint.

Well, you may think, that was most unfortunate but, because you are a professional, you carry on. And now let's say— and again, this is completely make-believe—you have a reputation for being a trifle late with manuscripts (Note to current hypothetical editor: Um . . .) and so in your contract, to avoid this problem, which, apparently, causes much mayhem and stress for editors, copy editors, designers, basically everybody in the Central Office, you have this peculiar obligation to submit a first draft of a number of chapters every few months, as a means for ensuring that steady progress is being maintained on The Work, as contractually defined. So you submit the first sixty pages of a first draft—and you know what those first sixty pages are like, of course, the grasping in the dark, looking for the light switch—to your newly assigned imprint, who has inherited you and your contract during the reorganization. And then *kaboom*, your life is destroyed.

Let's say—hypothetically, needless to say—that your previous book's sales did not justify the size of the *loan from people who will gouge out your eyeballs.* And now they're looking at these few pages of a first draft and the consiglieres will decide that they want their money back, and they will find a way to shred that contract, Louis, and they will hunt you down. They will demand immediate repayment of this *loan from people who will gouge out your eyeballs*, which, of course, has already been spent. And now they will suspend all royalty payments from your previous books. Suddenly, in an instant, you have gone from being a modestly successful writer to beyond broke and onward to heavily indebted to an organization that from time to time sends threatening letters in spine-tingling legalese threatening personal ruin and eternal damnation. You will beg and plead and send them revisions and new book proposals, promising to work off this *loan from people who will gouge out your eyeballs*, but the decision, as they say, is final. And now you are financially ruined.

Now, for the fun of it, let's say that you are an alcoholic who only recently quit drinking and was presently on the Marijuana Maintenance Program. I don't know about you, Louis, but I'd think now would be a good time to start hitting the vodka. If such a thing were to occur, I suspect I'd be nearly suicidal for a good long while, but in the end, Louis, I'd think I'd be grateful to the consiglieres for hastening the inevitable. Best to have your world collapse all at once rather than draw it out, don't you think?

But, Louis, these Fakarava chapters? What were you thinking? I know how you spent your time here. Sailing through the channel on board the *Casco*, you noted that the "water, shoaling under our board, became changed in a moment to surprising hues of blue and grey; and in its transparency the coral branched and blossomed, and the fish of the inland sea cruised visibly below us, stained and striped, and even beaked like parrots. I have paid in my time to view many curiosities; never one so curious as that first sight over the ship's rail in the lagoon of Fakarava." You took to a little cottage on this narrow band of land, a house with "three rooms, three sewing-machines, three sea-chests . . . and a French lithograph with the legend: '*Le brigade du Général Lepasset brûlant son drapeau devant Metz.*'" Fanny, the ever-industrious American, managed to rescue a rusty stove from the beach and return it to life, cooking hardy breakfasts. During the day, you wrote in a letter: "I am in the water for hours wading over the knees for shells." And you spent your evenings hosting the French-Tahitian Monsieur Donat-Rimarau, the acting vice-resident, who regaled you with stories about the islands. The moonlight cast shadows of the rustling palm fronds "so sharply defined that one voluntarily stepped over them," as Fanny observed, and you slept on the verandah, the lagoon breeze offering a respite from the heat of day.

But do we read of any of this in The Book? Hardly. Instead, for reasons known only to yourself, you abandoned the flow of narrative and instead offered the reader, what? Ghost stories? Observations about the occult? Third-hand tales told to you in the Marshalls? Boring, Louis, boring. And yet, right there at the top of your chapters on, ostensibly, Fakarava, you observed the true curiosity of this magical place. And it lies in the water.

The lagoon in Fakarava is an officially sanctioned UNESCO Biosphere Reserve. Typically, once someplace is deemed special and worthy of preserving by UNESCO, it is ruined forever. See, for instance, Lijiang in Yunnan, China, which was once a lovely village in the foothills of the Himalayas, but now gets 16 million tourists a year, shattering all that was idyllic and distinctive about the place. Fortunately, no such ruination seems imminent for Fakarava. There can't be more than two dozen *fales* on the atoll, and what tourists there are head straight for the water. Nearly every visitor I encountered was a hardcore diver, and with these people, the tattoos get really interesting. Everyone begins with a shark or a turtle, but I met one Dutch couple who between them had an octopus, three clown fish, a sea horse, two rabbit fish, a bunch of angelfish, a manta ray, and a moray eel. Just talking to them felt like being inside a Pixar movie. They're a peculiar crowd, some of these divers, and few things are more discombobulating than listening to people get all rapturous about their encounter with a ten-foot tiger shark and a twelve-foot hammerhead, in Dutch, during the morning's dive.

I spent a couple of days waiting for my cut to heal. The dog's teeth had broken through the skin. I treated the wound with antibiotic cream and let it close before doing any serious snorkeling—and incidentally, I do very much like the phrase *serious snorkeling*. If I could somehow figure out a way to incorporate the sentence *I'm a serious snorkeler, bitchezz* without it seeming like a gratuitous aside, I would. And I guess I just did. It's magic, really. But getting back to our tale, no, I was not concerned about rabies. They were merely island dogs, semi-wild, semi-cared for, and I had startled them by being a stranger who was running in the late afternoon torpor, a time when all should be still. Their instincts had kicked in and they just did what island dogs do, which is to make one think back fondly to *Old Yeller* and its delightful ending. If those dogs had been truly rabid, the islanders themselves would have long ago disposed of them. Biting strangers was fine; biting locals not so much. Dogs are smart and they know this.

Once the cut closed, I tested things out by wading into the lagoon in front of my *fale*. In the hour or two before sunset, the inshore waters were alive with ripples and dorsal fins as dozens of reef sharks swam languorously by. The scent of my blood failed to stir them, and soon I found myself becoming strangely accustomed to their presence. When Shark Boy asked if I wanted to snorkel the Tumakohua, or the South Pass, home to, literally, thousands of sharks, I surprised myself by saying yes.

It was more than twenty miles distant from Rotoava, a long journey over water on the dive boat. The water was incandescent and reminded me of the lagoons I had come to know in Kiribati. But Fakarava is different in innumerable ways. The tides go in and out twice a day, and while on the ocean side of the atoll it was noticeable as low tide revealed a barren reef shelf, a stony wasteland of jagged coral and tidal pools, on the lagoon side of the island the flow of water seemed to pass with hardly a murmur, the land barely expanding or contracting at all, reflecting the depth of this inland sea. Away from the village, the coconut palm trees, the fruit trees, and the casuarinas gave way to an arid shrubbery, the natural flora of draft-ridden atolls, suggesting it has been some time that the people of Fakarava lived a purely subsistence lifestyle, unlike Kiribati, where nearly every precious acre contains a family's food trees.

On the boat, as everywhere in Polynesia, were a few more European pensioners, Italians and French. They're all, like, fifty-five and spend their time traveling the world. I spoke to a Frenchman who had been a ship's pilot on Réunion Island, retired, and now was traveling with his wife for two months throughout French Polynesia and ruminating on whether or not to take a house on Moorea for another three. Meanwhile, one of the Italians on board was forever standing and falling on the rest of us as he tried to take pictures from a speedboat that was rocking along as fast as its twin engines could take it. Rarely have I seen anyone so clumsy or oblivious of other people or common sense. He was of the type who dawdle on the sidewalk, five abreast, at 6:00 P.M. as everyone else rushes to catch a subway, or who drive thirty-five mph in the fast lane, making phone calls and texting, as others swerve around him, giving him the bird, which he never ever sees. I'm not sure why these thoughts occurred to me. Was I becoming a type-A kind of person?

The Tumakohua Pass is narrow, perhaps three hundred yards across, and lies next to an abandoned village, the ruins of dwellings and an old church lying forlornly in the sun, its inhabitants long ago forced to depart due to the absence of freshwater. As we stepped off the boat and made our way to a small cove, sheltered by a reef, a swimming-pool-size lagoon of its own jutting toward the depths of the channel, we were immediately greeted by an enormous three-foot napoleon fish with a bulbous head and a friendly disposition.

"That is Jojo," Shark Boy informed me.

I blinked a few times. "And are you on a first-name basis with all the fish around here?"

He simply laughed and returned to the boat, vowing to reappear in a short while with the fish that would be our lunch. And in the meantime the sharks gathered. First one. Then another. Then three more. Another six. We hadn't been here but ten minutes and already roughly thirty sharks, all black-tip reef sharks, had gathered in a semienclosed area not much larger than a backyard pool. Naturally, Capitano Oblivious was the first to wade in, donning a mask and flippers, and I stood by, watching with baffled curiosity. Don't you think we ought to wait for Shark Boy? I thought. He could probably tell us which were the alphas, the nippers, and the bullies. He probably knows their nicknames. The translucent water was now swarming with sharks, and they seemed a jumpy lot to me, like oversize piranhas sensing that it was feeding time. They circled and darted and squabbled with each other as the Italian dunked his head and kicked himself forward, and now I waited for the real carnage to begin. Capitano Oblivious swam blithely onward from the sandy shallows through a school of sharks who grew increasingly jittery, as if they knew a meal was coming and could barely contain themselves. But they parted for the Italian, who made his way forward, searching for an opening in the coral headlands that would lead to the deep water. Lagoon channels, particularly narrow ones such as the Tumakohua Pass, are notorious for their powerful currents. Did we even know what the tides were doing? Was it ebbing or flowing? It certainly wasn't slack water, that much I could see. But soon, Capitano Oblivious had found his way to the deep blue of the channel, and now everyone was in the water—experienced divers all—putting on snorkeling gear, sharks swirling around their knees.

I stood there, pondering the bandage on my Achilles tendon. I peaked inside. There was the faint remains of a scab. Just how sensitive were sharks to the scent of blood? Should I flick off what remained of it? By now, all the others were swimming toward the channel, and I thought, better get in the water quick before I was all alone, to be picked off like a stray lamb by a pack of wolves.

Have you ever shared a tight, confined space—say, about six feet wide, a watery alleyway—with a half-dozen sharks? Exciting doesn't even begin to describe it. It's more like *Holy Fuck Holy Fuck Holy Fuck*. Never in my life had I been so close to sharks. Visibility was about a hundred miles, enough so that I could see every tooth, the brownish-gray tint of their toughened skin, the black tribal markings on their fins, and the unblinking, startled expression of their eyes, as we shared this aquatic thoroughfare from the beach to the . . .

Holy Mother of God. There were hundreds of sharks swarming below me now, over the edge of the reef, a wall of multihued shimmering color, a palisade of coral, descending into a blue-black void, where eagle rays, giant trevally, big fat groupers, a lone barracuda, our friendly neighborhood napoleon, and a gazillion tropical fish, schools, no universities of them, hugging the cliff wall, and all around were the sharks—blacktips, whitetips, vast amounts of greys, and a few massive, beefy silvertips. I swam, floating like chum, with eyes as big as dinner plates, over the steep precipice. *Holy Fuck Holy Fuck Holy Fuck*. It was shark nirvana, hundreds—*hundreds!*—of primeval, carnivorous, saw-toothed vessels of destruction, emerging from the darkness beyond, their shadows taking form, as they glided silkily past. And soon I felt . . . strangely calm, completely blissed out by the spectacle below. It is not very often that you behold a true wonder of nature, but this surely was one of them, an expressway of aquatic marvels. I dove as deep as I could, immersing myself in this astonishing world, next to soft coral that swayed in the current, among multitudes of vividly colored fish, and just yards away, always, from the sharks. To my surprise, I saw the Italian pirouetting below, so elegant and aware now, as he swooped into the depths, holding his breath forever, getting up close and personal with an eight-foot silvertip shark that loomed beside him, each studying the other.

I've snorkeled all over the South Pacific, but nowhere have I seen a place more bewitching than the South Pass of Fakarava. We emerged, speaking a Babel of languages, all expressing our amazement, as Shark Boy, who had returned with his catch, stood cleaning fish while the blacktip reef sharks stirred themselves into a frenzy. He threw a rock from time to time to keep them at bay, but otherwise remained in the shallows, unconcerned. This guy, a kid really, needs his own TV show. He lit a fire and grilled the fish, and soon, after lunch, we were back in the water, following Shark Boy as he led us on a drift snorkel, where we floated like aquanauts, flying with the streaming current around the headland of the channel, as the tide ebbed toward the ocean. It was a fast current and as we flew over the curiosities below, we got a sense of a fish's true character. Did it go with the flow, or did it fight it? Some just glided alongside us, and others struggled mightily, titanic manifestations of fishy willpower, as they resisted the current. And the sharks? They did whatever the hell they wanted. Up-flow, down-flow, whatever. A shark goes where it wants to go. But there were fewer now—dozens, rather than hundreds—and I wondered where they all went, until later, when we hopped in the boat, and launched ourselves over the sides in the middle of the channel, and there they were, the grays at least, circling forty feet below, in water that descended into a stellar, inky blue void, their forms still glittering with sunlight, like ferocious stars of the deep.

I was captivated. I didn't know what was coming over me. Tattoos. Sharks. And I wanted more. Well, that part was familiar. I have a head for *more*, of course. The following day I borrowed a bicycle from Shark Boy, put my flippers and mask in a backpack, and peddled toward the Garuae Pass, a few miles past the airport, where I followed a dirt and coral track to the headland. What will I see there, I'd asked him. "Sharks," he'd said beatifically, and I was beginning to understand. Encountering a shark in its element is both strangely serene and extraordinarily bracing, and your mind doesn't quite know what to do, how to react, whether with a burst of adrenaline or a flood of calmness, so it gives you both. But as I beheld the Garuae Pass, I felt something else. It was far wider than the South Pass, at least a few miles, and the water was turbulent. The tide was going out and I could see different currents swirling and ripping. There was no beach available to enter the water, just mounds of dead coral, sunbleached white. I felt some trepidation as I made my way to the water, walking barefoot over the rocks, searching for a good entry point but finding none. I gingerly headed into the water anyway, trying not to cut my feet on the sharp coral, put my flippers and mask on, and was immediately swept by a strong current. I took a last glance at land to see how fast it was moving, and figuring I could swim through it, put my mask on and saw . . . almost nothing. The visibility was not more than ten or twelve feet, the current and tides having stirred the sediment, and all I observed was what was right there in front of me, branches of coral and numerous fish swaying and gyrating in the chaotic flow. Elsewhere, there was just a milky darkness, and I swam onward.

The shark emerged like a bullet. I knew immediately that it was bigger than I was, but I can't tell you much else because I swigged down a chest full of water and was busy dying of a panic attack. I surfaced, coughed, and broke speed records as I swam with all my might back to shore, where I staggered onto dry land and collapsed, gulping air, enjoying the feel of shards of dead coral beneath me, content, very simply, to be out of the water.

Approximate length of swim: three and a half minutes.

Desire to swim with sharks again: lifted.

Chapter Fourteen

Is Tahiti really that bad?

This was the question I was determined to settle. Perhaps no place has suffered a greater rise and fall in the imagination than Tahiti. There was a certain inevitability to this precipitous decline, of course. Think of De Bougainville and Captain Cook and their lush prose, their quills shivering as they describe the scenes they encountered—the lovemaking, the churning of the dancers, the fragrant smell of blossoms. Think of *Mutiny on the Bounty*, casting an island so alluring that both Marlon Brando and Mel Gibson—er, for you younger people, there was a time when Mel Gibson was thought of as sexy, and not as, well, a bloated, wild-eyed, narcissistic, creepy dude who leaves scary messages—felt the need to commit treason, to risk the hangman's noose, in order to quench their ardor for the life they'd tasted in Ole Tahiti. With that kind of press, Tahiti was doomed to be proven an illusion, a fabrication, a chimera summoned from a storyteller's febrile mind. It could only be so. There are no other narrative possibilities. If something can end, then it will do so.

What I found surprising, however, was how little love there was for Tahiti among the French Polynesians themselves. On Fakarava, I met a Polynesian woman named Nani who spoke a near-flawless American-accented English.

"My mother sent me to the Cook Islands when I was twelve," she explained. "She felt it was important to learn English."

"But the Cooks aren't American," I noted. "They speak English with a New Zealand accent."

"Yes, but I didn't like it there. I spent all my time watching American television." Score one for cultural imperialism. "I like it here. Life is simple. You can live . . . I don't know how to say it in English. *La vie sauvage.*"

"Close to nature," I offered.

"Yes. Unlike Tahiti, with its pollution, its crowds, its noise, its traffic."

"Well, naturally, this is where you are from so . . ."

"No," Nani said. "I am from Tahiti. I came to Fakarava to escape Tahiti."

Robert Louis Stevenson left for Tahiti to escape Fakarava, and so I dutifully followed with dimmed expectations and heightened curiosity. My journey, by prop plane, was far easier than Stevenson's, however. He'd caught a cold on the atoll, which soon worsened into the Bluidy Jack. Fearing for her husband's life, Fanny insisted on sailing onward to Papeete, where, after a stint in a hotel as doctors tended to him, they settled into a small cottage with a garden of mango trees. Stevenson didn't get out much. Indeed, it was expected he should die here as he was convulsed by hemorrhages. He was stoic about this turn of events, and continued to smoke as others made plans for his funeral. It was left to his mother to observe: "I don't much like Tahiti. It seems to me a sort of halfway house between savage life and civilization, with the drawbacks of both and the advantages of neither."

I settled into a small guesthouse, where a couple of nurses from Lausanne were lodging, determined to find jobs here, *in paradise*, but no one would hire them. I suggested they try the outer islands, or perhaps New Caledonia or Vanuatu, where medical professionals such as themselves were needed, but they wanted to stay here, in Tahiti, *where the action is*, and as I went to bed, they went off to the nightclubs. I liked their pluck, but they'd be home in a month or two. They lived in a dream and it didn't take long to figure that in Papeete, at least, the roosters had long ago stirred and put an end to fanciful slumbers.

Papeete is an administrative city. And it is French. So it is like that. Of course, there are Polynesians here, many with distinctive tattoos, but much more common are mixed-race people, and you look into their eyes and see Macau and Honolulu and all the other ports where history swirled and danced and romanced. French is the lingua franca, and I heard one man say: "He wants independence? *Alors*, who will pay for his bread? Who will pay for his home? Independence? It is like kicking your mother in the head."

At exactly 5:00 P.M. the shutters came down and people retreated to the suburbs, to the *Tahiti Pas Cher* for groceries, to the Mobil station with the Stop and Shop to fill up their Renault, to the McDonald's with the jungle gym to pick up dinner, and the city center was left for the players, who at 5:15 are all magically dressed in their I-think-I-might-like-to-get-laid-tonight clothing, the women alluring in strappy dresses and heels, revealing a great expanse of legs, which I spent an inappropriate amount of time gandering because they offered the telltale clue as to whether the gams I was gandering belonged to a woman or a man, since this was Polynesia and these things are not always self-evident. The *mahu* are physically male but, since time immemorial, have been raised as females. Often it was the eldest boy, who was groomed to help with the household chores, including cooking and tending to the younger siblings. Some eventually grew out of being the designated *mahu* and eventually married and had children of their own. Many, however, whether due to nature or nuture, embraced the designation. Polynesians, notoriously, have a very elastic sense of sexuality and if a man hooked up with the village *mahu*, it wasn't a gay thing or a straight thing, but just kind of an island thing. In other cultures, of course, effeminate boys are bullied and jeered, but not so in Tahiti, which, like elsewhere in Polynesia, long ago acknowledged that some are men or women and some are neither and both. Today, the *mahu* are *mahu* by choice and many have breast implants and wear dresses and sashay and are so over the top in their femininity that they could only be really campy men. Try as she might, however, Ms. Coco cannot hide that she has the legs of a manly man.

Many *mahu* are servers in the town's cafés, which by 5:30 are full of people smoking and drinking and listening to sentimental Tahitian pop music. The fifty-plus crowd is strangely absent. I wasn't sure why. The atmosphere is not aggressively young, just people smoking and drinking. But no fifty-plussers. Maybe they're dead or something. Since this was France, you can't get dinner before 7:30. It's. Just. Not. Done. So I spent the interlude running on a seaside promenade, next to the Boulevard Pomare, where I was pleasantly startled to discover that I was hardly the only runner in Papeete. I wasn't sure what to make of this. I never see runners elsewhere in the South Pacific, and yet here in Papeete, there must be, I don't know, maybe upward of dozens of people exercising. Was this a good sign? Or was this indicative of our forthcoming global homogeneity, when we are all exactly alike, with the same habits and the same aspirations as those on the other side of the planet? And then, in the evenings, I would find a food truck and have me some *poisson cru*, a tuna ceviche with coconut milk and lime, a perfect culinary commingling of France with Polynesia, and I thought maybe this could work, this blending of cultures.

"We are destined to be the same. It cannot be resisted. It cannot be stopped. It is inevitable," said the Lithuanian sitting across from me one evening at the guesthouse. He had dropped everything—job, family—to spend a couple of months traveling around the world. Why, I had asked him? "Because it was cold," he said.

His name was Tomas and he was about my age, thickset and balding, and we talked about what Eastern Europe was like in the early nineties. While I was in Prague, he was traveling to Yerevan and Moscow, "to buy yo-yos," which he then sold on the streets of Vilnius. Now, he ran a software company. "You cannot defy corporate capitalism. No one can," he said. "It is too alluring. It knows what you want. It knows what everyone wants. Americans, Germans, Chinese, Indians, Tahitians, they all want Nike. Or Pizza Hut. Or a BMW. Everyone wants a flat-screen television and a MacBook. The difference between now and twenty years ago is that now everyone can buy a flat-screen television and a MacBook. Everyone," he said, stabbing his finger in the darkness, "wants the same thing. They want to *consume*."

"Well," I said. "I can think of some places that will hold out to the bitter end, that will always be *different*."

"Name one," he said.

"Kiribati," I said.

"I have not heard of this place."

"Exactly. No one has."

So there, Mr. Smarty Pants. And now I was feeling triumphant. I told him about the remote atolls, and how the I-Kiribati
will never become *consumers*, not least because there is nothing
to *consume*, and there will never be anything to *consume*, because capitalists like yourself have never even heard of Kiribati.
No one knows diddly about Kiribati.

"Excuse me," said a gentleman from the next table, an
American (yay, Americans in French Polynesia). "I heard you
mention Kiribati. We've spent some time there, and . . ."

And *poof* went my argument, to the great amusement of
Tomas. I was now speaking with John and Melinda, a friendly
couple from Oregon. They were sailors who had once built
their own boat and sailed it across the Pacific, stopping in Kiribati and numerous other islands. They'd since sold the boat,
but from time to time, they headed back to the South Seas and
chartered a sailboat, which they were now in the midst of doing. We spoke about Kiribati, and after a while John asked: "So
what brought you there?"

"Well," I said. "My girlfriend at the time got this job
and . . ."

"You're J. Maarten Troost, aren't you?"

I allowed that I might be.

"So what are doing in Papeete?"

And now I thought for a moment. "I have no idea."

The suburbs of Papeete extend all the way out to Venus
Point, toppling over hills and covering the expanse of land
that lies between the ocean and the towering, seven-thousand-
foot range of barbed pinnacles that anchor the island. I rented
a car, a little put-put manual Peugeot, the cheapest vehicle I
could find, and drove along the coastal road. Those mountains,

and the exuberantly ambrosial valleys they concealed, shrouded in mist, must be where the real beauty of Tahiti now lay, I figured, because it sure was ugly out here on the seashore, a cascade of minimarts, light industry, and graffiti-strewn apartment blocks and bungalows that goes on and on and on.

I set out with restless diligence early that morning, following the trail of Robert Louis Stevenson like a bloodhound on the case, and drove happily onward, content to leave Papeete in the rearview mirror. Everybody shits on Papeete, of course. It was once the fabled paradise, but now yadda yadda yadda. But ask most of the locals, and they'll shrug their shoulders, offer a few obligatory complaints about the traffic and the prices, and then they'll mention their job and how it's okay, it pays the bills, and their kids are doing well in school, perhaps they'll become doctors or lawyers, though, of course, they'll need to complete their studies in France, but in the meantime we have our *vin*. Have you tried this *Vin de Tahiti*? It's *pas mal*. Travelers don't like Papeete, I thought, because it reminds them of home, and who wants to spend a gazillion francs when they could have the very same experience by simply heading out to a strip mall followed by an evening downtown at the drag fashion show?

Fortunately, Robert Louis Stevenson did not stay long, which meant that I didn't have to either. He wasn't well yet when he left Papeete, but seeking to find more tolerable surroundings, the *Casco* sailed around the island to Taravao, near the isthmus with Tahiti Iti, which juts out like a spherical appendage to the main island. The captain soon discovered that the mast was rotting and eventually headed back to Papeete to be refit, leaving Fanny to hire a wagon and horses to carry Stevenson farther south, to the village of Tautira, when the mosquitoes proved unbearable. It was here that he convalesced and exchanged names with the local chief, Ori a Ori, who took care of all his needs, because Stevenson, like everyone who goes to Tahiti, soon ran out of money as work on the *Casco* dragged on from one month to the next. "You are my brother," Chief Ori a Ori told him. "All that I have is yours."

In a letter from Tautira, Stevenson wrote: "You are to conceive us, therefore, in strange circumstances and very pleasing; in a strange land and climate, the most beautiful on earth; surrounded by a foreign race that travelers have agreed to be the most engaging." Tautira was, he said, heaven, the garden of the world, a place that he would whimsically call Hans Christian Andersen–ville. I found it on the map and was pleased to note that it was located at the very end of the road, some forty miles distant from Papeete, at the tip of Tahiti Iti, which even today is said to contain the last remaining vestiges of Old Tahiti.

But first, I wanted to have a look at Venus Point. It was here, on Matavai Bay, that Western dreams of Tahiti were made, the beach where both Captain Cook and Captain Bligh strode ashore, mighty emissaries of the Royal Navy, whose words and deeds became the embers of fantasy. Of course, this place should be called Venus Point. It is only right. Cook observed the transit of the planet Venus in 1769, when he alighted upon Tahiti as captain of the *Endeavour*, during his First Voyage Round the World. There is a small white obelisk near the black sand beach, next to a glorious nineteenth-century lighthouse, that commemorates the occasion.

But it is Captain Bligh's landing and all that followed that casts Venus Point in soft, radiant hues. Venus, of course, is the Roman goddess of luv and sexy times, and She cast Her spell on all who landed upon Her shores. William Bligh was a master on board the *Resolution* during Cook's Third Voyage, but will forever be memorialized as the captain of the *Bounty*, the despot who, obsessed with order and the well-being of his bread-fruit seedlings, lost his ship to Fletcher Christian and a mutinous crew. They too have a memorial here, with bas-relief portraits of our main characters, foisted upon a volcanic rock ringed by pebbles. I studied their images; the mean, stern-faced taskmaster, balding, with a sneering mouth, next to the Golden Boy, long-haired with heavy-lidded eyes and pouty lips. We have always been conditioned to root for Fletcher Christian, the romantic lead, who, casting off the shackles of tyranny, led his men to freedom, eventually landing upon the shores of lonely Pitcairn Island with the women they loved, distant now from the lash of the wicked Bligh.

Me, I think Captain Bligh was the hero. Perhaps it is my destiny to become a grumpy, old man, or maybe it's because Anthony Hopkins is sober and Mel Gibson is . . . well, not my place to say, but now, whenever I see or encounter the tale of *Mutiny on the Bounty*, I cheer for the man in blue. Think of their respective legacies. Acting Lieutenant Fletcher Christian, having abandoned Bligh and the remaining loyalists, the shipmates for whom he was responsible, to the mercy of the seas and near-certain death, returned to Tahiti. Some of the mutineers remained there, but Christian, together with eight other shipmates, eleven Tahitian women, six local men, and one child, sailed onward to Pitcairn, where they burned the ship to avoid detection, and lived happily ever after. But the story doesn't end there, of course. Within four years, all the Tahitian men were murdered. The mutineers turned on each other, including Fletcher Christian, and soon there were just four left, together with ten women and a few children. One of the crewmen, William McCoy, learned how to distill alcohol from the ti plant, and now they were perpetually drunk. The women fled for their lives and erected a fort. McCoy, in a drunken stupor, hurled himself off a cliff. Another went insane and had to be hacked to death. Finally, one of the two remaining mutineers destroyed the liquor still, and, after enduring a prolonged withdrawal, an unsettled peace reigned over the island. Today, some of their descendants are imprisoned on the island, locked up for abusing children, but since Pitcairn now falls under E.U. jurisdiction, their prison, conforming to European norms, is said to be the loveliest building on the island. There are plans to turn it into a hotel once the last prisoner is released.

And Bligh? He and eighteen loyalists were set adrift on a twenty-three-foot launch without a map or a chronometer. He sailed at once for nearby Tofua to obtain supplies, where one of the men was killed in an attack by the locals, and then proceeded to sail for forty-seven days across 3,618 nautical miles to the relative safety of Timor, losing not a single soul during this jaw-dropping feat of seamanship. Bligh was exonerated of all culpability in the *Bounty* affair, and went on to become a vice admiral. There are seventeen family trees who owe their existence to Captain Bligh. Hero or monster? You decide.

I stood watching the kite-boarders and the beachgoers, taking in the verdant panoply of green rising above, following the ridges of soaring mountains, and its startling contrast to the black sand where it meets an aquamarine sea gently cascading upon its shores. Squint and you can see everything. Listen and you can hear the noon bell and the creaking of masts. Breathe and you can smell the . . . sunscreen of French vacationers.

Moving on, I entered the world of SILENCE CULTE. This is what the road signs now said. I believe it means WORSHIP SILENCE. So I did. I did not toot the horn. I did not grind the gears. I turned the radio off. I was as quiet and stealthy as I could be, rolling over speed bumps in villages that suddenly, shockingly, were quiet hamlets with perhaps a few tin-roofed bungalows, a general store, maybe a school or a church, and gardens with banana and papaya trees, enclosed within walls of trimmed hedges and flowering blossoms. Elsewhere all was wild and beautiful, where primeval mountains tumble as if a green torrent into a glimmering ocean. I made my way to Taravao, on the isthmus, thinking that I might stop here, but forged onward the moment I saw three tour buses pulled up in front of a McDonald's, and continued on to Tahiti Iti, *little* Tahiti, where I saw a sign pointing toward the Taravao Plateau. I followed it and soon discovered myself on a rugged, meandering single-lane road, tree-lined and shaded, climbing from the tropics to a pasture in the Alps, with cool, crisp air, farmhouses, and bovine herds, missing only the clinging of cowbells and the echo of Heidi yodeling in the mountains. I whistled, *The hills are alive with the sound of music*, until I came across a lookout, some 1,800 feet above the sea, where I could see all of Tahiti, its breathtaking beauty, and wondered what I would have done during that searing, mutinous moment on board the *Bounty*, when you have beheld *this*, and now were confronted with nothing more than the harsh tedium of naval life. Which vessel would you choose? Which life?

It was getting late and I had yet to find a place to stay. I followed the coastal road, nary a vehicle to be seen, passed a few slumbering villages, until I ran out of road. This must be it, I thought, Tautira, *Hans Christian Andersen–ville, the garden of the world, heaven.* The road looped through the village, and I rolled with it, once, twice, three times, seeing nothing but unkempt homes, a lovely stone church, people who gave me hard, unfriendly stares, and packs of mangy dogs that roved through the village like gangsters in heat. Nowhere did I see a sign promising a room or *fare*. I stopped in front of the general store, walked in, and noted the smell. It is the same odor one finds in nearly every village emporium in the Pacific, musty and damp, a suggestion that something dead herein lies, an aroma that immediately causes your brain to signal: *Might be a good idea to avoid the meat.* I asked the Chinese shopkeeper if there was a pensionne or *fare* in the village. He assured me there was not, and that there wasn't a room available within twenty kilometers of here, whereupon I hung my head, returned to my sputtering Peugeot, and drove back from whence I came, thinking it's the beach for me tonight, until some miles away I saw a precious little handwritten sign taped onto the stem of a coconut tree, announcing the availability of a *fare*.

It was a French-Tahitian family with an extra bungalow. *Oui*, I could stay. Here was the *fare*. Here was the outdoor kitchen. Supplies could be had just down the road, so I picked up some eggs, salad, a baguette, and some cheese for fifty smackeroos and cooked an omelet as the surf ebbed and flowed, the *shoosh* and roar of the sea accompanying a setting sun, the crashing waves lending a faint haze, distributing glimmers of radiant light as if refracted through a diamond.

I was joined by Jean-Michel, who lived here with his Tahitian clan, and we spent some time talking about the Pacific navigators of yore, agreeing that Western schoolchildren are inadequately served by this fixation on Magellan, Columbus, and Cook, and that the early explorers of Oceania are their equivalent and more. He noted the similarities of traditional sailing canoes with those found in Southeast Asia, of which he seemed to have some knowledge. He had been a social welfare officer, he said, arriving more than thirty years ago from his home in France.

"What I like about Tahiti is that you can have the best of both worlds—*la vie sauvage* and civilization."

How differently he sees that glass from Ma Stevenson. He sees the best; she the worst. It is the difference between a Latin temperament and a Scot's. I mentioned that I have seen mostly the French world and not much of the Polynesian in Tahiti. He acknowledged that this was increasingly true. "The percentage of people speaking French at home is increasing, while those speaking Tahitian is decreasing. In the end, most people speak neither language well."

In the morning, I hastened back to Tautira. It was a Sunday, a day for church. I figured services would begin bright and early like elsewhere in the Pacific, and so I arrived before 8:00 A.M. only to find a village still snoozing. I did, however, see a woman dressed immaculately in white—definitely a churchgoer—who informed me that Mass wouldn't begin until 10:00, so I had a couple of hours to kill. I headed to the black sand beach, at the mouth of the Vaitepiha River, which led into a deep valley tightly confined by mountains that reared up like a series of perfect, interlocking triangles. Stevenson spent much time here, noting the children and the games they played, as Princess Moe, a relation of Chief Ori a Ori, prepared him dishes of raw fish in lime juice and coconut. I felt so very happy for Stevenson, envious even, that he was able to enjoy such fine company. No such luck for me, however. I met the Village Psycho.

There were garbage cans on the beach, though not nearly enough of them, judging by the bottles of beer and rum that tumbled over their rims. The man who appeared to have con-sumed it all staggered over to me and pronounced himself the Angel of Mercy. His eyes were wild and bleary and when he said that he was crazy, I had no reason to doubt it. To prove the point, he did the crazy-man cackle, and proceeded with a long discourse about his attributes as the Angel of Mercy, which I am not even going to attempt to translate, since it would force me to try to make rhyme or reason of his words, and really, there wasn't any. He proceeded to put his hand on my shoulder, which I didn't like, since, at least on my end, we were not yet buddy-buddy. So I asked him the perennial conversation-killer—what do you do? What's your job? I love that question for its somno-lent power. It's the blanket you can throw on any verbal fire. And here it worked, because whatever runaway train of thought he had been on now crashed, and he blinked a number of times and scratched his matted hair and after a good long while con-cluded that he didn't actually have a job. To keep this train derailed, I asked him, So what do other men do around here? Well, let's see, he said. There's the gas station. And the store. And the school. And, hey wait a minute, buster, are you some kind of policeman? You are, aren't you? Why, you . . .

And I walked back to the car. Fucking alcoholics.

Church was a tasteful affair, with a cheery priest whose sermon reminded us that it's best not to worry, to be *heureux*, to remind ourselves of our blessings and to celebrate all that is joyful in life. The congregation skewed old, with just a few families attending, as in France. Afterward, people were very polite, and I shook hands with everyone, including the *mahu* who led the choir, and then they wandered onward, back to their lives, and I spent a desultory hour walking around the village, mindful of nasty-looking dogs and noting the flip-flops and shorts garb of the vast majority of Tautira's inhabitants, suggesting that Sunday church was not on the day's itinerary for them.

Concluding that I had pretty much exhausted the village's entertainment options, I headed back and joined Jean-Michel and his family for their Sunday repast. We sat outdoors, in the kitchen *fare*, as he introduced me to everyone, a dozen or so family members, Tahitians all. It was a birthday party for a three-year-old boy, who sat happily singing as the ocean shimmered behind him. There was a long rigmarole about wine, and the superiority of light California wines for the noontime meal. French wines are too heavy for the afternoon, don't you think? Well, I'm not real particular anymore. We could just dispense with the wine altogether and go straight to the vodka and then I could join my friend, the Angel of Mercy, but I thought that would be impolite to say, so I said that I was *bon* with just water.

I felt relaxed and happy here, grateful to have been invited to the family meal. There were grilled meats and fish and salad and the conversation flowed easily.

"When I am in France," Jean-Michel said, "my battery dies. Everyone is so depressed, always complaining about politics or the economy. They are always talking about the past. Here, it is about the present. My battery doesn't die here. No one complains or speaks of the past."

We were interrupted by a little boy who wanted to know if I spoke Tahitian. I said that, alas, I did not. He told me that this was very sad and I agreed with him. And then we watched the three-year-old open his gifts—a puzzle and a tot xylophone. Parents might regret that xylophone, I thought, as he began to hammer away.

"But I also like Asia," Jean-Michel said. "Europe lives in the past, Tahiti in the present, but Asia lives for tomorrow. I love the energy there."

The woman across from him snorted with laughter. Her name was Camille and she was radiantly beautiful, a young Tahitian woman seven months pregnant with her first child. "Tell him why you love Asia," she said to Jean-Michel.

"There's a woman." He shrugged.

"With lots of energy," finished Camille, to her great delight. And then she turned to me. "Are you married?" Yes, I said. She nodded and turned the conversation to where one might find a good woman these days, and I watched this table of French-Tahitians debate the relative merits of the globe's female population. If you want to find love, the table concurred, you should head to Southeast Asia, and somewhere above, I noted the sparkling gleam of Venus transiting from one orbit to another.

Chapter Fifteen

In a world of ceaseless change, it can be gratifying to know that some things remain forever the same. Take the simple act of getting oneself to Tarawa, a sliver of coral on the equator that functions as the capital of the Republic of Kiribati. I'd worried that in the years since I'd lived there that the world had somehow caught up to Kiribati, enveloping it in its familiar arms, quickly transforming this peculiar, isolated country into just another facsimile of our homogenous global culture. I feared that instead of traditional I-Kiribati dancing, of which even Stevenson had said: "Gilbertese dance appeals to the soul: it makes one thrill to the soul; it makes one thrill with emotion; it uplifts one, it conquers one: it has the essence of all great art," I'd now find a nation doing a Gangnam Style horsey dance. Instead of a staple diet of fish and breadfruit, I worried that the I-Kiribati may now have discovered chicken tenders and onion rings—of which, I'll concede, I would have trampled over the maimed elderly to consume, such was the meagerness of the local diet that I had come to know and abhor. And what of the island's youth? Back in my day, they'd discovered La Macarena. What would it be now? If I heard a peep of Justin Bieber, I'd know that the end was nigh.

Fortunately, it's still a pain in the ass to get to Tarawa, so this boded well. From Tahiti, I flew to New Zealand and then onward to Nadi, Fiji, where I hoped to find a plane to Kiribati. You'd think there'd be a direct flight between Papeete and Nadi, the two busiest airports in the South Pacific, but this turns out not to be the case. The Pacific is essentially divided into three concentric circles and they have nothing to do with each other. There is the French Pacific, of course, where the people, by and large, look like Pacific Islanders. And yet the moment someone speaks, or you turn on a television, or read the local newspaper, or otherwise engage in some form of communication, it is apparent that you are in France, which may seem self-evident, it being called French Polynesia and all, but still, even after all this time, was something that struck me as so discordant that I didn't quite know what to make of it, just that it felt odd, like it was some kind of affront to the natural order of things.

To the north lay the American Pacific, a sphere of influence that stretched from Hawaii to Guam, composed of chains of islands all dependent on the largesse of the US government, which in turn uses these remote locales to conduct its really spooky, supersecret activities. Biological weapons? Chemical weapons? Check and check. Nuclear weapons? Of course. Kwajalein Atoll in the Marshall Islands, proud home of the Reagan Test Site, is where the US military conducts its ballistic missile testing and what it calls "near-earth and deep-space surveillance," as well as . . .

Okay, I'm just speculating here, but I happened to be on Kwajalein in 2006 (why can't I shake the feeling that right at this very moment the NSA has locked on to my laptop) and I noticed that right there on the runway (some kind of Code Red Alert is presently pinging through the ECHELON Inter-

Service Counterintelligence Communication System) was a Royal Thai Navy plane (Joint Special Operations Command has been alerted to possible real-time threat) as well as an unmarked Gulfstream V (Delta Force operators are being deployed), which the CIA has been known to use for its rendition operations (did I just see shadows pass outside the window?), wherein terrorism suspects are kidnapped and taken to third-party nations for enhanced interrogation (multiple red laser sight tags are presently dancing on my forehead) . . .

. . . So in conclusion, the US presence in the Pacific has been overwhelmingly benign and devoted entirely to the well-being and happiness of the islanders themselves, and it is for this reason that the northern Pacific—Hawaii, the Marshalls, the Federated States of Micronesia, Guam, Palau, the Marianas—has essentially zero contact with their southern brethren. They are content, filled with joy, their bellies full and their hearts bursting with mirth.

Then there is the independent Pacific, and it is vast and disparate. There are Melanesians and Micronesians and Polynesians, but this doesn't even begin to describe all the fissures and complexities of these itsy-bitsy, tiny little countries. You can be in a village in Papua New Guinea, walk five miles to the next village, and you have essentially traveled from one nation to another, each with its own language and customs. Ditto for Vanuatu. And the Solomon Islands. In Tonga, you have a feudal society. You're either a noble or a commoner and this determines whether you can vote or afford a moped. In the more remote islands, like those of Tuvalu, you can spend an entire life—forty or fifty years even—without having left the twelve square miles of your sun-drenched atoll. Fiji, of course, is ever combustible with its chiefly rivalries and military coups and the mostly poor, unhappy Indians that comprise 40 percent of its population.

There are islands in the Pacific so peaceful as to be nearly Edenic and others so violent and crime-ridden that you wouldn't dare lay your head to sleep until you were safely tucked behind walls laced with shards of glass and patrolled by night watchmen and vicious mongrel dogs loyal only to the hand that feeds them. It is true that in each of these countries you will find coconut palm trees, sandy beaches, and warm translucent water—every single one of them a postcard advertisement of the same dream—and yet, despite commonalities in geography and ancestry, perhaps no region on earth is as unneighborly as the independent South Pacific.

Nowhere does this lack of, let's call it, esprit de corps manifest itself more clearly than in the simple act of trying to get from one island nation to another. And thus the hopscotching around the Pacific. In Fiji, I showed up at the airport early one morning to catch a scheduled flight to Tarawa only to be informed that the plane had already left.

"Um," I said. "It says here on my ticket that the plane was scheduled to depart at eight thirty." I looked at my watch. "It's presently six A.M."

"They decided to leave at five thirty," said the counterperson.

This left me baffled. It wasn't so much the discrepancy between the plane's scheduled time of departure and its actual departure, but rather that someone had been in a hurry to get to Kiribati at all. Looking around, I saw half a planeload worth of passengers similarly perplexed. Something actually left early? For Kiribati? It was like an affront to the space-time continuum. I asked the Fijian woman at the counter when the next flight to Tarawa would be.

"Maybe next week," she said.

Excellent, I thought. That was more like it. *Maybe next week* was the official motto of the Kiribati I had come to know.

It took a month for Stevenson and his party to sail from Tahiti to Hawaii, a difficult journey full of "calms, squalls, head sea, waterspouts of rain, hurricane weather all about." They sent the *Casco* back to San Francisco and spent another six months in a cottage on Waikiki Beach, then inhabited by a mere twenty souls. Even this proved too much for Stevenson, who, catching up on work and correspondence, complained bitterly to Charles Baxter that "the care of my family keeps me in vile Honolulu, where I am always out of sorts, amidst heat and cold and cesspools and beastly HAOLES. What is a haole? You are one; and so, I am sorry to say, am I." Clearly, this was a man not yet ready to return to continental life, and so when the opportunity arose to obtain passage on a pygmy trading schooner to Kiribati and Samoa, Stevenson seized the moment and, together with Fanny; Lloyd Osbourne; his son-in-law, Joe Strong; and his "China boy," Ah Fu, departed Hawaii in June 1889. The *Honolulu Advertiser* wryly observed: "It is hoped that Mr. Stevenson will not fall victim to native spears; but in his present state of bodily health, perhaps the temptation to kill him may not be very strong."

The night before my departure I essentially camped out at the airport. No way was I going to let some eager-beaver pilot leave without me again, and in the predawn darkness, we took off, heading toward the end of the world. There was another foreigner sitting next to me, and curious, I asked what drew him to Kiribati.

"I come for the leprosy," he said in a peculiar French-Australian accent. "And the tuberculosis." Then he coughed violently.

I gave this the full attention it deserved. He made it sound like a spa treatment. Some go for the aromatherapy and an enzyme peel, while others choose the all-inclusive leprosy/

tuberculosis option with a cholera treatment thrown in for free. He was a doctor, and he informed me that he made this trip four times a year.

"And are there still many cases of leprosy on Tarawa?" I asked.

"Yes, many," he said, wiping his nose on his sleeve.

"And how does one go about acquiring leprosy in this day and age?"

He sneezed. "It is very contagious," he informed me as he searched for a tissue. "It is in the air." I looked at him, saucer-eyed now. "And you must have a certain gene. I have been treating leprosy for thirty-five years and I have never been infected." I observed him closely. He was gnarled and misshapen.

I hadn't informed anyone in Kiribati that I was coming, of course. Imagine that you live in Barton County, Missouri, and that for two years some city boy from downstate came and lived among you. Everyone was very kind to him, but sometime later, you discover that he wrote a book called *The Moral Depravity of Barton County*. What would you think? Exactly, which is why I thought it best to keep things hush-hush. People can be so sensitive about book titles.

And then I saw the islands, the first of the Gilberts, palm fringed and lonely, the forgotten crests of undersea volcanoes. No place looks more intriguing than an atoll rising from the great depths of the ocean, curving around a luminous lagoon like a sea serpent coiled around a sparkling jewel. There are about 100,000 people now living in Kiribati, on thirty-two low-lying islands dispersed over an area as large as a continent, though nearly half reside on Tarawa. We flew low over the northern part of the atoll and I could see that the tide was out, revealing a vast expanse of sandy lagoon flats and the desolate reef shelf. We landed and . . . was that a wrecked plane in the bushes? And, wow, there still isn't a fence next to the runway. But there were people, and I waved, good morning, Kiribati.

They say that you can never go home again. You look for everything to be the same and when you find that things have changed, you are left reeling, crestfallen and dazed. Fortunately, this didn't seem to be a problem on Tarawa since as far as I could tell everything remained exactly like it had been, as if it were frozen in a teardrop of amber. It was, even at 9:00 A.M., staggeringly hot, a kind of heat that seeps into your bones, crumbling them into ash. I walked across the tarmac, breathing in the heady humidity of the equatorial Pacific. The terminal was exactly as I remembered it, made of cinder blocks, wood, and tin, with hand-painted signs. One sign informed us that it was for TRANSIT, and I looked around and wondered to where. I was a trifle worried about getting through Immigration. I dimly expected to be greeted with a raspy voice saying, *We've been waiting for you to come back*, and then I'd be hustled on board a Royal Thai Navy plane and flown to Kwajalein, but the immigration officer was too busy cracking jokes with the other passengers to give me anything other than an arrival stamp.

I'd called a guesthouse the previous day from Fiji. Teetang and her husband, Titi, had arrived at the airport to pick me up and I followed them out to a pickup truck and tossed my bag into the back. I asked them about the changes to the island. What's new?

"There are many Chinese now," Teetang said, as we drove over a potholed causeway that had my teeth rattling.

"I thought the Chinese were gone. Didn't the government decide to recognize Taiwan instead?"

"Yes, but many Chinese stayed and started businesses."

Yes, of course they have. "Has any other country come to open an embassy?" I wondered. Sometimes the Great Game is played at the very margins of the world. That Kiribati kicked out the Chinese and invited in the Taiwanese was unsurprising. Pacific Island countries often switch their fealty from one to the other depending on the size of the aid offered. But I was curious if there was a new player in town.

"Cuba."

"I'm sorry," I said. "I thought you said Cuba."

"Yes," Teetang confirmed. "Cuba. They have an embassy here and all the doctors now are from Cuba."

"Really. Well, that's awfully nice of them."

"But many people think it's very strange. They say why would a small country like Cuba open an embassy in a small country like Kiribati? So they think the Cubans are here because they want the body parts."

"The body parts?"

"Yes, they take the body parts and sell them."

She said this very matter-of-factly, as if discussing a recent change in shampoo preferences. I didn't think for a moment that the Cubans were gouging out kidneys in Kiribati and selling them on the black market—at least not for the fun of it—but I liked that people were talking about it. When I lived on Tarawa we were all convinced that the Chinese were bringing in heavy armaments to the island. It's what one does on atolls. You see something that interests you and you create a story, and if it happens to be dark and scary, all the better.

It had rained in recent weeks and the island exuded an unexpected lushness, a greenery that far exceeded that of my memory. Unlike Fakarava, the lagoon here retreats like a vanquished army during low tide, leaving behind a desolate desert that reflected a blinding, piercing sunlight as if it were a mirror casting signals. There were more people. Parts of the island that I remembered as unsettled now beheld an array of homes, nearly all done in the local style, with a platform raised on stilts, a thatched roof, and mats made of pandanus leaves that could be rolled and unfurled and used as walls. The Mormons too had been busy building more schools and churches. In the South Pacific, no church is more aggressive in its missionary activities than the Mormons. People don't wear much on the islands, but you'd be surprised how many are wearing magic underwear. Then I noticed the seawalls. These were often built to extend a family's available space a little farther into the lagoon or to protect what they had from erosion. They were nearly all ruined now, like the walls of some ancient fortress that could not withstand a siege. And the island's lone road had all but dissipated, leaving a cratered moonscape for drivers to navigate.

The guesthouse was located in the middle of South Tarawa, the populated lower axis of the atoll, and it faced the lagoon. It was two stories, which was very exciting, making it sort of like the Empire State Building of mid-South Tarawa. Upstairs, I looked out the window and saw the thatched roofs below, where, to my amazement, I noticed cats nestled in the dried leaves. So that's where they lived. I'd always wondered where the cats hung out. No one kept them as pets. Kittens were generally scooped up and drowned. You need to be resourceful to survive on this island if you're a cat.

I dropped off my backpack and immediately headed to the road and flagged down a passing minibus. I wanted to indulge my memories. There were only nineteen people inside this minibus, which meant that I didn't have to sit on someone's lap, a luxury akin to hiring a Lincoln Town Car. And the music? It was familiar. Old. What was this again? It was on the tip of my tongue. It's . . . Cat Stevens. It's not the sort of thing I'd want to listen to every day, but I was expecting a brain-melting, techno-electronica bastardization of a Katy Perry teeny-bopper anthem, so this was akin to scoring tickets to La Scala. I hopped off in front of a familiar dirt-road cul-de-sac leading toward the ocean and saw a recognizable store, Angirota Enterprises General Merchants, which had been our go-to shop for our everyday needs when my wife and I lived nearby. Of course, after two years on Tarawa our everyday needs had been reduced to those of a single-cell organism, and I remembered with fondness the simplicity of our lives back then. *Really, you didn't throw up once today? Me too.* And we celebrated and called it a good day. The shop was exactly as I remembered it, a sky-blue cinder-block storehouse with a tin roof and a counter behind which lay cans of corned beef and bags of rice. I took a gander at the fridge, which contained the familiar boxes of Longlife Milk, stacks of Victoria Bitter and XXXX Gold, and a few wilting vegetables. I left feeling strangely elated. It's. Exactly. The. Same.

I followed the curve of a muddy track, instinctually picking up rocks in case I was pestered by dogs, and followed it toward our old home. Was it always this derelict looking, I wondered? These were all government-owned cinder-block houses, and even shrouded with a verdant foliage, they looked like the grim remains of the Battle of Stalingrad, with gaping holes in the roofs and crumbling walls. They were invariably surrounded by a constellation of well-crafted traditional dwellings, which encircled the Western-style house like mourners at a funeral. I walked on, waved a friendly howdy to the kids who were yelling *i-matang i-matang*, the local word for "foreigner," as if Bigfoot were walking past dressed in a clown costume. Then I saw two familiar casuarina trees, which leaned over, offering shade to a family of pigs snorting in the bush, and I knew I had found our old home.

I had to stare hard to recognize it. Our house was green,

but this one was yellow. Of course, I thought, as I stood there withering in the heat. The sun had cooked the paint. And I knew we had two cement water encasements, which collected rainwater from the roof. But here, there was simply a pile of shattered gray cement. The door was missing, and as I approached, I announced my presence with a genial *mauri*, the I-Kiribati greeting. The interior of the house was barren of all furnishings. There were two naked children sitting on the tile floor, staring blankly at me, next to a woman who was on her side snoozing, and as I spoke, she opened her eyes. I tried to explain that I once lived here, that I had heaps of fond memories, that right where you happen to be napping there had once been a dining room table, upon which a volunteer vet had operated on a dog, and it sure is swell to be back, reliving all those sweet recollections, and . . . she merely grunted and went back to sleep.

So it went that day. I crisscrossed the island, visiting the relics of bygone years. My wife Sylvia's former organization, the Foundation for the Peoples of the South Pacific, used to have an office with a well-tended demonstration garden and a staff of ten. The office was now used as an Australian visa-processing center and the garden was no more. FSP had been reduced to a two-person operation, inhabiting a small office above a store, and I recognized neither of the employees. The Otintaai, a government-run hotel where we used to gather for Cheap-Cheap Fridays, had really intriguing signs plastered over its walls. DANGER. THIS BUILDING IS UNSAFE. U.N. STAFF NO ADMITTANCE. SINCERELY, U.N. SECURITY. What made this particularly interesting, as I soon learned, was that the stickers had been placed there immediately *after* a visit by Ban Ki-moon, the U.N. Secretary-General. I don't know why, but this tickled me. Good, I thought. For once, someone from the U.N. is denied the option of a room at the Four Seasons, and is forced to endure a night or two of reality. Well done, government of Kiribati. The rest of the world thanks you.

It was only later, as I gathered behind the guesthouse, standing on a seawall to enjoy the sunset, that I sensed profound change. There is not a more spectacular sight than that of the sun descending in crimson and orange grandeur along the equator, its wispy light casting radiant flares across the expanse of the lagoon and the cascade of palms following a sliver of land to the horizon. A gathering of fairy terns fluttered near shore, diving into the lagoon and singing melodically. I could hear the songs from the boys high up the coconut trees, which they had climbed to gather toddy, the tree's nectar. The tide had come in and I watched it rise. And rise. And rise. Soon, it was bubbling beneath me, seeping into the seawall, and escaping like babbling fountains. The seawall was but a soggy, collapsing peninsula, suddenly surrounded on three sides by ever-surging waters. I looked around me with particular interest, and noted the trees and bushes that just an hour or two earlier had been dry and undisturbed, but now lay immersed in the lagoon. Many of the coconut trees, I now saw, were dead, standing like mute sentries above the encroaching water. The island was sinking, its destiny foretold in the great beauty of the gathering sea. And then I saw a dead cat float by in a gentle current and I exhaled. This, at least, was familiar.

Chapter Sixteen

When I was in Fiji, I saw a newspaper with the headline: ENTIRE NATION OF KIRIBATI TO BE RELOCATED OVER RISING SEA LEVEL THREAT. The article went on to say that the government of Kiribati was in the process of purchasing five thousand acres on Vanua Levu, the second-largest island in Fiji. Initially, the plan was to use the land as a farm to secure Kiribati's food needs, but as things got more dire, it would be a place for the I-Kiribati to settle after rising sea levels made their islands uninhabitable. "This is the last resort, there's no way out of this one," Anote Tong, the president of Kiribati, was quoted as saying. "Our people will have to move as the tides have reached our homes and villages."

I don't know about you, but if I heard that we would soon be leaving our country because fish were about to swim through our doors, I'd think this would be a news story I should probably pay some attention to. There's a difference between emigrating and abandoning the motherland. Emigrate, and you still retain the option of one day coming back. Perhaps you didn't like the food, or the weather, or they didn't have your favorite cereal, and you decide to return home. This, however, was something far more apocalyptic. There's no going back after a family of octopuses has moved into your kitchen drawer.

To prepare for this eventuality, the government launched an Education for Migration program. Again, I noted the doomsday language, even though *education* rhymes with *migration* as if it were a verse in a limerick. It sounded so final, like one of the things you check off as you prepare for some seminal event that will forever mark the boundary between before and after. I met with one of the instructors, Mary, an I-Kiribati friend from the good old days, when sinking below the ocean was not on our list of pressing worries. After the usual flurry of news and gossip, I asked her about the program.

"We teach the youth vocational skills so that when they leave Kiribati, they'll have something to do," she said.

"But how do people feel about being forced to leave Kiribati?"

"They are resigned to it," she said.

This struck me as an unsatisfying answer. How could anyone be resigned to losing a country, *an entire country*, to rising sea levels? It's not as if you can just conjure up a replacement nation out of thin air. There are worse places, of course, than Fiji, but the I-Kiribati will never become *Fijian*. Many people, for one reason or another, become expatriates or immigrants, finding themselves in a new land, but when they pack for a trip home, they don't usually include scuba gear. Losing a state to the ocean is not quite the same as losing your accent.

"What is that English expression?" Mary wondered. "The canary in the coal mine. Kiribati is the canary in the coal mine."

But because canaries are small and cute, just like Kiribati, they're easy to dismiss. Of course, in the past few years, parts of both New York City and New Orleans have spent time underwater, albeit due to storms and not tides, so perhaps it will take the loss of Denver before it finally occurs to some that maybe it's not such a good idea to pump so much carbon into the atmosphere. I know, I know, mustn't do anything to stifle *growth*. The important thing is to expand the gross domestic product. There must always be *more*. This is how we measure our well-being. I understand the sentiment very well. I am wired for *more*, understand it intuitively, deep in my bones, can see its allure, that equation that says if I *consume* just a little *more*, the world will be suffused with sunshine and unicorns. But honestly, I don't think it's a great idea for nations to do things my way. Nation-states should be measured and thoughtful and prudent. They should not, under any circumstances, be allowed to behave like a junkie in pursuit of a fix. There are consequences to be dealt with, victims even, such as a nation of low-lying atolls like Kiribati, which will soon become nothing more than a modern Atlantis, a sunken underworld that lives on only in legend.

Was it really that bad, though? Or were the tides that I was seeing, so high that they swept over causeways and inundated homes, an anomaly? I tracked down Atenati, who used to work in the demonstration garden at FSP. I visited her at her home, in the center of the island, equidistant from both the ocean and the lagoon. She told me that even here her well water was becoming brackish. "But I still have my garden," she said. "For the people that live near the lagoon? They lost their gardens. Nothing grows anymore because of the seawater."

Since I had last seen her, Atenati had spent a few years in Australia, where her daughter lived. She had married an Australian, and when they had their first child, they pleaded with Atenati to move to Brisbane. "I didn't want to go," Atenati said. "I like my island, but my daughter, she begged, she said that she needed her mother, so I went. I lived in Australia for two years. But I didn't like it. No smiles. No laughing. Everyone always very serious. No one friendly. I like it here, on my little island. Here I speak and laugh with everyone around me. When I want to talk to my neighbor, I just raise my voice, like this." And here she bellowed, which was immediately met with a dozen replies floating over her traditional fence. "I like it *here*," she said with a laugh.

Bwenawa, however, was far less cheery. He too had worked in the FSP garden with Atenati and he had guided me through the history and customs of the islands. He lived near the hospital, where, apparently, the Cubans were busy harvesting human organs, and I took a minibus to find him. His home was located nearer the lagoon, in a densely populated swath of land, where crumbling cinder-block structures and wood-and-thatch homes competed for space with mangy dogs, pigs, chickens, and some really agitated roosters. Soon, I saw the source of the roosters' distress. A cock fight. A group of men were busy sending their birds into battle.

I found Bwenawa's two-room house nearby. He was already an *unimane*, or respected village elder, when I lived on Tarawa. Now, he was an *unimane emeritus*, and as I noted his hunched posture and his swooped-back gray hair, I suddenly felt the passing of years. He now worked with the other elders, digging deep into records from the 1947 Land Commission, to discover who the true owners of the land on Tarawa were. As the capital atoll, and the only island with electricity or formal cash-paying jobs, Tarawa attracted wave after wave of outer islanders, and as a result of the overpopulation, the indigenous population could no longer forge a livelihood or maintain a sustainable existence using customary means. Many had sold their land, believing that they were getting a tidy sum of money, but money inevitably disappears and now they discovered that they were both poor and landless.

"But see, Bwenawa," I said, "pretty soon it won't matter. You'll be off to Fiji. Plenty of land there for everyone."

Bwenawa sighed. "You see that *kie-kie*," he said, pointing to a small wooden platform raised on stilts with a thatched roof. "The tide came to there." This was about eighty yards inland. "No one here can grow food anymore. All the gardens die. The coconut trees are dying. And there is much more erosion of the land, also on the ocean side."

We stopped for a moment to listen to the squawking of unhappy roosters. I asked him, in all seriousness, about his thoughts about uprooting the entire nation and moving to Fiji.

He thought for a long time. "I don't know," he finally said. "We will leave it to the government to decide."

I went to look for the government. For a brief moment I thought I might even get to speak with President Tong, who, nearly alone among Pacific leaders, has used his perch to voice the alarm. Rising sea levels are not some abstraction, he has said. It is our reality today. So I went to the Ministry of Foreign Affairs, which shares a small two-story building with the Ministry of Public Works, whose staff, I was pleased to note, was busy doing Zumba when I arrived. I watched as a dozen public employees did a little meringue, a little salsa, with a dash of mambo and heaps of chachacha, following the instructions on a television that had been rolled into the office. There are moments when you realize just how much you truly love a country, and this was one of them. I joined them because when offered a chance to salsa dance with a Ministry of Public Works, how can anyone say no? "We do the Zumba every day," a young woman informed me, a sheen of sweat on her forehead. "For the exercise," she added, like anyone needs an excuse to Zumba.

The Ministry of Foreign Affairs, alas, was not nearly so fun-loving. I walked upstairs and asked the first person I saw if it might be possible to chat with the Secretary of Foreign Affairs. The secretary was out of the country, I was told, but I could speak to her assistant, and so I did. I told her that I had once lived here on Tarawa, wrote a book about it even, and that I was presently visiting in a kind of quasi-journalistic type capacity and might it be possible to arrange an appointment with the Secretary upon her return.

"You wrote a book?" the assistant inquired. "What was the name of this book?"

"Uh . . . The *cough cough cough* lives of *cough cough cough.*"

"I'm sorry, but could you repeat that?"

"The *cough cough* of cannibals."

"I still didn't catch that."

"Thesexlivesofcannibals. So, looks like it's another sunny day today."

She pursed her lips, and in an instant I knew that no one would speak with me. So if you're looking to see what the government of Kiribati finally decides to do, when do they wave the flag and say the last good-bye, I'm afraid I can't help you. But look around, follow the news, Google it, bear witness. The very least we could do for the canary is acknowledge its demise.

On Sunday, I went to church. It's something I'd never done before on Tarawa, possibly because when I lived here, I was still at that age when sleeping until noon on the weekend seemed like a sensible and natural thing to do. One of the surest signs of advancing years, of course, occurs when you begin to regard 8:00 A.M. as a provocatively late hour to rise from your slumbers, a wanton disregard for the preciousness of time.

But I wanted to go to church because it's a good place to mull things over, and I was confronted with a dilemma. Robert Louis Stevenson spent several months in Kiribati, traveling from island to island on board the *Equator*, though he only wrote about two, Butaritari and Abemama. These chapters, coming toward the end of *In the South Seas*, are the book's liveliest, and it is no wonder. Butaritari was then the commercial hub of the Gilbert Islands, so visited by copra traders that the island supported not one but two bars, The Land We Live In "being tacitly reserved to the forecastle," as Stevenson described the clientele, "and the Sans Souci tacitly reserved for the afterguard." Typically, the I-Kiribati were forbidden to drink, but the king of Butaritari, Tebureimoa, attired in "pajamas which sorrowfully misbecame his bulk," had lifted the taboo on alcohol to commemorate July Fourth, the American Independence Day, and for the previous ten days "the town had been passing the bottle or lying . . . in hoggish sleep."

It was a perilous time for the Stevenson party. The entire island was consumed by brawls and danger, and even Fanny took to carrying a pistol, brandishing it on the beach as she impressed everyone with the accuracy of her shot, blowing apart bottle after bottle, of which there was no shortage, during her target shooting. From the bushes, people flung rocks at Stevenson's head or loitered threateningly around his compound, next to the king's thatched palace. No one dared to turn off the tap, to deny the pouring of another round: "too surly a refusal might at any moment precipitate a blow, and the blow might prove the signal for a massacre." He let it be known that he was the son of Queen Victoria, a man not to be trifled with, and finally, after the carnage and mayhem threatened to unspool the last fine line of order on the island, prevailed upon the king to reimpose the taboo on demon alcohol.

Today, Tarawa serves as the fulcrum where alcohol and trade, what there is of it, intersect in Kiribati. Most of the bars are in Betio, near the Making Cigarettes Factory, one of the new Chinese businesses to have opened on Tarawa. Betio is the islet where the Battle of Tarawa was fought during World War II, and people today live among the detritus of war, rusty Higgins boats and Sherman tanks that reveal themselves at low tide, and the heavy guns and concrete pillboxes used by the Japanese, which sprout like mushrooms amidst palm trees and people—lots of people. Betio is one of the most densely populated spots on earth, a warren of shanties and traditional housing, ringed by beaches brimming with rusty tins, garbage, and innumerable canine skulls bleached white by the sun. The scent of shit prevails. This is where the harbor is, and offshore I could see sunken freighters and Korean purse seiners, their industrial rigging offering a bewildering contrast to the blueness of an unblemished sky seamlessly converging with the lagoon.

To stay true to Stevenson's travels, I figured I should do some pith-helmeted exploration of Tarawa's alcohol subculture. I'd been to Butaritari when I still lived in Kiribati and knew it well enough to know that The Land We Live In and the Sans Souci had been closed for nearly a century. It is a soporific outer island now, as peripheral to Tarawa as Kiribati is to the world, and an unlikely scene for alcohol-driven fury or drama. Tarawa was where that action was now.

And yet, blithely crawling from watering hole to saloon through the maze of Betio presented obvious difficulties for me. I was very pleased to have made it this far without succumbing to the voice that says *just one* or *just today*, and I was wary of pressing my luck. I was conscientious about avoiding bars. At 5:00 P.M., I typically went for a run and let my endorphins carry me through the hours when I was most likely to have a wandering mind, and I hesitated to alter a routine that had served me well. I was becoming superstitious about my travel habits. Besides, what's that saying? Spend enough time in a barbershop and eventually you're going to get a haircut.

So I went to church to ponder my next step. There must have been eight hundred people packed inside this white sanctuary with more spilling out of the doorways. The interior had a groovy seventies feel to it, all browns and oranges, though the Mass seemed to come from an even earlier era, pre-Vatican II perhaps, because it went on forever. From time to time, I looked at my watch. Sunday became Monday and then Tuesday. *Tick-tock* went the clock. Why was this dragging on so, I wondered? There were no pews inside this church, just a bare, splintered concrete floor. Maybe it was the pain. Could be. There sure was a lot of it during this Mass. Pleasure is fleeting; misery endures. I kneeled in prayer, observing the other parishioners, bare knees on jagged concrete. There was no slacking or sitting on heels here. But what was the priest doing? Why was the Apostles Creed taking so long? The floor was stained with quarter-size dollops of blood. They were everywhere, the gruesome outpourings of faith, crimson testaments to our suffering. My back was throbbing; my knees splintered; the skin torn. I looked up at the crucifix. You can always tell you're in a Catholic church by the depiction of the cross. Catholics don't go for abstractions, which is why you'll always see the nails and the wounds and crown of thorns, which puts things in perspective when your bones are cracking, your muscles are straining, and the skin on your kneecaps is splitting open on a concrete floor. Would Jesus complain? That's invariably what you think when your eyes gaze upon a foot-long nail hammered into his feet. And so we suffered the pains of the flesh silently, on a hard floor stained with rivulets of blood. A few began to buckle, slid-

ing flip-flops under their knees, but the truly devoted continued on, holding a pose of penance, becoming one with eternity,
because that's what it felt like, an eternal torment. In Islam, you
can tell the really devout Muslims by the knobs on their forehead. In Kiribati, you can spot the pious Catholics by the
gnarly scabs on their knees. But I continued to meditate. What
should I do from here?

Find thee a nun, a voice said.

Which is how I found myself in island rehab.

Was this the voice of God? Or a memory of my last communication with my wife, who had heard of a Catholic charity
that helped alcoholics in Kiribati and thought I might want to
have a gander. Do I sometimes confuse the two voices? Probably, but both usually lead me to good places so I don't spend a
lot of time parsing. I found the nuns next to the runway, in a
Robinson Crusoe–like compound made of plywood and thatch.
I had taken a blaring minibus to the airport, and then, making
sure to look both ways for approaching aircraft, wandered the
length of the runway until I found a smattering of jolly sisters
in blue frocks and white habits, and the next thing I knew I was
addressing twenty I-Kiribati alcoholics on Day One of their
treatment. They were as mixed as any group of alcoholics—
young and old, male and female—and they had introduced
themselves with the same tales of woe and misery that are common to rehabs everywhere, except it was followed by laughter
and much conviviality, because that's how they deal with un-
pleasant things in Kiribati—with a smile. I told them my little
story, how I'd ended up in a place much like this, except it wasn't
on a runway, and there weren't mangy dogs sauntering about,
and it didn't ask random strangers who just ambled by to get up
and speak, as far as I know, but otherwise it was very similar.
Things are going to suck for a little while, I said, as if I had any

wisdom to offer, but eventually it gets better and you'll enjoy seeking out others like ourselves, that we are all of the same tribe, and that life is way better when you can actually remember it.

Actually, during a break, I decided that this was far better than my rehab. These sisters can *bake*. There were trays of doughnut holes and pancakes filled with coconut shavings and doused with coconut syrup. Alcohol has heaps of sugar in it, of course. Take it away, and what emerges is a sweet tooth that will not be denied. And these nuns, bless their hearts, stepped into the breach, and while we spent the rest of the afternoon in diabetic shock, we were sated.

I spent much of my time at Island Rehab with Sister Matarena, a whip-smart nun of about sixty-five with twinkling eyes and a seen-it-all disposition. She ran the program, had been doing so for twenty-three years, which meant that she had seen it all. It was a three-week program, she explained, focused on alcoholism, the family, and spirituality. Most of the participants were from Betio. The islet was divided into thirteen sectors and every month they scooped up the neighborhood's alcoholics, one sector at a time, calling to my mind that scene from *Monty Python and the Holy Grail*. "Bring out your dead! Bring out your dead!" They didn't have many resources, she said, but they do what they can. "It's a terrible disease," she said. I hear you, Sister.

When I lived on Tarawa, I had no idea that this place existed. Of course, I wasn't looking for it either. I was similarly surprised to hear Sister Matarena discuss the scourge of kava on the islands.

"Haven't you seen all the kava bars?" she asked me.

I admitted that I had not, but, of course, I wasn't searching for them either.

"It's a big problem now," Sister Matarena said.

"But, Sister," I said, "how can kava be a problem? People who drink kava simply get sleepy, they relax, they don't start fights and cause trouble. And it's cheap, unlike alcohol, so it doesn't take so much money away from food and school fees."

"It's a different kind of problem than alcohol," she said. "It is a problem for the culture. People sleep all day and drink kava deep into the night. They are served by teenage girls called the flowers of the *yaqona*. It's on the outer islands now too. It's very difficult to get alcohol to the outer islands, but easy to bring kava. Then no work gets done as they sleep all day. No fishing, no gardening, no sweeping, no building. And it's not just the men. The women drink it too."

I was happy to have been informed about the presence of kava on Tarawa by Sister Matarena. In any other context, and my brain would have lit up like a Christmas tree, and started to babble about how this intoxicant should be fine, no worries, and why don't we mosey on down to the kava bar and have a flower of the *yaqona* serve us up a shell or two. What's the worst that could happen?

Oh, I know. I hadn't thought of it in ages, but during one of my quitting attempts I went on the Kava Maintenance Program. Someone with a kava bar in the United States had looked me up and very kindly sent me a box of powdered roots. Needless to say, I drank it every evening, making a colossal mess in the kitchen with a blender and a bowl, and the moment I finished the kava I headed out to find a drink. I let that thought linger in my mind, and when Sister Matarena asked if I wanted to come back the following day, I said I did. I was among my people here. Robert Louis Stevenson may have found more drama in Kiribati, as undoubtedly I would have had I spent my evenings in the bars of Betio, but when an island offers up a little serenity I reach for it with both hands now.

Chapter Seventeen

So I was wrong. Much, in fact, has changed in Kiribati since I was here last. Take, for instance, the presence of a sandbar off Na'a, the northernmost tip of the island. It wasn't there before. At no point during my years on Tarawa did I recall the existence of a long, elongated sliver of sand extending far to the south, at least a mile, following the contours of a submerged reef, the rim of an undersea volcano that separates the lagoon from the ocean. And now, here it was. Over the years, surging tides had extended their reach, scraping off soil that the island could ill afford to lose, and depositing it in places where before there was only water. The atoll was in motion, changing with startling rapidity, as the ocean toyed with it like a cat fiddling with a mouse. At some point, of course, the mouse would be no more.

I found myself on a . . . what, exactly? A boat? A sea-bus? Driftwood? A floating junk pile? It was yellow and it had an engine that coughed and sputtered and strained against the incoming tide. It had two plywood hulls, a squat wheelhouse, and a kind of awning over the weathered deck. In any event, I was on the water, chug-chugging toward Abaiang. This was now the only outer island that people could reach by sea. There was once a similar ferry to Maiana, but a year earlier, it capsized and sank and thirty-three people drowned.

As we passed through the channel, we were buffeted by lazy swells. Few sights are more visually stunning than that place where the lagoon meets the ocean. There is a riot of color, hues of blue so radiant that you'd swear someone slipped you a tab of acid, and below, just beneath the surface, were clumps of coral in ardent bloom surrounded by schools of darting fish. I was in the wheelhouse, sharing a bench with a woman nursing an infant. The captain lay sprawled beneath me on the floor, snoozing through the torpor of midday. At the helm was a one-eyed sailor wearing hot-pink Capri shorts. A gold hoop dangled from his ear. Another crew member offered me a plastic mug of sweetened tea, and I sat contentedly watching this wonderland go by.

Stevenson alighted upon Abaiang but didn't write about it. Instead, it was Tembinok, the king of Abemama, who caught his eye. "The last tyrant," he wrote of him, "the last erect vestige of a dead society." They hadn't meant to land upon Abemama. Ships avoided the island and the terrifying despot who ruled it. But a wind caught their sails and they entered its lagoon. Tembinok was a gift of the gods for Stevenson, a character so unique, menacing, and charming that you could almost feel the writer's pen lurching across the page, scribbling furiously as he sought to capture every nuance, every detail of the great king: "a beaked profile like Dante's in the mask, a mane of long black hair, the eye brilliant, imperious, and inquiring . . . Where there are no fashions, none to set them, few to follow them if they were set, and none to criticize, he dresses 'to his own heart.' Now he wears a woman's frock, now a naval uniform; now (and more usually) figures in a masquerade costume of his own design . . . The masquerade becomes him admirably.

In the woman's frock he looks ominous and weird beyond belief."

A flying fish leapt and soared a hundred yards and more. On the bow of the boat, people stirred in the languorous heat, aware suddenly that we had visitors. I moved forward and joined them. We were accompanied by a dozen spinner dolphins, surfing the bow waves, just inches from our noses, as we lay flat peering over the front of the boat.

"You ever eat the dolphin meat?" the man next to me said. "It's very good."

Swim, dolphins, swim, I thought. Do not lurk here. What did we look like? A whale-watching cruise? You've got the wrong boat. Swim away.

But they didn't, and as we crossed the open seas they tumbled up front like eager scouts on point, blazing a trail across the great depths of the sea. It was a crowded boat, with families clustered on mats in the shade of the awning, finding space amidst crates of canned food and old bicycles, with more people gathered up top, absorbing the full blast of the sun. The crew had cast a couple of fishing lines off the stern of the boat, and when hours passed without a bite, no doubt due to the enormous Asian fishing vessels lurking around Tarawa, they pulled the lines back in as we approached the channel into the lagoon at Abaiang. A green turtle swam near and I gave my tattoo an affectionate pat. You're not alone, crooked turtle. The acid really kicked in here, because Abaiang's lagoon shimmered with such breathtaking displays of color that even Gauguin's paintings seemed monochromatic and dull in comparison. There was a village on the southernmost tip of the island and I could see its thatched-roof dwellings and *maneabas*, the meeting-houses where the I-Kiribati congregate for events large and small, and then the atoll marched toward the horizon, a long display of coconut trees and white sandy beaches and all around turquoise water so dazzling and lustrous that you'd think you'd died and gone to heaven. Except, surely God offered a better meal than this. The chase boat was unhooked from its perch on the side of the vessel, and the crew filled it with boxes of Fabulous Pork Luncheon Meat, MJ China Cabin Biscuits, bags of rice, and fruit-flavored bubble gum. And so we moseyed down the length of the atoll, hopscotching from village to village, where people and the grim fare of the islands were unloaded, as local sailing canoes, lean and swift, carried fisherman across the lagoon.

Sister Matarena had radioed the Catholic high school on Abaiang and informed them that they'd have a visitor. I hopped off the chase boat in the shallows of the lagoon and waded ashore. The school was like a village. Students from throughout Kiribati boarded here, and I saw them sweeping and transforming a field of coral and scrub into a track, complete with lanes delineated with sand. In a *maneaba*, a group of teenagers sang one of the old songs, a high-energy number that shook coconut trees and caused the water to ripple. The I-Kiribati can *sing*. It's one of those countries—maybe Jamaica and Mali are comparable—that breathes music.

Nearby, there were a number of gravestones announcing that here lay Father Leon Marquis (1902–1942, killed in the Marshall Islands) and Brother Louis Latour (1875–1919) and Sister M. St. Pierre (1874–1952) as well as a dozen small unmarked graves that I presumed held the remains of students who have died here. A sister came to fetch me and took me to the kitchen to show me the rainwater tap while a piglet and a puppy played and wrestled on the floor, and then she marched me to the guesthouse, which looked like an L-shaped thatched *maneaba* with beams of coconut timber lashed together with coconut fiber. Inside, there were plywood partitions separating four rooms. Mine had a small wooden bed frame with a foam mattress and a mosquito net. On the wall, there was a picture of Jesus praying. The sister returned a short while later with dinner—fish, rice, breadfruit, both boiled and fried, and bitter green *bele* mixed with onion—and as I ate, I was briefly joined by the headmaster, a kindly man with hangdog eyes, who had once been a ship's captain.

"What's the strangest place you've been to?" I asked.

"Antarctica on an icebreaker."

This made me laugh. An ice cube seemed to challenge the reach of one's imagination on Abaiang, never mind an iceberg. Many I-Kiribati men trained to become seamen, but very few rose through the ranks to become a captain. I asked if he missed it.

"It can be difficult to be on land. I miss the sea. But I am a graduate of this school, and when they asked me to come back, I couldn't say no."

"What's your biggest headache here?"

"The kids," he said with a roll of the eyes. "Typical teenage behavior."

He needed to attend to his duties, and I stayed up for a short while reading my Kindle with the aid of a flashlight, and then once I turned it off, spent much of the night being feasted upon by ravenous mosquitoes. Somehow, they had managed to find every hole in the netting, and when finally I did fall asleep, I was soon awoken to the *CLANG-CLANG-CLANG* of the bell rustling everyone up for predawn Mass.

And that's when I stepped on my Kindle. It was like two worlds colliding—the pre-electric past, wherein there are no light switches to help guide your feet when you are suddenly and noisily awoken—and the whiz-bang gadgetry of the present. Here, the past won. The Kindle gave a desolate croak and could not be roused. Curses, I thought. A real book wouldn't do this to me. I resolved to go back to print until the brainiacs in Silicon Valley fixed this fatal flaw in their hardware. What good is a book if you can't step on it?

I hobbled to the *maneaba* just as Mass commenced. The students were in uniform and divided into neat rows, boys on one side, girls on the other. I sat quietly in the back, picking pieces of Kindle out of my foot, and was pleased to discover that the service would be in English.

"Life is about living, not dying," said the priest, a stern-faced man with a helmet of black hair and flowing purple robes. Fair enough, I thought. We should focus on life, not death. "But what is the meaning of life?" the priest bellowed. I waited with eager expectation. It seemed only right and true that I'd discover the answer during predawn Mass on a remote atoll in the South Pacific. "What is it?" the priest repeated. Yes, I thought, what is it? "You don't know?" he suddenly hissed. No, Father, I don't. What is the meaning of life? "You really don't know," he said, his voice dripping with bitterness. "I am very disappointed in you."

And then he segued into the blessing of the sacrament. Wait, I thought. You're not going to tell us. At least offer us a little guidance, or a clue, or at minimum, a parable for us to deconstruct. C'mon, not even a hint? But he kept the meaning of life to himself and proceeded on with the Blessing of the Eucharist. We responded in English with the words used in all Masses since time immemorial, and as we did so, he lowered the Eucharist and glared at us. "Why do you reply so softly?" he said. I dunno. It seemed plenty enthusiastic to me, given that the sun hadn't even risen yet, and some of us were plucking shards of plastic out of our feet. "Why?" he said. "Do you not know the words? Is that it? Is that why you speak so softly? YOU DO NOT KNOW THE WORDS."

His voice echoed off the lagoon and now there was a long moment of silence. The students shifted uncomfortably, heads down. The few dogs that had been lingering outside the *maneaba* shuffled off. A rooster's bluster broke the still air. Finally, the priest picked up his chalice and bowl of wafers, lowered his head and exited the *maneaba*, striding to the old stone church and disappearing into the nave and whatever dark lair he had constructed for himself.

We sat stunned. First you deny us the meaning of life, and now you march off in a snit with billowing robes, forbidding us the sacrament? I'm not sure if you're aware of this Father Cranky-Pants, but all through the islands there are missionaries—Mormons, Baha'i, Seventh-day Adventists—just looking for disillusioned Catholics. You've got to at least try, don't you think? But no, instead you give us "the last tyrant," storming off "in a woman's frock." That just won't do these days. People have options, you know? It's like my Kindle. I have a library's worth of choices . . . Oh, that's right. We're back in ye olden days now.

Fortunately, the Church also has nuns, who, while certain petulant clerics stewed in a sea of resentment, were busy running rehabs, cooking meals, tending to the sick, teaching kids their math lessons, and otherwise cheerfully going about their business of making the world a better place. And you can't fool a nun. Over a breakfast of sweet, stale bread and expired peanut butter I watched them happily make mincemeat out of the kids trying to talk their way out of school.

"He said he left his books in the village," Sister Teetang said with a smile, after dismissing a boy. "He wanted to walk to the village and get it. All day walking to the village. All day walking back from the village. I sent him to class."

I explored the island on a bicycle borrowed from the sisters. There is a coral and sand path that follows the length of the atoll, next to the lagoon, undisturbed by vehicles since there are but three working trucks on the island and not a single car. In between villages there are long, serene stretches and I often stopped to have a quick swim. Toilets are mostly unknown on the outer islands so it's best to avoid the beaches near settlements. The sand there is thick and slimy and often fertilized. But away from the villages what you find is a beach of such languorous beauty that you can't believe that such a place still exists, uncorrupted and untainted by tourists, its rhythms as immutable as dawn and dusk. I watched reef herons wade through the shallows of the lagoon, stealthily hunting. Swimming some distance from shore, I was astonished to see that the beach itself was alive. What I had taken as a smattering of inanimate shells and rocks, were in fact tribes of crabs, all marching and scurrying as if this were rush hour in Times Square.

More serene were the villages themselves, where subsistence living still predominates. Subsistence living, of course, is the technical term for men sitting on their asses all day while the women do all the work. Sure, at some point before nightfall the men will catch a fish or two. And from time to time, they'll build a wood and thatch home or repair a *maneaba*. But that's pretty much it. Meanwhile, the women are hacking open coconuts and laying them out to dry. They're weaving mats and entwining palm fronds. They cook, tend to the fires, sweep the day's dust and leaves, take care of the kids, and otherwise keep the whole edifice of island society standing upright and firm.

I passed a village with the second-largest *maneaba* in Kiribati—think of an aircraft hanger made from the remains of coconut trees—and another, Koinawa, that offered a cathedral, built under the guidance of a Belgian missionary who failed to notice that big stone churches are really uncomfortable on the equator. The exterior is lovely; the interior gutted and ruined. Even Father Cranky-Pants recognized this enduring truth of the tropics. It's hot out here, which is why the giant *maneaba* gets love and tending and the stone church does not.

But I was looking for another village. On Tarawa, Sister Matarena, a native of Abaiang, had told me about Tebunginako. "The sea, it swept it away," she told me. "The people who were out, they came back to find their possessions floating away." The village is located near the northern end of the atoll, a pit of land wide enough to encompass a freshwater lagoon, where milkfish once thrived and fed the village. That lagoon was the first to go as it flooded with saltwater that soon killed the milkfish and nearby coconut palms. There were once *babai* pits, sunken depressions where locals cultivated taro, and in a few short years the encroaching ocean turned the water lens so brackish that nothing could grow. As spring tides, or king tides as they're sometimes referred to, began to flood homes, the village picked itself up and moved fifty yards inland. But it wasn't far enough. The ocean continued to surge, lapping at the edge of the village. The inhabitants built seawalls. The ocean tore them down. Finally, as sea levels continued to rise, the village was abandoned and the people dispersed. All that remains of Tebunginako today are the ruins of a *maneaba* and the skeletons of homes surrounded by a great flood of water. It is a haunting sight. And it is different and it is new. This was not the past or the future. This was today, the land receding under the waves.

Chapter Eighteen

Why Samoa?

This is a question that has vexed readers and biographers since Stevenson first planted his flag in the hills above Apia, building what would become the only true home he'd ever know as a grown man. Reading through his letters, one searches in vain for a clue, some foreshadowing of his decision to settle here, far away from the bustle and glare of the continental world, on an island stirred by little else than trade winds and rumors. On board the *Equator*, as he toppled down the latitudes from Kiribati to Samoa under a glaring sun so hot that the wood on the ship's deck buckled, Stevenson betrayed no hint or promise of his fateful decision to remain in the South Seas. Indeed, from his pen, one senses a longing for London. "I can hear the rattle of the hansom up Endell Street and see the gates swing back, and feel myself out upon the monument steps—Hosanna home again." And yet, a few weeks after writing those words he will have purchased four hundred acres of land and begun work on what would become Vailima, his haven, abounded by five streams, where he would become known as Tusitala, the teller of tales, in a place where "headhunting, besides, still lives on my doorstep."

I spent a few weeks in Samoa, traveling between Upolu and Savai'i, the less populated of the two islands, where I hoped to encounter the *fa'a* Samoa, or Samoan Way. It is a pious country, with speed bumps enforcing a go-slow mandate in front of churches belonging to Congregationalists, Methodists, Mormons, and Seventh-day Adventists. The buses are painted in trippy colors and have God-fearing names such as Kingdom Transport, Paradise in Heaven, God Bless Samoa, Forever Strong, and Jesus—I Trust in You. Then there is the Bon Jovi bus, which together with the It Wasn't Me bus, prowl Samoa like a couple of young hoodlums playing hooky. Invariably, the buses are crowded and it is common to see passengers sit in each other's laps. Samoans are among the largest people on earth, and it is no wonder that buses seek divine protection, because God only knows how they manage to roll without shattering the suspension.

On Savai'i, near the village of Manase, I found a small beach *fale* with a thatched roof and walls of flapping mats, modernized only by the presence of a mosquito net, where I watched the squalls lining up on the horizon like tornadoes on the Great Plains. Samoans fear the water. You rarely see kids swimming or men fishing from canoes. Life seems very much turned inward here. The myth about the South Pacific is that it is a great, open expanse where escapism can run amok. But it's not like that at all. The appeal of the South Seas is really about how small you can make your world. It's not about broadening your possibilities; it's about reducing them until all that is left is sustenance and family.

The beach *fale* was owned by the high chief of Manase, who every evening would drive on the sand in his pickup and offer a regal wave. I liked him. I could only speak a few words of Samoan but despite the language barrier I sensed he was a wise and sagacious chief. I know this because in an act of dictatorial might, he had banned dogs and so I ran freely from village to village, past tin-roofed shops featuring murals of Jesus and Bob Marley, and designated bus stops where locals left clusters of bananas to be eaten by any with a hankering for a snack. It was a runner's paradise. In the village of Avao, I came across some men building a church and a stone monument and as I paused to have a look, I was joined by a barefoot man in a lavalava who spoke as if his voice box was stuck on fast-forward.

"ItistocommemorateJohnWilliams," he said all at once. "HewaswiththeLondonMissionary-Society. HecometoSamoain1830. In1844hegaveusthefirstBibleintheSamoanlanguage."

I absorbed this. "Do you drink kava here?" I asked, genuinely curious.

"Ohyes. ItisSamoansfavoritebeverage."

Obviously, he didn't drink enough of it.

The hyperkinetic kava drinker aside, Savai'i seemed as sedate an island as any I'd ever visited in the South Pacific. Life moved easily between church and farming, where people cultivated land so lavishly bountiful that everything grew here, from coffee to cocoa to vanilla to taro to coconuts. I hiked deep into the hills, to the summit of Mount Matavanu, a volcano that had last erupted in 1911, burying forty square miles and a few villages under lava flows so thick that in some places they measure nearly four hundred feet in depth. Near the top, a path had been cleared by Da Craterman, a bushy-headed guy with a massive wart on his chest, who bedecked his trail with a plethora of signs commemorating all those who had sojourned here.

"I have been visited by people from one hundred and twenty countries," he said.

"So which countries are you missing?"

"I don't know," he said. "I have no map."

Near the top, Da Craterman's signs displayed a touching concern for the hiker's well-being. 3RD WARNING. VERY DEEP DOWN. VERY DANGEROUS. At the edge of the crater, I beheld a Lost World, a steep and lushly overgrown cavern alive with the songs of birds. It was difficult to imagine that this had once been a lively and active volcano. It was difficult to imagine that anything on Savai'i was once lively and active at all.

On the ferry to Upolu, I met an Australian fishing captain on his way to Pago Pago in American Samoa, where his boat was being prepped for another run. He had a license to fish the Cook Islands until May, he said.

"We're going to fish the snot out of it until our papers expire," he exclaimed. "I've seen more fish in the past four years than I've seen at any point in my life. But the bloody greens closed the fishing grounds around Australia and New Zealand. Bloody prancers."

"But aren't rising ocean temperatures changing fish migratory patterns?" I asked.

"Yeah," he said. "But we can still find them."

Upolu is said to be the bustling heart of modern Samoa. Most of its people reside in Apia, the capital, which lies below the imposing summit of Mount Vaea. It is a town where wooden buildings from the colonial era still stand amidst a smattering of garish office buildings and a peculiar parliament that seems to have been lifted straight from the desert in Abu Dhabi. Land disputes seemed to be the issue of the day, as they are on most islands, their very nature causing one to value dirt above all else.

"No one wants to farm anymore," a Samoan woman told me. "They want to work in an air-conditioned office. But what happens to the village boys? Some chief gets them drunk and sends them off to burn property in a land dispute. Samoans, they often take things too far."

Walking around town, I find it difficult to imagine Stevenson settling here. There were plenty of *palagis* in Apia during that era, playing the colonial game, which Stevenson wrote about extensively in his *A Footnote to History: Eight Years of Trouble in Samoa*. In 1889, seven ships from Great Britain, the United States, and Germany played a game of naval chicken in the harbor, daring each other to leave and seek safety in the open seas as a typhoon bore down on them. Six ships were sunk during the storm, killing more than two hundred sailors. That was the sort of continental nonsense that Stevenson scorned. True, by living here, on an outpost on the far side of the world, he avoided the petty backbiting of literary society, for which he had even more contempt, but Samoa was hardly untouched by Western concerns. Combine the meddling of imperial powers with a rapacious cast of *palagi* beachcombers, deserters, and felons, and Apia featured the very worst of the social orbit he'd known in the West. Indeed, his son-in-law, Joe Strong, would soon join this dissolute mob, having robbed and cajoled Stevenson out of every penny he could find, and eventually settling in town with a local woman, leaving his wife and child to fend for themselves in Vailima.

Some, Paul Theroux among them, maintain that Stevenson settled in Samoa because of its excellent, for the time, links to the outside world. There were regular mail ships that called on Apia, linking it to London, San Francisco, and Sydney, no small thing for a writer. And Stevenson needed to keep working. He was supporting a large family now, and once he purchased Vailima, building the grandest home in Samoa, its upkeep demanded a steady flow of funds. From time to time, he entertained the idea of giving up the pen to become a South

Seas trader. In more melancholic moods, he wished he'd followed the family tradition and become an engineer. "Were it not for my health," he wrote in a letter, "which made it impossible, I could not find it in my heart to forgive myself that I did not stick to an honest, commonplace trade . . ." But write on he did, continuing the prodigious output that had become his habit.

And yet, the presence of a mail ship casts Stevenson in a practical light that he himself rarely displayed. Certainly, he took his responsibilities seriously, but he had always had an air of improvisation about him. He made do, no matter what the circumstances. Something as prosaic as the convenient presence of a mailbox or a telegraph seemed an unlikely justification for building his hearth.

Misa Telefoni, the affable former deputy prime minister of Samoa and a Stevenson aficionado, advanced another theory as to why the author chose to remain here, in the temperate hills above Apia.

"I believe Stevenson was influenced by H. J. Moors," he said. We were sitting inside Aggie Grey's, an illustrious hotel from the 1930s once frequented by James Michener and Marlon Brando. "He was very persuasive and he had his own interests in wanting Stevenson to stay."

Misa's grandfather had worked for the postal service and helped introduce the telephone to Samoa, which is how he acquired the family name. We had a mutual friend, and what I liked about the Pacific is that this alone is enough to elicit an invitation for coffee from a highfalutin official. Imagine if you knew someone who went to high school with Joe Biden, and then visiting Washington, DC, you get a call from the vice president inviting you for a ride in his Camaro. Misa was speaking about H. J. Moors, an American trader and businessman who soon befriended Stevenson and provided the building materials that would go into Vailima. He sold the timber to Stevenson for a premium, marking up the price substantially, causing the author much stress and worry over the ever-escalating costs of his home. Moors, I thought, saw Stevenson as an easy mark, a meal ticket, another *palagi* to be charmed and cajoled into spending money he could ill afford.

"I think Moors viewed his relationship with Stevenson as a way to ensure that he will always be remembered. Stevenson was famous; Moors was not. By establishing a deep connection with Stevenson, Moors knew that he too would be written about."

This hadn't occurred to me. I couldn't imagine anyone seeking a claim to fame through their acquaintance with a writer. But Stevenson lived in a different era, of course, one that predates radio, television, and movies, a time when the only popular entertainment available was that which was found between the covers of a book. Today, of course, people are famous for doing nothing at all. I'm looking at you, Kim Kardashian and Paris Hilton. Back then, you needed to earn it, and fame was gifted or cursed to very few. Stevenson, at the peak of his career, was the proverbial shiny object, a designation that ill suited him. The crowds that followed him in New York and Sydney, while massaging his ego, stifled him and made him uncomfortable. He was most at home on a poorly charted island, wearing pajamas and a dapper sailor's cap, free in his anonymity, the only calling card his wit and curiosity. His renown baffled him. The only person who didn't know he was famous was Stevenson himself.

"Once he settled here, he began to love this place," Misa continued. "He became ensconced in the local culture. And this was very unusual for a foreigner. The Samoans grew to love Stevenson, and when he died, they worked all night to clear a path to the summit of Mount Vaea. Can you imagine?"

I couldn't since I had not yet been to the gravesite. I was still trying to get inside Stevenson's head, to try to figure what had made him hang his hat here, in Samoa, rather than in Hawaii or New Zealand or Timbuktu. My own personal theory was that he simply grew tired, that on the cusp of forty he became weary of even the sweet rigors of travel, and that with this temperament it was only a matter of time until he found the right circumstances to furl the sails and settle down. He felt healthier in the tropics than he did in more distant latitudes, but that still encompasses a large swath of this planet. That he settled in Samoa, I thought, was coincidental. If he had sailed the Indian Ocean, I felt, he might have called Madagascar home.

And yet, the moment I approached Vailima I sensed something else. The house is exceedingly large, nestled on a tended lawn a couple of miles up into the hills above Apia. There is a grand luster to the manse, which was painted white with a red corrugated-iron roof. There is Stevenson's room, the single bed, the writing desk, and a window that opened to the verandah and a lawn where a couple of banded rails happily wandered. Next to it was Fanny's room. They did not sleep together, apparently. Was it the hacking and coughing? No, for there was a sick room too, with mosquito nets and bottles of potions and medicine, where Stevenson convalesced. It was a house of bedrooms. His mother had the grandest, next to that of young Austin, Fanny's grandson, who would be the last to carry the Stevenson name. On the wall was an etching of RLS teaching Austin a history lesson, as well as many photos of him hosting kava ceremonies or elaborate feasts with the Samoans he'd adopted as his extended clan. Perhaps this house, this life, satisfied Stevenson's cravings for both the Bohemian and the homespun. There were personal touches like a sewing machine, a few engravings from his days in France and England, as well as a lion skin hoisted onto the wall, near his safe. Vailima had the only fireplace in Samoa as well as a library and a piano.

He would live here on the hillside for four years, long enough to make it home, and as I looked at the photos of Stevenson, his eyes intensely alive, I couldn't help but feel that this was the only place for him. There was nothing calculating about his decision to remain in Samoa. It was intuitive. He knew, seemingly from the moment he stepped ashore, that this was the place for him, finally, after all those years of roaming the seven seas. Here, the restless gleam in his eyes gave way to an air of contented bemusement. Like all islanders, he was attached to his land, and it was here, in faraway Samoa, that he felt the pulse of his ancestral roots, the Scotsman's bond with the soil. In a letter to a novelist, he wrote: "For the first time, near my fortieth year, I find myself a landholder and a farmer: with paths to hew in tropical bush, weeds to deracinate, weeders and diggers to supervise. You at least will sympathize when how I tell you that this work seizes and enthralls me; I would rather do a good hour's work weeding sensitive—our deadliest enemy—than write two pages of my best."

For all his adult years, Stevenson lived separately, in an ethereal universe of his own creation, detached from the toils and pleasures of conventional life, floating airlessly from story to story, island to island, never alighting long enough to be anything more than a wanderer, a visitor among worlds. It is not without its allure, such an existence. The world is ceaselessly interesting when no day resembles another. But invariably, the bliss of the novel gives way to the yearning for the familiar. It was as if Stevenson had awoken from a dream, and now he seized the morning in gratitude, anxious to be back among the real, the tangible, the finite, the small daily connections that bond us with life. He took to the land with the zeal of the newly converted. In a few years, he hoped, his plantation would earn enough and he would "be released from the obligation to write." Nowhere else would this be possible than on a South Seas island. Stevenson, the *famous* Robert Louis Stevenson, would never be allowed to retire wordlessly to a farm in upstate New York or Yorkshire. The world would clamor on his gates. In Samoa, he could write "The End" and make it so.

As these thoughts occurred to me, I felt a bond with Stevenson. I understood the siren song of the itinerant traveler, followed its tune to distant shores and faraway lands. It is what drew me to Stevenson. Here, I thought, is a fellow traveler. But now, wandering among the grounds of Vailima, I felt an even greater affinity still. I can't swing a four-hundred-acre farm, perhaps the bottle cost me that too, but if I could, I would. Every journey has its end. The trick, of course, is to recognize it. I followed the lure of the drink for far too long, never seeing that, invariably, it always took me to the same miserable place. Finally, hopping off that steamer to nowhere, I felt the same profound need to make up for lost time, to establish a root somewhere, to put a declarative end to one life and to immerse myself, both feet in, into another. I wanted the clean slate and the fresh start. It takes a lot of weeding and tilling of the soil to create a Vailima, but I knew how to do that. You do it one day at a time.

I stood on the lower verandah and breathed the scented air and listened to the songs of birds. It was here that Stevenson suddenly turned to Fanny. "Do I look strange?" he asked, and then he collapsed unconscious, dying shortly thereafter from a cerebral hemorrhage. He was forty-four.

The climb to his grave leads through a tangle of rain forest, then up a steep promontory, where foot-long lizards scampered over roots among foliage so dense that not even a passing burst of rain punctured the canopy. I emerged from the forest and beheld the tomb. It stood on the edge of a ridge. Below was a sweeping panorama encompassing all of Apia, the harbor, and beyond the ocean that had carried Stevenson for so long. The grave site is made of white cement blocks, upon which a plaque displays his epitaph, written fifteen long years earlier, when, as so often with his sickness, he was confronted with the potential imminence of his own demise:

> *Under the wide and starry sky*
> *Dig the grave and let me lie:*
> *Glad did I live and gladly die,*
> *And I laid me down with a will.*
>
> *This be the verse you grave for me:*
> *Here he lies where he long'd to be;*
> *Home is the sailor, home from sea,*
> *And the hunter home from the hill.*

The tomb was extensively defaced by people who had carved their names into the stone. HOWARD said the most prominent etching. I spent a moment looking for a sharp rock so I could add IS A FUCKWIT, but then, with a sigh of regret, let it be. Here, my travels would end. I rested for a few moments at the base of the tombstone and marveled at the view, the cascade of hills tumbling toward the sea, a hint of mist swirling around their ramparts. The air was clamorous with birdsong and carried the scent of hibiscus. Of course, Stevenson felt at home here, I thought. I could not think of a more enchanting place to lie. This was no desolate memorial. It was, in its own way, a pinnacle to a life well lived, a reflection of Stevenson's quest for the transcendent, a place that called to mind faraway adventures and tropical fairy tales. Stevenson could only be here on an island in the South Seas. Anyplace else would be wrong, an affront to the natural order of things. And as I stood and began my journey onward, I felt alive to the possibilities of life, alive to the turn of a good yarn, alive to the long voyage, alive to home, alive.

Notes, Sources, and Flotsam

The author would like it to be known that he is not a scholar. He, in fact, relied heavily on the work of others, in particular *Louis: A Life of Robert Louis Stevenson* by Philip Callow (see, especially, Chapter Seven), *Robert Louis Stevenson: A Biography* by Frank McLynn, and *Robert Louis Stevenson* by Claire Harman. The introduction to the Penguin Classics edition of *In the South Seas*, written by Neil Rennie, was invaluable. Many of the quotes from Robert Louis Stevenson were lifted from *Selected Letters of Robert Louis Stevenson*, edited by Ernest Mehew.

The author is also aware that the map provided herein is an old map, that the New Hebrides are now known as Vanuatu, that Abaiang is spelled with a *b* and not a *p*, and that Tonga is no longer Friendly. He decided to include the old-timey map because he felt that it would lend the whole enterprise an air of gravitas. It would make the book seem classy. He may have been mistaken about this. And so to the citizens of the Navigator Islands, he apologizes. He acknowledges your modernity.

Also, as seasoned travelers to the South Pacific may have

surmised, it's not possible to visit the islands in the order de-scribed herein when traveling commercial. For organizational purposes, the author decided to structure the book so that it followed, more or less, the guiding principles of *In the South Seas*. The author also changed a few names. Just because.

Acknowledgments

To the good people at Gotham Books: my very patient editor, Lauren Marino, Emily Wunderlich, Susan Barnes, and Bill Shinker.

My agent, BJ Robbins, for sticking through thick and thin.

For all those who helped me out on a long journey: John Cox, Joe McClean, Lelei Lelaulu, Eric Weiner, Misa Telefoni, Nynette Sass, Linda Uan, John Anderson, Jack ("I did not order the Long Island Iced Teas") St. Martin.

And my family, of course.

Also available from
J. MAARTEN TROOST

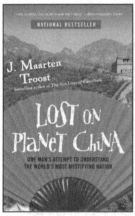
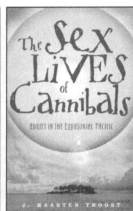
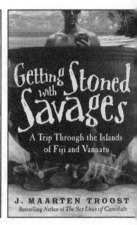

"Troost has a command of place and narrative that puts him in the company of some of today's best travel writers."

—*Elle*

B\D\W\Y

Available wherever books are sold

Printed in the United States
by Baker & Taylor Publisher Services